Fact in fiction

Fact in fiction

The use of literature in the systematic study of society

Joan Rockwell

Department of Sociology
University of Reading

Routledge & Kegan Paul
London

First published in 1974
by Routledge & Kegan Paul Ltd
Broadway House, 68–74 Carter Lane,
London EC4V 5EL
Printed in Great Britain by
Ebenezer Baylis & Son Ltd
The Trinity Press, Worcester, and London
© *Joan Rockwell 1974*

ISBN 0 7100 7877 3

PN
51
R65

Contents

For my parents and children, including Maria

Preface

When academics are born (not just sociologists), a Good Fairy at the christening promises them that when they grow up they will be able to read and understand books. Hardly has she finished speaking, however, when a Bad Fairy interrupts to say, with a threatening gesture, 'But you must never, never look out of the window!'

This is not the only possible explanation, but I offer it as an hypothesis, to explain the extraordinary proliferation of books based on books, theories breeding theories, footnotes giving rise to footnotes, with very little attention paid to the real world surrounding the matter under discussion.

There are difficulties, however, in the way of capturing the real world and using it as proof. The first and greatest of these is that it is impossible: as Weber points out, we can never know *all* the facts about any phenomenon, within or outside ourselves—even 'the smallest slice of reality' (Weber, 1949):[1] and this makes proof by quantitative demonstration ultimately invalid. I have attempted in this little book to consider rationally some sociological principles relating to the place and function of literature in society, with particular reference to narrative fiction. But I have made no attempt to review or summarise theories of knowledge, 'the sociology of literature', 'Structuralism' or the like, nor have I attempted to make a quantitative survey, except in the most general terms—no graphs or mountains of data will appear, in an attempt to 'prove' my notions by body-count.

My basic premise is that literature neither 'reflects' nor 'arises from' society, but rather is an integral part of it and should be recognised as being as much so as any institution, the Family for instance, or the State. Narrative fiction is an indicator, by its form and content, of the morphology and nature of a society, just as the specific structure and function of the family in a society will be an indicator of how that society differs from others. Two hundred years before Marx and Engels made their claims for the class and economic determination of the 'cultural superstructure' of society, Giambattista Vico in *The New Science* (1744) stated that 'The order of ideas must follow the order of institutions'. He was arguing against Descartes's claim of rationality as a universal human trait, arguing that, on the contrary, rationality is historically acquired, an order of ideas which suits a certain order of society.

Fiction, to be sure, is a social product; but it also 'produces' society, because it has a normative effect on its members, perhaps especially in childhood. Nursery rhymes, folktales, religious observances such as those connected with Christmas and Easter, comicbooks—all of these, which set ideals of behaviour and a picture of the world before the child, are necessarily conveyed in narrative form. The same is true of Science in its initial presentation: the Apple of the Garden of Eden reappears in connection with the Law of Gravity.

Max Weber, in the discussions of scientific methodology referred to above, says plainly that the 'absolute infinitude of this multiplicity' [of objects and events in the world] must be ordered by the observer, according to the ideas he brings to the object of his scientific enquiry. Scientific enquiry, however, is both rare and recent in human affairs. It seems to me that 'narrative fiction' has always been, not a falsification of reality but a necessary ordering of it. 'Real' reality cannot be apprehended as it is: an infinite, equally existent number of discrete and ever-changing entities and events. To see the universe in those terms might be accurate, but would be impossible to absorb, and meaningless in human terms. A selection of events on the basis of chronological sequence, causality, and value judgments has always been necessary; that is to say, information about reality has been presented to and by the human species in the forms of narrative fiction known to us as History, the Law, Religion, Epic Poetry, the Novel, the Drama, and the statements of politicians and journalists. In one sense, everything is fiction; in another sense, fiction is reality.

I hope I have succeeded in writing in clear language. I have tried to avoid the cement-like opacity of regular sociologese, assuming that the eyes of other readers bounce off the page with boredom as mine do. I have tried to keep notes and references to a minimum, assuming a certain literacy in the common reader; but I hope the notes will be read, as they contain a lot of interesting stuff which would impede the argument if it was in the text; they are mostly illustrative asides, as in lecturing.

The present book derives from a lifetime of reading, interest in the social sciences, and the experience of developing and teaching a course called 'Analysis of Literary Sources' (not 'Sociology *of* Literature' but on the contrary, 'Sociology *through* Literature', in Lewis Coser's phrase (1963)) at the University of Reading. I owe great thanks to my students, whose scepticism and protests—'Why should fiction *prove* anything?'—forced me to consider and make articulate what I had always supposed to be generally accepted truths. Also to Professor S. L. Andreski, for his willingness to entertain new approaches to sociology, and for defending the course before it was well-established, thus probably preserving me from 'remaining as a Trophy to the troops of Error' (Browne, 1643).

So far as writing the book itself is concerned, the very greatest thanks and gratitude are due to Professor Bernard Rosenberg, whose encouragement and enthusiasm on seeing a small part of the original MS. were the impetus without which nothing more would have been done. I also wish to thank several people for their kindness in taking the time to read portions of the book and make valuable suggestions: Professor A. W. H. Adkins of the Classics Department, University of Reading; Iris Andreski; Dr David Crystal of the Linguistics Department, University of Reading; Dr Maria Hircowicz of the Sociology Department, University of Reading; Professor Richard Hoggart of the Birmingham Centre for Contemporary Cultural Studies; and Anne and Kate Lynch.

Also, grateful thanks to Mrs Mava Quinlan, for her patient disentangling and constructive and aesthetically pleasing typing of the script.

The errors, as usual, are my own.

Note

1 Three essays, two from *Archiv für Sozialwissenschaft und Sozialpolitik,* 1904 and 1905; and one first published in *Logos,* 1917.

The number and types of causes which have influenced any given event are always infinite and there is nothing in the things themselves to set them apart as alone meriting attention. A chaos of individual judgements about countless individual events would be the only result of a serious attempt to analyse reality 'without pre-suppositions'. And even this result is only seemingly possible, since every simple perception discloses on closer examination an infinite number of constituted perceptions which can never be exhaustively expressed in a judgement. (p. 72) . . . as soon as we attempt to reflect about the way in which life confronts us in immediate concrete situations, it presents an infinite multiplicity of successively and coexistently emerging and disappearing events both 'within' and 'outside' ourselves. The absolute infinitude of this multiplicity is seen to remain undiminished even when our attention if focused upon a single 'object' for instance, a concrete act of exchange, as soon as we seriously attempt an exhaustive description of all the individual components of this 'individual phenomena' to say nothing of explaining it causally. (p. 78)

J. E. T. Eldridge, to whom I owe these two citations, sums up Weber's point on the impossibility of complete causal explanation (1971, p. 11): 'One cannot in the nature of the case, Weber argues, give a causal explanation of even an individual fact in any final sense, nor even exhaustively describe "the smallest slice of reality".'

Part I

Principles and methods

Chapter 1

Language and literature

Fiction, as we may infer from the word itself—something 'made' or 'made-up'[1]—is not identical with fact. Virginia Woolf speaks with scorn of those who 'expect fiction to be true and poetry to be false'. Others proclaim a positive incompatibility between literature and reality; thus Mannoni begins his study of Freud (1971) with these words: 'Despite its outstanding literary qualities, Freud's work cannot really be treated as literature: it is concerned with truth.' This statement is the more remarkable in view of Freud's consistent use of paradigms from literature, and his self-identification with the most famous of these, with Oedipus, 'who solved the riddle of the Sphinx and was a man most mighty'. And also in view of Freud's insistence on the central importance of language and the dream-story in plucking up the truth from the subconscious.

There seems to be some relationship between fiction and society which is definite enough for fictional characters to be regularly used as prototypes of social roles and social attitudes. A Micawber, a Shylock, Crusoe on his Island—these names are quite unselfconsciously invoked as shorthand descriptions of social classes and social interaction by writers of every kind, including social and psychological scientists.

I intend to go much further than this, as I think the patterned connection between society and fiction is so discernible and so reliable that literature ought to be added to the regular tools of social investigation. I think it can be shown that literature is a product of society rather than the crystallised result of private fantasy (as Diana Spearman contends in *The Novel and Society* (1966)). Neither is it simply entertainment, welcome in all societies to pass the time and because of the universal fascination of a story, as Somerset Maugham states in *Ten Novels and Their Authors* (1963, p. 17),

3

(but without saying why a narrative *should* be universally fascinating: a point raised by Ernst Fischer in *The Necessity of Art* (1963)).

Fiction, I say, is much more than this. I would like to offer the proposition that fiction is not only a representation of social reality, but also a necessary functional part of social control, and also paradoxically an important element in social change. It plays a large part in the socialisation of infants, in the expression of official norms such as law and religion, in the conduct of politics, and in general gives symbols and modes of life to the population, particularly in those less easily defined but basic areas such as norms, values, and personal and inter-personal behaviour.

The implications of this are that fiction can give us two types of information about society: first, in a descriptive way, facts about the state of technology, laws, customs, social structure and institutions. Second, more subtle and less easily obtained information about values and attitudes. These last become most visible when they are brought to the surface as the themes of literature in nodal periods when great changes are taking place in the basic institutions of society. Changes, for instance, in the structure and formation of the family or of economic life—changes which produce a conflict of values which finds its expression in literature. I would follow Lucien Goldmann (1967, pp. 511-12) in his contention that:

at any given moment, social and historical reality always presents itself as an extremely complex mixture, not of structures but of processes of structuration and destruction, the study of which will not have a scientific character until the day when the chief processes have been made clear with a sufficient degree of rigour.

Now, it is precisely on this point that the sociological study of the masterpieces of literature acquires special value for general sociology.

But, it may be contended, the masterpieces of literature have a universal validity for human-kind at all times—we go back to the Greek dramatists because 'the stable, the permanent, the original human being is to be found there' (Woolf, 1966, p. 4). In that case, they may tell us something about 'human nature', but little about Greek society, and we may dismiss at once the idea of using literature for this purpose. If human nature can be said to be original, permanent, and stable at all times and places, literature which puts it before our eyes in this or that society can give us no basis of social comparison, as every action and attitude may be readily transposed from one period to another. (Such notions give rise to such literary fiascos as T. S. Eliot's Oresteian pastiche, *Family Reunion*, in which he disastrously imagined he was bringing Aeschylus to life in modern dress.) The RSC, on the other hand, was able to transpose *The Merchant of Venice* successfully to the nineteenth century, as the same bourgeois norms were operative in both periods, with the single exception of the (literal) pound of flesh, which could not survive translation from the medieval ghetto.

If we compare the actions and the values recorded in classical Greek literature, we cannot help seeing that they are very different from the actions and values we might expect to find in fiction now. If we believed in curses, we could not wonder that there was a curse on the House of Atreus, since it contains a man who slew his brother's children and gave him their flesh to eat; a man who, to get a good wind for the fleet, ritually sacrificed his daughter by cutting her throat before the assembled army; a wife who ritually killed her husband in revenge for this; a son who killed his mother to avenge this death and was declared no murderer. In our time, drenched with blood though it is, all of these deeds would be considered the acts of criminals, and would be so treated in literature. And yet for the Greeks, the Homeric poems and the classical drama derived from them were the standard of morality. We must conclude either that the classical Greeks were psychopathic criminals *en masse*, or that their nature, neither stable nor permanent, was very different from ours, like their society, and that their literature can, at least in part, tell us how, if not why.

It is germane to this study to consider the importance of the Homeric poems in Greek society. H. D. F. Kitto in *The Greeks* emphasises the almost total saturation of the Greek people with Homer, and the influence of the poet in social behaviour (1967, p. 8):

> a citation from Homer was the natural way of settling a
> question of morals or behaviour. Homer could be quoted in
> diplomatic exchanges, like a Domesday book, to support a
> territorial claim. A kind of Fundamentalism grew up: Homer
> enshrined all wisdom and all knowledge.

The belief in the 'divine wisdom' of Homer was revived in the Renaissance, and it was Giambattista Vico in *The New Science*

(1744) who first enquired why, if Homer was all-wise, he repeatedly depicted the vile actions of the gods, kings, and heroes, making them a sort of pattern for imitation. The reason he gives is that which occurs immediately to common sense and sociological reasoning: that the poet is limited, by his audience and his own conditioning, to the norms and values of his own society (ibid., book 3, section I, para. 781):

> Let us concede to Homer what certainly must be granted,
> that he had to conform to the quite vulgar sensibilities and
> hence the vulgar customs of the barbarous Greece of his day,
> for such vulgar perceptions and vulgar customs provide the
> poets with their proper materials.

Having stated that the content and manner of literature is determined by society, Vico refers to what he assumes, and what most people have always assumed, to be the normative function of literature (ibid., para. 782):

> Nevertheless, if the purpose of poetry is to tame the ferocity
> of the vulgar whose teachers the poets are, it was not the part
> of a wise man, versed in such fierce sensibilities and customs,
> to arouse admiration of them in the vulgar in order that they
> should take pleasure in them and be confirmed in them by that
> pleasure. Nor was it the part of a wise man to arouse pleasure
> in the villainous vulgar at the villainies of the gods, to say
> nothing of the heroes.

We have here the kernel of the use of literature in the study of society: the poet and his material are produced by society, and therefore necessarily contain information about it. Also, the poet is 'the teacher of the people'; fiction gives patterns for behaviour, and is thus not only a source of information but a normative force in society.

To enquire why this should be so, I am afraid we must go the whole distance, and ask first about the functions of language in society, before even considering that particular use of language which we call story, fiction, or literature (extending the term to include also oral or non-written narrative).

Language

Language is apparently necessary to the existence of human society, since no society we know of has existed without it. Literature, like pictorial art, is also apparently universal, and it is a sociological truism that what is found universally must be of some social use. When I say literature is universal, I mean to include, of course, such primitive and direct forms as proverbs and 'folk-wisdom', folktales and ballads, which, though simple, have a pattern and a tradition; as well as productions on the gigantic scale of the Athenian drama, the plays of Shakespeare, or the novels of Dostoievski.

We may begin by asking ourselves why language is so important. The short answer is that it is a complex and infinitely flexible means of communication, with evident practical superiority to the relatively simple signals of animals. Engels, in *The Origin of the Family, Private Property and the State* (1884), offers the hypothesis that language became necessary when the first human beings began working together co-operatively (the 'yo-heave-ho theorem'). Marxists in general are infatuated with the idea that the origin of language lies in the demands of one human activity alone, namely *work*. Following Engels, Ernst Fischer in *The Necessity of Art* (1963, p. 23) says:

> Animals have little to communicate to each other. Their language is instinctive: a rudimentary system of signs for danger, mating, etc. Only in work and through work do living beings have much to say to each other. Language came into being together with tools.

He also derives the concept of *concept* specifically from the early making of tools: 'making-alike', i.e. imitating, one hand-axe to make more (ibid., p. 28):

> Thus the first abstraction, the first conceptual form, was supplied by the tools themselves: prehistoric man 'abstracted' from many individual hand-axes the quality common to them all—that of being a hand-axe; in so doing, he formed the 'concept' of a hand-axe.

But recent studies in primate and other animal ethology force a modification of these views. Surely it is 'social relationships' in general, and not specifically the relationships involved in 'work', which are the origin of language. What have previously been thought to be purely human characteristics—'Man is the tool-making animal' —are no longer exclusively human property. Tools are now known

2

not to be specific to man or hominids or even primates: birds have been filmed winkling out insects with a bit of thorn. Primates have been extensively recorded using branches as weapons, and tearing them off to do so. Animals certainly communicate skills to each other, as English birds, in ever-widening geographic rings, have taught each other (they had no other teachers) to peck through aluminium milk-bottle caps to get at the cream.

John Napier, in *The Roots of Mankind* (1971), sees, as indeed anybody must, a connection between the origins of culture and of language, but not the necessity that language must come first, or be *derived* from 'work'. (Whatever 'work' might be to prehistoric man. We may safely say that he did not arrive in the world like Crusoe on his Island, with 1,800 years of European civilisation behind him and full of prudent thoughts of financial gain.) Napier, discussing the transition from primate to man, says (ibid., p. 204):

> The essential ingredient of cultural tool-making [as distinguished from *ad hoc* improvisation] is the element of tradition by which a skill is passed down from one generation to another, and it is possible that evolution of cultural tool-making, the final stage of the tool-making saga, followed close on the heels of the evolution of speech and language. Speech, however, is not the only means by which information can be passed from one individual to another. Learning by example would be a perfectly feasible way in which one hominid could teach another an activity as simple as pebble-tool making. Indeed it has never seemed to me that lack of language and speech would be any bar to the development of simple cultural traditions, although it has for long been implicit that speech and culture are so reciprocally linked that one is not possible without the other.

The work of modern animal ethologists, such as Tinbergen, Lorenz, the Russells, and especially Jane Goodall, has brilliantly revealed the existence of vocal signals, and others based on elements other than sound, such as touch, sensation of heat or cold, involuntary responses such as bristling hair, mimetic communication by grimaces and gestures, and perhaps telepathic communication, in inter-animal behaviour. These signals are sufficient to touch off appropriate social response in quite complex situations requiring recognition of danger, aggression, relative status, need for comfort and reassurance, and reconciliation. One might then claim for animals, at least for those which live in social groups, simple cultural traditions in the sense of learned behaviour regularly used in certain situations, without the use of language.

But it is true that animals have nothing which even approaches what Chomsky calls the 'open-ended' quality of human speech, with its stock of words which any speaker can put together in a literally infinite number of combinations which will be instantly understood by any other speaker of the language.

The essential difference is that it is the *words themselves* which convey the meaning, not an imitation of an action or an affectively toned transmission of the sense of a total situation.

Words are capable of far more precision than gestures can have in the communication of concepts, although they are frequently less expressive and vivid: an actual sigh is better than the word. Words are also arcane, in that understanding of them is limited to those who know their specific meaning, and in this they differ from most gestures. Communication *in words*, unlike most gestures, includes some people and excludes others.[2]

Communication, however, essential and noticeable a function as it is, is not the only use of language. There is also the highly important function of *demarcation*. Language includes some and excludes others: it acts as a social bond and also as a social barrier.

These two functions are of course related: the social barrier reinforces the social bond. 'Consciousness of kind' (alikeness) is felt with those with whom we share speech, and difference, sometimes revulsion, felt towards those with whom we do not. H. D. F. Kitto points out in *The Greeks* (1967), and this is universally agreed so far as I know, that the Greeks of the classical period felt akin to all who spoke the language: their word *barbaros* meant literally 'those who do not speak [Greek] but make meaningless sounds (bar-barbar) instead'. Such people are evidently outside the cultural boundaries and perhaps less than human; common language equals common culture and common understanding.

But even within a common language there are demarcations: regional differences in intonation, nuances or special uses of words, perhaps words peculiar only to a certain area, variations in meaning, alternate syntax and alternate pronunciation—these are dialects, correct speech within a cultural territory.

There are also class demarcations. Class membership is marked, to be sure, by intonation and accent, but also by variant usage and choice of content, some of which is clearly indicative of class characteristics and values. Erich Auerbach in *Mimesis* (1953) has an interesting discussion of this class content of language (ibid., pp. 242–3):

> When we read: *Monseigneur le cappitaine de ceste place, nous, comme officiers d'armes et personnes publicques, de par le prince de Galles, nostre très redoubté seigneur, ceste foiz pour toutes à vous nous mande, de par sa clemence de prince, vous signiffier, adviser et sommer . . .,* it is unmistakable that, even at a moment when he is deeply moved and horrified by the Prince's cruelty, La Sale derives supreme pleasure from getting this emphatic but syntactically confused display of class pomp down on paper. And there we have it in a nutshell; his language is a class language; and everything determined by class is non-humanist. The stable class-determined order of life, in which everything has and keeps its place and its form, is reflected in this solemn and circumstantial rhetoric, with its abundance of formulas, its superabundance of conventional gestures and invocations. Every person has a proper form of address. Madame du Chastel calls her husband *Monseigneur,* he says *m'amye* to her. Every person makes the gesture which befits his rank and the circumstances, as though in accordance with an eternal model established once and for all *(à jointes mains vous supplie).* When the Prince forces the commander's herald to witness the boy's execution (the scene is described twice), we hear this: *. . . alors, en genoulx et mains jointes je me mis et lui dis: 'A! très redouté prince, pour Dieu, souffrez que la clarté de mes malheureux yeux ne portent pas à mon très dollent cuer la très piteuse nouvelle de la mort de l'innocent filz de mon maistre et seigneur; il souffist bien trop se ma langue, au rapport de mes oreilles, le fait à icelui monseigneur vrayement.' Lors dist le prince: 'Vous yrez, veuilliez ou non'.* The tradition which we have here reentered is most strikingly to be felt in outstandingly solemn passages where, as we said, the matter at issue is surrounded by a defense in depth of solemnly introductory formulas. From such passages it becomes clear that we are dealing with formations of the late antique period of decadence, formations which, from the early Middle

Ages onward, were absorbed and developed by class-determined cultures. In the vernaculars this tradition extends from the compact and magnificent rhetoric of the Strasbourg Oaths to the preambles of royal edicts (*Louis par la grâce de Dieu,* etc).

Shaw's Professor Higgins was absorbed in the phonetic content of class dialects, but was brought to the realisation that there was a class difference of content and point of view as well. Taking as a constant the concept of the speaker's own self, we see in England a consistent variation in the term used to express it, and one might hazard a guess that the variation corresponds to the content of the norms of various classes. In England, members of the individualistic and competitive upper and middle class (especially professionals) call themselves 'one'. One reads, as a matter of course, in, for instance, *The Times Literary Supplement*, phrases such as 'The whole point, one had thought . . .' And Nancy Mitford, nicely discriminating as she is in these matters, allows her aristocratic characters in *The Pursuit of Love* to chatter incessantly about themselves as 'one'. Thus Captain Warbeck (p. 37):

'It's the acid from port that makes one so delicate now.'

Linda, on the practical difficulties of suicide (p. 58):

'You know what it is,' she said, 'trying to kill rabbits. Well, think of *oneself*.'

'Darling, darling Mummie,' said Linda, 'the meet's at Cock's Barn, and you know how one can't resist.' (p. 64)

'I'm in love,' said Linda proudly.
'What makes you think so?'
'One doesn't think, one knows.' (p. 84)

Linda said, hurriedly and guiltily: 'Well, I may seem to laugh at the comrades, but at least one knows they are doing good not harm. . . .' (p. 128)

And Linda again (p. 159):

At dinner she said 'Could one know your name?'

And Fabrice, duc de Sauveterre, answering Linda's question (p. 161) 'But why should you despise them?' replied:

'Oh really, my dear, one does, that's all.'

Mitford was an upper-class writer, a rarity compared with the number of novelists of bourgeois middle-class origin and speech, and she was a conscious observer of the nuances of class diction, as will be seen by any reader of *Noblesse oblige: an enquiry into the identifiable characteristics of the English aristocracy.* The bourgeois professional, such as the Oxbridge academic, notoriously aspires to an aristocratic manner, including this one, which of course reinforces the occupational individualism indicated by 'one'.

The English working class, on the contrary, consistently refer to the single self as 'us'. Perhaps this is mere accident, but it is so consistent that it is certainly tempting to see—when a hairdresser, for instance, explains how easy it is to get to work from her near-by home by saying 'It's just around the corner and *we're* there'—a significance in the plural, a connection perhaps with those constant appeals for solidary agreement with which British working-class speech is sprinkled—'innit?'—'dunnit?'—'didn' I?'—as justification and explanation. A call is made, by this usage, for agreement, and thus an elementary emotional support, even when, or maybe especially when, the speaker is relating something the interlocutor cannot know. Consider this exchange from a TV police serial:

P.C. Why are you sleeping rough?
Girl I had a falling-out with me old fella, didn' I?

The cosy togetherness of British working-class speech is also exemplified by the consistent use of endearments to strangers: 'Sorry, love!' says the drunk who bumps into one in the street; and 'Thanks very much, dear!' says the man who has just read the gas-meter.

While class dialects are a fascinating study, we may as well assume that this ground has already been covered by Professor Higgins and Nancy Mitford (1963) and other researchers, and merely note that to speak the same language, and especially the same class, occupational or local dialect, is to be a member or claim membership of a social group. Class dialect *may* be regional (Boston), but in England it crosses regional boundaries and is superimposed everywhere (Wyld, 1920, pp. 2–3).

Good English, Well-bred English, Upper-class English . . .
sometimes too vaguely referred to as Standard English—this
form of speech differs from the various Regional Dialects in

many ways, but most remarkably in this, that it is not confined to any locality, nor associated in anyone's mind with any special geographical area; it is in origin . . . the product of social conditions, and is spoken as essentially a *Class Dialect*. Received Standard is spoken within certain social boundaries, with an extraordinary degree of uniformity, all over the country.

The relative value of class dialects may change. Walter Nash points out in *Our Experience of Language* (1972) that it is no longer necessary to talk 'posh' in England to get into an upper-class occupation (or anyway an academic job), but nevertheless I think we may say that dialect is still a means of identifying those who should be accepted and those who should be excluded, whether on grounds of talking 'common' or talking 'la-di-da'. Ants are said to recognise members of their own nests by the collective smell, present on each individual, and to kill those who don't smell right. Speakers of dialects kill, or at least they are anxious to exclude, those who don't talk right: 'Whenever an Englishman opens his mouth, he makes some other Englishman despise him.'

One aspect of the so-called 'mass society' of modern industrial countries is the attempt, only partially successful, to impose Standard speech (so identified) on the whole population. It is intended to supersede all dialects, is taught in the schools and used in the mass media—except for the fictional representation of special social groups, who are differentiated by a stereotype of their dialect. Shakespeare, for one, used this method. 'Standard speech' is, of course, a class and degree-of-education dialect, and Robbins Burling in *Man's Many Voices* (1970) discusses the discriminatory injustice which results from the down-grading by the educational system of all other dialects (ibid., pp. 156–8):

> *Street Talk.* Urban Negro children are sometimes imagined to be so verbally deprived as to be almost tongue-tied, but any serious examination of the language of Negro youths when speaking with their contemporaries suggests that admiration of fluent and innovative speech is as marked among them as among any other group. In a remarkable study, based partly upon observations in Chicago and partly upon an examination of literary sources, Thomas Kochman has described some of the terms used by Negro youths for various expressive forms of language.

Rapping for instance, describes a distinctively fluent and lively way of talking, one that is always highly personal in style. It can be a way of creating a favorable impression when first meeting a person, though it can also become rather competitive and lead to a lively repartee. *Rapping* to a woman implies a colorful way of propositioning her, but otherwise it is simply a lively way of projecting personality when style is more important than the information exchanged.

Shucking (or one of a number of synonyms such as *jiving*) is the kind of language used when facing authority, particularly white authority. *Shucking* describes a kind of speech that hides the speaker's true feelings of indignation or pride, masking them behind an apparent innocence and deference. *Shucking*, therefor, describes the role of shuffling ignorance that whites have forced upon Negroes, and it can cover not only speech and intonation but the gestures and facial expressions by which one feigns repentance and evokes the sympathy of those in power. Naturally, the more militant black leaders now look upon *shucking* with little favor. The term *shucking* can also describe a style of speaking to other Negroes who are not in a position of authority. Here it refers to attempts to create a false impression and can include anything from an outright lie to a more subtly misleading variety of discourse.

Running it down is used for straightforward communicative speech, where the purpose is to convey information, narrate events, give an explanation or offer advice rather than to display personality in some particular way. *Gripping*, apparently a fairly new term, refers to the speech and facial expression that go with a partial loss of face and even some fear. In a street code that emphasizes being fearless and tough and 'keeping one's cool', *gripping* can hardly be much admired, but it is not as bad as *copping a plea*, which amounts to complete surrender to superior force and a pleading for mercy.

Signifying refers to teasing or taunting speech. It may include some boasting, and it may be used to goad another into an aggressive act. *Signifying* can arouse feelings of embarrassment, shame or futility, but it may help to stir up a little excitement on an otherwise dull day. *Sounding* is an even more direct verbal insult, and the term refers specifically to the insults that are hurled back and forth in a rather stylized game called *Playing the Dozens*. *Sounding* refers most specifically to the initial remarks that test whether or not another person is willing to play the game. The game of *Dozens* involves competitive slurs upon one's opponent and upon his family, and it is often encouraged by *signifying* of onlookers.

The recognition of these distinct modes of speech suggests that verbal skills are by no means neglected in the street culture. It even seems that the ability to use words is as highly valued as physical strength. Perhaps it is even more highly regarded, for a youth may resort to fighting only when he feels he can no longer hold up his reputation by verbal means alone. Violence may be an admission of verbal defeat. Language is used in the ghetto streets for self-assertion, competition, and when trying to manipulate others. Kochman concludes, 'by blending style and verbal power, through "rapping", "sounding", and "running it down", the Negro in the ghetto establishes his personality; through "shucking", "gripping", and "copping a plea", he shows his respect for power; through "jiving" and "signifying" he stirs up excitement. With all of the above, he hopes to manipulate and control people and give himself a winning edge.'

It is these same Negro youths whom educators sometimes imagine to be verbally stunted and so inarticulate as to be incapable of expressing themselves clearly in the classroom. No doubt the educator would be just as inarticulate were he to try playing the *Dozens*. Each may be fluent in his own sphere, and each may equally admire verbal skills.

The importance of dialect-allegiance is shown by the fact that social mobility, both upward and horizontal, requires an effort to leave behind the original dialect and acquire either Standard or the dialect of a group further up the social scale. *Downward* social mobility, on the other hand, makes no such demands, and one of the protective devices used to ward off realisation of its genuineness and finality is the effort to retain the former speech. This applies, of course, only when the mobility is unintended and undesired: people who 'snob-downward', as the Danes say, make great efforts to pick up working-class accents and lower-class expressions.

It is impossible to over-estimate the importance of language in the social bond, both as means of communication and as means of identification. But there is another function which is so obvious as to be almost invisible. A very large part of the 'humanising' of infants is done through language. One of the most remarkable proofs of the quality of human intelligence is the ability to learn a language by the age of two or three years; and it is worth noting that a great part of the initial socialisation of the infant is accomplished through the *use* of language. The young child, striving and eager to learn (and the intense drive to learn at this age has often been noted), finds out how to behave and what his attitudes should be, partly through verbal instruction: 'Do this, don't do that, do as I say, stop that this minute!', and through verbal descriptions of action desired or in progress: 'Now we have a bath, eat our supper, go to bed.' Much of the communication between mother and child is certainly emotive, non-verbal, based on repetition of total situations, perhaps telepathic. But, as he develops, increasingly *talk* becomes a factor in the child's social universe. He talks himself, practising and using words and expressions. He has always been able to get action to satisfy his demands by vocal gestures such as bellows and whimpers: he now learns that he, too, can instigate action and effectively manipulate his social group, through the use of words. Children who are deprived of verbal interaction lose the chance both of learning and of acting through articulate speech, are socially deprived, and may be retarded in their mental development.[3]

In society, the *sacred* nature of language has always been recognised. Language has always, rightly, been regarded with awe. One might perhaps offer a wild Jungian speculation as to whether this might be due to a deep collective 'memory' of the truly great step forward when the species acquired language. However that may be, many, perhaps all, religions give it as one of the first deeds of their Deity that *He gave language to the people*. 'In the beginning was the Word, and the Word was with God.'

The sacred books of various religions are written in sacred (archaic) language, and efforts have consistently been made to keep it that way. The first linguistic studies (400 B.C.) were directed to the preservation *unchanged in its purity* of the Vedic Sanskrit, the sacred language of the Vedas; the same efforts have been made on behalf of the Koran, from the ninth century onwards; and in Talmudic studies from the sixteenth century. It is understood that the *language itself* is sacred, not merely the religious themes and devotional content of the texts. The language is felt to have a magic-emotive power, which depends partly on being archaic and thus traditional, partly on being somewhat mysterious through the difference from modern usage. It is feared that this power is lost when the language is changed to conform to modern usage, hence the efforts to retain the old wording. An excellent expression of this feeling is seen in this letter to *The Times* (25 September 1971):

From Canon C. B. Armstrong
Sir,
Isolated phrases in the Series Three order for Holy Communion have been rightly criticised, but a more serious misapprehension underlies the whole revision. It is simply that liturgical and everyday languages are the same.

In the latter we are speaking to our fellowmen in reasonable and factual communication between equals. In the former we are daring to approach God in worship and prayer. Liturgy therefore requires a large element of the numinous. This is provided by dignity of language, by a perennial character to which tradition and antiquity give some weight and colour, and by a touch of rhythm suggestive of the musical. Further it is designed to express the aspirations of many worshippers whose spiritual experience and thoughts are varied and only partially concordant. And accordingly an element of comprehensive imprecision must be retained, instead of the explicitness desirable in common speech: the latter may alienate, offend, or feel discordant, and effectively prevent the 'lifting up' of many hearts.

Yours, etc.

Catholic dissatisfaction with the new Vulgate Mass, now officially in use everywhere, has found organisational expression in the creation of the Latin Mass Society, which aims to restore the Latin Mass as more suitable for religious use, for substantially the reasons stated by Canon Armstrong. Here 'imprecision' may be extended to mean actual non-comprehension of the Latin language by almost the entire Catholic population of the world.

While one of the proclaimed aims of the Protestant Reformation was to make the Bible available to everyone by putting it into the Vulgate (common, local, non-Latin) language, a point is always made of retaining at least the semblance of contact with the archaic language, in the interest, no doubt, not only of accuracy but of maintenance of the 'power' of the original. Translations have always been 'with the original language diligently compared and revised'. It is certainly arguable that increased availability, in every sense, of the sacred books has led to, or at least accompanied, more secularisation, not more religion. A highly secular country like Denmark has an impressive list of fourteen major translations of the Bible since the Reformation.[4]

A practical demonstration of the recognition in high places of the societal importance of language is the eagerness of conquerors to extirpate the language of the conquered and replace it with their own.[5] Language in this context is seen as a social bond, symbolic of national identity, a focus of loyalty, and a potential source of trouble. As Irish nationalists say in Gaelic, *gan teanga, gan tir*—'no language, no nation'. To replace the native language with that of the conqueror is not only to secure convenience of administration, but is to establish a symbol of the dominance of an alien culture. Speakers of the native tongue, including the natural leaders of the people, must learn the language of the conqueror and are at a disadvantage in it. Use of the native language may be forbidden and it may disappear—numerous examples of this in the British Isles will occur to the reader—taking the native culture with it into oblivion. Or use of the native language may be proof of social inferiority, as in Finland, where the upper and the educated classes have been Swedish-speaking since the thirteenth century, when Christianity and the Swedish language were forced on the Finns.

The linguistic stratification is also evident in Sweden itself. These contiguous areas form a cultural unity in this respect. *Grube* by Sara Lidman (1968) is a documentary study of miners in two mining villages in Sweden, Kiruna and Svappavaara; both lie north of the Polar Circle, and the majority of the miners are Finnish or Lapp speaking. They are perfectly conscious of the disadvantage of not speaking the dominant language. The book consists of tape-recorded interviews; a typical one, in rough translation, is as follows (ibid., p. 122):

It's better for young people growing up now, they know Swedish before they go to school. I couldn't speak a word of it when I began school. I was nine years old. It was strictly forbidden to speak Finnish on the playground, but it slips out anyway, and then we got belted. . . . It was a fine thing to speak Swedish . . . We always looked up to the Swedes . . . we always thought we were not nearly so good in Tornedal [as they were] because we couldn't speak Swedish. But the next generation won't have these feelings of inferiority, we hope.

Some respondents say they have a feeling that even in the Union Hall there are invisible signs saying 'Swedish ought to be spoken at work'. On the other hand some Swedish-speakers feel that they are kept at a distance by their Finnish-speaking workmates. Education, good jobs, and the ability to manœuvre (in union negotiations, for instance) depend on the ability to speak Swedish, and Finnish (not to mention Lapp) is a sign of social inferiority. This was spelled out in the plainest terms in an Edict of 1850—when Finland belonged to the Tsar of all the Russias—forbidding the publication of any literature at all in Finnish (Finnish Tourist Bureau, 1971, p. 24):

It was feared that creeping radical ideas would spread among the masses if they were given reading matter in the only language they understood.

The Decree stated that 'persons who understand only Finnish belong solely to the working or farming classes'. Thus the 'uneducated reader who belongs to the lower classes may misunderstand books that are not dangerous for the educated citizen'. 'Needless reading' was to be eliminated because it 'alienated' the working population from their labour.

Nothing was to be published except for purposes of 'religious elevation or commercial gain'. The same reasons which make conquerors eager to degrade and uproot the language of the conquered, make nationalist and liberationist movements eager to reinstate and legitimise it. This happened in Finland and it has frequently happened elsewhere. Language is a focus of national consciousness around which loyalty can readily be mobilised, especially when a whole class or nation which speak it are conscious of having suffered for doing so. The Danish peasant class, in its difficult but inexorable rise to social visibility and political and economic influence in the nineteenth century, brought up with it the Danish language and forced it into use as the language of the Court and the Law, the Parliament, the theatre, business, and polite society. This was not unopposed ('What, shall learned men be forced to speak this peasant tongue?'), as German had been the polite language of the country ('I speak French to my mistress, German to my friends, and Danish to my dog'—Frederick V, King of Denmark from 1746 to 1766) since the Reformation in 1526 brought an imported German Protestant King to the throne and a German aristocracy into power. Nevertheless, the triumph of the Danish language was accomplished in a very short time. Without belittling the conscious efforts of the Nationalist movement to this end, there can be no doubt that this was chiefly due to the rise of the class which spoke it; the peasant class, ousted from Parliament in 1570, returned to it in 1882, with the *Systemskiftet*. But even long previous to this, great educational efforts had been made to educate the common peasantry, especially in the use of 'standard' Danish rather than dialect. Thus in 1814 every village was required by royal decree to provide a school house and a schoolmaster for the village children. The High School Movement later in the nineteenth century provided education for young adults of the peasant class (chiefly sons and later daughters of owners of farms) in cultural subjects, specifically the national cultural past: pre-history through archaeology, correct Danish speech and especially the 'living' (i.e. spoken) word, and the study in translation of the literature of the Danish 'folk'—that is the literary record of the pre-Christian, prefeudal 'heroic' society of Scandinavia, as depicted in the sagas.

Literature

It has been assumed almost unanimously (except by Plato, who would put a wreath on the poet's head and then banish him from the Republic, for misleading the people by telling them lies) that literature in some way *reflects* society, so that to know the literature of a society is to know what sort of stories please them, and also, more significantly, to find in this mirror a reliable image of a number of hard social facts. This does not mean that we may reasonably expect to find in fiction everything in miniature which exists in the society which produces it. Such expectations lead to critical monstrosities such as those criticisms of Jane Austen, that most sociological of writers, which excoriate her for 'leaving out' the Napoleonic Wars, or for failing to have her protagonist express what the critic would like to see said about the true nature of the socio-economic system (Kettle, 1962, vol. 1, p. 122):[6]

After all, the important question is not whether Emma recognises the existence of the poor at Hartfield, but whether she recognises that her own position depends on their existence.

Emma was a clever enough girl, but surely it is unreasonable to expect her, a fictional character, to expound the Theory of Surplus Value some forty years or so before Marx developed it!

Literature has no such ideological errands. It is not obliged to be more committed or topical about economics, politics, or anything else, than the people in it might naturally be. They must be measured by their own (the author's) yardstick, not ours, and in their own world they might be enthusiasts for communism, Christianity, or anything else, just as the temper of the time, as experienced and recorded by the writer, makes it likely. This in fact is what makes literature valuable as social document: it is written *then*, from *that* point of view, containing matter that we perhaps could not conceive of from our different angle of vision. This is why it tells us new and solid facts. It is mere idleness to scold the writer for writing what he must write, and idiocy to want everything written down into a porridge of 'correct' attitudes.

The attraction of fiction is the personal element: it is a story about people, they have adventures or something happens to them, we become interested in their fate. For some reason, their actions and expectations have a moral or normative value, their behaviour in some way makes manifest the values of society.

It seems reasonable to ask, why should values and norms be represented in fictional form? In strictly logical terms, there seems no reason why a story of persons doing anything whatsoever should represent the values of society, or, to put it the other way round, why the behaviour of fictional beings should be taken as a model of behaviour by real beings; this last will be discussed at some length in Chapter 2. But meantime we may ask why norms should not be clearly and simply stated in abstract terms; why should they appear dressed up as symbolic persons in symbolic situations? There seems no logical reason for this, but empirically there does seem to be a human tendency to deal with any idea whatsoever, no matter how abstract, in terms of human personification, envisioned human action, or human sense impression. This extends from Socrates— who could find no better definition of Virtue than 'that which a good man does'—to modern nuclear physics (Deutsch, 1959, p. 122):

> The human imagination, including the creative scientific imagination, can ultimately function only by invoking potential or imagined sense impression. I cannot prove that the statement I have just made is true, but I have never met a physicist, at least not an experimental physicist, who does not think of the hydrogen atom by evoking a visual image of what he would see if the particular atomic model with which he is working existed on a scale accessible to sense impression.

A specific example of this reification of scientific concepts in a visual image, and the casual acceptance of the process, is shown in this obituary from *Time* of 6 March 1972:

> DIED. Maria Goeppert Mayer, 65, only woman besides Madame Curie to win the Nobel Prize in physics; of a heart attack; in San Diego. A German-born scientist who emigrated to the U.S. in 1930, Mayer visualized the atomic nucleus as a series of onion-like layers of neutrons and protons. That insight was developed into the Jensen-Mayer 'shell theory' of the nucleus, for which she shared the Nobel Prize with fellow physicists Hans Jensen of Heidelberg and Eugene Wigner of Princeton.

Even more striking is the breakthrough in the conceptual world of nuclear physics which led to the atomic bomb, caused by Niels Bohr's description of the molecular nucleus as 'similar to a drop of water', which forms a 'waist' and then separates. Professor Frisch in an interview on the TV programme 'Horizon' of 29 October 1973 declared: 'If Bohr had not described it in this way, we [Lise Meitner and himself] could not have developed the idea of nuclear fission.'

It is probably useless to enquire why the human species should have this trait of requiring the personification, or at least the figuration, of abstracts. They can be understood, literally 'visualised', it seems, when they are likened to something else, to a solid fact we already know. Whatever may be the origin of the trait, it is impressed on the infant from his earliest life. It comes into the first verbal experiences. The infant is surrounded by various kinds of care: the necessary physical care of course, but also the humanising contact with the mother. A great deal of this communication is simply the diffuse expression of affection through sense impressions such as warmth, tactile pleasure, rhythm, and repetitive and musical sound and movement, such as rocking and carrying. But lullabies and 'swaddling songs' are not only necessary to preserve the life of infants, as Frederick II discovered in his infamous experiment,[7] but they have, besides the affective content, a didactic fictional content. Persons and situations, radiating outward from a recognisable baby-centric viewpoint *(Bye, Baby Bunting)* are invoked, and soon whole codes of conduct are impressed on the child by simple exemplary tales, songs, and proverbs, in which people, or animals functioning symbolically as people for the time, teach a lesson through a statement of desirable or undesirable conduct: ' "You *bad* little kittens, You've *lost* your mittens!" And they began to cry.'

To a greater extent than is generally realised, the lessons of socialisation—how should the baby behave? what should he believe?—are taught by presenting a series of fictional actions and their consequences. The inference, which may never have been formulated but is justified empirically by the universal use of the method, is that a fictional model is an effective guide to action, whether through imitation or avoidance.

The didactic function of the 'literature of initial socialisation' is a key to the values of the society which produces it: it is intended to influence behaviour to conform to the norms, and this tells us what the norms are. But there is also a general seepage of norms into the total fictional product of a society, whether or not the particular literary work is intended to be didactic or entertaining, a work of art or the outpouring of the innermost self of the writer. The Little Red Hen is certainly a prototype of the character traits and activities required by the Protestant ethic: self-reliant, hardworking, passionless—she maintains her good humour through all rebuffs—practical, using foresight to make reasonable predictions and act on them, and selfish; she is motivated solely by self-interest in appropriating entirely for her own use the entire product of her efforts (' "No, *I'll* eat it," said the Little Red Hen, and she did'); she must be a model of individualistic 'bourgeois' behaviour, just as surely as Robinson Crusoe, rightly hailed by Marx and others as the embodiment of these same characteristics. Crusoe, who has these traits to an extreme degree, plus a love of adventure and travel which he rationalises as the best way to get the greatest amount of the money for which all his sufferings are undergone, is a model whose form and character are determined by Defoe's saturation in bourgeois norms,

3

so that he must express them if he is to write at all. It would be
hard to say which of these tales, written consciously to amuse, but
unavoidably pointing a moral, is the more expressive of bourgeois
morality. Both are exemplary.

In tribal and peasant society, folk-wisdom, which is the practical
knowledge of desirable (= useful) behaviour and attitudes, appears
in tales, proverbs, sayings, and jokes. The message is quite likely
to be a cynical recipe for 'beating the system': a realistic appraisal,
looking up the stratification ladder from a peasant's-eye viewpoint,
of the state of the world and human relations, and advice on how to
deal with it. This counsel is not given in abstract terms. Even if
persons are not named as characters, social situations are conjured
up, as in the Spanish proverb: 'With the rich and mighty, always a
little patience.' Undoubtedly, a little patience is necessary: both for
survival (of the peasant speaker) *vis-à-vis* their wealth and power;
and also because their protected life makes them so obtuse that one
cannot expect quick understanding from them. Centuries of feudal
relationships are contained in this proverb: the tyranny of power,
and, in the ruled, the sense of their own moral superiority and
ability in manipulation, which makes it tolerable to people who are
actually powerless but who claim *pride* high on their list of social
values. In Germanic-speaking countries and in Yiddish, on the
other hand, similar advice is given more directly and more cynically:
'Cap-in-Hand goes through the Land' (*Hoot-im-Hand, geht durch
die ganzen Land*), meaning: 'Servile politeness is one way to get
around', referring to horizontal and (potential) upward mobility.
This general observation is presented in the person of an actual man
named *Cap-in-Hand* (who snatches off his hat at every contact with the
rich and mighty and because of this) *goes* (travels with the expendi-
ture of nothing but servility) *through the whole land* (personal
advancement seen as an actual journey through the countryside).
This echoes the real experience of countless poor and peasant people
of all time, who have had to leave home to better their fortunes, and
can only move upward by moving away. What makes this an
effective proverb is, first of all, the personification of a mode of
behaviour, which makes it easy to 'see'; second, the implicit
description of psycho-social power-relationships, appealing to the
experience of the 'consumers' of the proverb; and third, the fact
that it taps the social and historical experience of the class which
made it and consumes it: in other words it is true.

Personification is also much in use in other norm-imposing parts of the social network, such as the law. The law, in a way, also gives advice as to the best way to behave. At least it says what must, and more particularly what must *not* be done by certain persons ('The peasant shall not hang his own thief, but shall bring him bound to the Thing, with two witnesses' (*Den Aeldre Vestgötalag*, cit. Rosenberg, 1878–85, vol. II, p. 156).) Here the law specifically excludes self-made justice, in the early Christian period in Scandinavia when the crucial movement was being made towards establishing the impersonal punitive power of the State; the peasant is named as a member of a class in a class role. However, when the laws are devised to cover everybody and are thus more abstract, it is paradoxically necessary to resort to fictional personification to identify an individual who belongs to a large category. The law has a hypothetical but visualisable person in mind when it sets a standard, similar in type to that of Socrates, of what might be expected of a *reasonable and prudent man* or *l'homme moyen sensuel*. The reasonable-and-prudent one is he who acts according to the prevailing norms in the situation; it would thus seem logical to say so plainly, but this is impossible, as people find it easier to see an example than an abstraction, and so the fictional person is created to be the standard of behaviour.

In politics, a great deal has been said and written about the effect of the mass media on political life. Probably most people would agree that there are two ways in which politics is daily growing more falsified. One is the fictional presentation of politicians, and the other is the fictional presentation of events.

The media, and especially television, bring the image of politicians within the intimate visual range of the citizen and potential voter. Aristotle, discussing in the *Politics* the optimal size of cities for the best choice of leaders, said no polis ought to be so large that all voters cannot see one another face to face at one time. He felt this was a guarantee for the real character of politicians to be known, as indeed it was in a face-to-face, small-scale society contained within a series of primary groups: every clan and every individual could be placed and known by personal reputation at least. The television image of politicians attempts to recreate this personal knowledge, but of course it is a pseudo-image; the politician is not really known to the viewer, but presented and marketed in the form that his managers think the viewer wants to see. The public reacts to his looks, his apparent 'niceness' or charisma, and he himself remains really unknown. Considering the collective nature of decision-making in modern industrial society, it is doubtful, however, whether this makes much difference.

In a similar way, television falsifies events, not merely by selecting what to show, by creating pseudo-events by being present with camera crews to record them, and by lying about them, but more essentially by giving the public an illusory sense of participation, and even of decision-making, in events which they have really only been shown or told about.

And yet it is wrong to blame all this on the media as such. It is part of the general fictional content of politics, as practised literally from the dawn of history. The praise-singer, bard or skjald had the function of recording and praising the deeds of chieftains, and in this praise and its acceptance by the people lies the actuality of their reputation and consequently their power. Politicians of all time have been concerned to impose a fictional version of their deeds and character, to obtain the consent of the populace to their continued power. Machiavelli's advice to the Prince is concerned with the maintenance of this fictional *bella figura* in the grand style.

Charismatic leaders, who by definition have no institutional power, are able to influence social events through the real belief, which they inspire in their followers, that they personally embody the most desired values. Thus they have the potential of genuine power, and may eventually acquire it through their followers. It accounts for their very high rate of death by assassination: they attract very strong emotional affect in persons who know them not at all, but for whom they embody a social value which it is imagined may be removed by destroying the human personification of it.

Lastly, it is also necessary to remember that religion, the essence of those transcendental values which society claims to value most highly (or, according to Durkheim, the essence of society itself), presents these values consistently in the form of fiction. The content of all religions is *stories of the deeds of the Gods*. The rituals of religion are symbolic re-enactments of these deeds, in which the people are shown again and again: What happened when the world was new, how the God was born, his acts and miracles, how he was destroyed ('It is necessary for one man to die for the people') and how he rose again. From these stories the people are to partake of the experience of what is good, what is evil, what should be imitated and what

abhorred. All this instruction is to be inferred through the perception of a series of events, a narrative. We cannot be surprised to find
that the Greek drama is directly derived from religious ritual, the
Chorus remaining as a cultural vestige from the time when all the
people were participants in the rites.

In so far as the poets teach the people, 'whose teachers they are',
according to Vico, they teach them by fictional narrative. The
human race requires to be instructed in parables.

Notes

1 FICTION, ME (a F. ad L. fictionem, F. fingere; see FEIGN)
   1. The act or product of fashioning or imitating—1784.
   2. Feigning; deceit, dissimulation, pretence—1609.
   3. a. The action of feigning or inventing imaginary existences, events,
   states of things, etc. 1605. b. That which is feigned or invented;
   invention as opposed to fact ME. c. A statement proceeding from mere
   invention; such statements collectively—1611.
   4. Fictitious composition. Now usually prose novels and stories
   collectively, or the composition of such works—1599.
   5. A supposition known to be at variance with fact, but conventionally
   accepted: a. in *Law*, b. *gen.* (chiefly trans.) 1828.

   From *The Shorter Oxford Dictionary*, Oxford University Press, reprinted,
   with corrections, 1964.
2 But there is also a culturally variable language of bodily signals, brilliantly
described by Hall (1966).
3 There is extensive material on this point, some of the most interesting being
descriptions of cases of extreme deprivation through isolation. See, for instance, Malson (1972); also Gesell (1941); Davis (1940 and 1947); this
material is condensed in Chapter VIII of Davis (1966). Recent studies of
deprivation by poverty in ghetto children, while not so extreme, support
these findings, although some US researchers claim to find evidence of racial
inferiority in the same data.
4 The Institut for Dansk Kirkhistorie sent me a list of fourteen separate
translations.
5 This must be qualified by saying that the imposition of the language of the
conqueror seems to be most noticeably a feature of modern imperialism, or
the imposition of the rule of a more technologically advanced culture on a
more simple one. When more primitive and aggressive societies—warrior
clans such as the Achaeans, Tartars or Vikings—attacked rich and highly
developed, but militarily inferior societies, they tended to acquire the
culture, including the language, of the conquered.
6 '*Whether she recognises that her own position depends on their existence.*' This
question is important, according to Kettle, because it illustrates 'the in-
adequacies of Jane Austen's social philosophy' (p. 113). However, Austen is

writing a novel, not sitting an examination in correct social philosophy in which she may legitimately be given marks; it is absurd for the critic to feel as aggrieved as if he had hired her to write a pamphlet, and she had done it wrong.

7   His second folly was that he wanted to find out what kind of speech and what manner of speech children would have when they grew up, if they spoke to no one beforehand. So he bade foster mothers and nurses to suckle the children, to bathe and wash them, but in no way to prattle with them or speak to them, for he wanted to learn whether they would speak the Hebrew language, which was the oldest, or Greek, or Latin, or Arabic, or perhaps the language of their parents, of whom they had been born. But he laboured in vain, because the children all died. For they could not live without the petting and the joyful faces and loving words of their foster mothers. And so the songs are called 'swaddling songs' which a woman sings while she is rocking the cradle, to put a child to sleep, and without them a child sleeps badly, and has no rest.

Cited by Chinoy (1967, p. 72) from Ross and McLaughlin (1949, pp. 366–7).

Chapter 2

The transmission of norms in fiction

Introduction

The universal existence of censorship tells us that there is a common opinion among the rulers of humankind that literature has some effect on people besides providing them with entertainment. The enormous sums which many governments willingly spend on the mass media, particularly radio and television, from which they get no measurable advantage,[1] might tell us the same. Whether or not they are right in thinking so, those who are in power and might therefore be in a position to influence the content of the mass media, and 'serious' fiction or 'high literature' as well (if, that is, it is possible to influence the content of fiction; those, like Diana Spearman (1966), who think that fiction is the product of private fantasy ought either to deny the possibility or concede that the content of 'private fantasy' is socially determined), prove by the establishment of censorship that they think it is important to control what people read and see and hear. This can only be because they think that the 'consumption' of fiction is not merely a pastime which perhaps temporarily excites the emotions, but that it may have a lasting effect on the opinions and values of the population and consequently affect their social behaviour. They demonstrate, by the existence of censorship, that they believe that fiction is normative.

Heads are turned, it seems, by novels. By exposure to the simulated life of imaginary people, by reading of scenes which lie far outside his real experience, the reader may become 'depraved and corrupted'. Children may be turned against parents, citizens against the State, moral attitudes and behaviour may be so affected that there is a general decline in manners and morals: society may be in danger of being unmade. Or, on the other hand, literature may set good examples, it may 'show us noble deeds and brave feats . . . and point the distinction between good and evil to those who wish to understand it'.[2]

The effect which is here assumed certainly seems disproportionate to the cause—why should anyone's behaviour be changed by a story?—and those who wish to abolish censorship deny that literature has any such power. Numerous studies[3] of TV violence seem to show with varying degrees of inconclusiveness that exposure to scenes of violence on TV does not create new tendencies to violence in children who are not unstable or potentially violent already. Unfortunately one detects a certain circularity in this argument—those who are violent now have been by definition potentially violent previously.

In any case the measurability of such phenomena as the effect of the 'TV experience of violence' is very slight. Children who are much exposed—watching for many hours a day—also suffer from other factors such as poverty, parental neglect, bad schooling, bad housing, lack of positive contact with peers and adults, and many other negative factors, which are impossible to disentangle from the 'pure' effect of television. Also, modern industrial societies are so saturated now with TV that it is no longer possible to find a control group which has never been exposed. South Africa, which alone of all large states has declined until recently to have television as a matter of policy, might be cited as proof that violence can certainly flourish without it. The reason for not having it—fear of the normative effect of programmes originating in other countries if they did not produce all their own programmes—is an acknowledgment of the felt power of the mass media to influence behaviour. And the principles under which TV will be introduced early in 1975 are a faithful reflection of the social structure and ideology of that country. Senator J. P. van der Spuy, the Minister of National Education, announced in the Assembly in April 1971 that the Cabinet had approved the introduction of 'a statutorily controlled television service' for South Africa, which would form 'an integral part of the Republic's broad educational scheme' and which would be designed 'to ensure that the Christian values of South Africa and the social structure of its various communities were respected' (*South African Digest*, 7 May 1971).[4] Scandinavian state TV is administered by the Departments of Education of the various countries, but the Christian values of South Africa are to be served by the South African Broadcasting Corporation, functioning through a technical advisory committee, 'consisting of an equal number of representatives from each of the following: the S.A. Broadcasting Corporation, the Human Sciences Research Council, the S.A. Bureau of Standards, the Armaments Board, the Industrial Developments Corporation, and the Departments of Commerce, of Industries, and of National Education (ibid.); and the 'social structure of its various communities' (apartheid) are to be respected by means of an ingenious juggle with languages, faithfully recorded in the British press as SOUTH AFRICA TO HAVE SEGREGATED TELEVISION. Senator van der Spuy explained that TV, so expensive, so demanding of resources, would necessarily have to be introduced in phases, at first one channel only in English and Afrikaans, with completely equal treatment of these, the two official languages. 'In the light of experience gained and results obtained, *a decision will be taken* on *separate services* in English, Afrikaans and *the main Bantu languages*' (ibid.; my italics). Later, that is, or *sine die*, or never, a decision will be taken as to whether to risk TV for the majority population, as to whether the normative effect will be worth the expense, or whether the danger of outside influence, if Africans have TV, would be too great for the maintenance of the wicked and zany system of apartheid values.

But the special case of South Africa takes us only a short distance in speculation as to the effect of TV on violence. We know already that TV is not the *only* causative factor in the incidence of violence, since there was plenty of it in the normal course of social life in pre-industrial societies. It might be worth looking at other forms of literature belonging to those societies.

In any case, it is clear that there is no one-to-one relationship between exposure to scenes of violence on TV and the re-enactment of them in real life. It has been reckoned (Larsen, ed., 1968: Black, 1972, pp. 57–60) that the average American child sees 13,000 killings on TV by the age of fifteen, and yet the average American child does not commit 13,000 murders, or even one. But who is to say that he and she have not become 13,000 times more callous, more habituated to killing, and tolerant of violence in real life? The indifference or approval of the US public to such authentic and well-publicised killings as those at My Lai or Kent State University may be the result of such habituation.[5] There is no way to test this, as there is no way to repeat the historical fact of the conditioning.

What *is* demonstrable, though, is that there is a high positive correlation between the amount of violence tolerated (or required or desired) in the ordinary life of a society, and the amount tolerated or required or desired in literature. The USA, which has the highest rate of homicide and violent crime of all sorts, of any industrial country, has also, according to Rees in *Encounter* (April 1972) an 'incidence of television violence [which] has been shown to be double what is on our own [UK] screens'. Rather more than double, if you ask me, although the image of tolerated (official) violence on British TV is increasing, a point which will be discussed later in this chapter. But in 'Z-Cars' on 15 August 1972 a policeman named Skinner said of a particularly nasty villain: 'I'd like to needle him— with a 25-pound needle', to which a sergeant replied: 'Careful, the public is listening . . .' with a glance towards the camera. This game of normative influence is not played sleeping, and it is certainly ambivalent.

In the USA, light entertaining fiction has always been very apt to deal in violent action, reflecting a violent society. Sam Clemens saw four separate killings in public in Hannibal, Missouri before he was ten years old, and grew up to write boys' adventure stories such as *Tom Sawyer* and *Huckleberry Finn* with a fairly large portion of corpses, murders, lynchings, and a regular blood-bath of a feud in which Huck's friends and protectors are ridden down and shot. Twain, however, does not present this as desirable action, he shows it as sickening slaughter; and Huck's comment on another occasion is 'Human beings can be awful cruel to each other.' Robert Louis Stevenson, on the other hand, defended himself against Henry James's criticism of the brutalising effect of the killings in *Treasure Island* by claiming that this literary violence was natural to children: 'Was there ever a child which did not imbrue its little hands in gore —except Master James, of course?' Certainly the English, as Orwell pointed out in 'The decline of the English murder' (1940), despite their gentle manners and low homicide rate, delight in murder mysteries, and produce the best ones, which typically treat murder as exceptional—the outbreak of murder in the quiet village, the unknown corpse in the library. American thrillers are more apt to present a violent milieu, where killing is normal—the old dime novels, dealing with the Wild West, bandits, Indian raids; gangster thrillers; the sex-and-violence classics of the thirties by Chandler, Cain, and modern film escalations of these: *Straw Dogs, A Clock-*

work Orange, The French Connection, Dirty Harry, The New Centurions. Julian Symons in his important recent book, *Bloody Murder*, cites Howard and Haycraft (*Murder for Pleasure*, 1941), who say that 25 per cent of all fiction sold in the United States in 1940 was crime and detection thrillers (1972, p. 13). Much earlier, D. H. Lawrence in *Studies in Classic American Literature* (1958 edn), where he discusses the frontier novels of James Fenimore Cooper, remarked that Cooper established in literature the typical American man—*the man with a gun* (instead of a penis), and with an intense relationship to another man of a different race.[6] A notion developed at some length by Leslie Fiedler in *Love and Death in the American Novel* (1966).[7]

By comparison, popular fiction in Denmark at the present time, even the crime-thrillers, has not the same preoccupation with violence. The same cannot be said, however, of the sagas, the literary product of the Viking era. The Viking society of pre-feudal Scandinavia was a clan-based warrior culture in which the basic condition of stability and justice was the readiness of the armed men of the clan, its personnel and defence, to engage in the blood feud. Loyalty to the clan was the basic virtue, honour (reputation) the basic value. Security was maintained, status and wealth achieved, inheritances and lawsuits settled, by the violent deeds of competing warriors, who had to be eager to take the very real risks of such a life if stability and justice were to be maintained. The sagas accordingly present the savage pleasure of fighting with double-headed axes as infinitely desirable, and also show how the men are goaded into action by wives, mothers and sisters, if the attraction of gaining reputation by fighting is not enough. A mother says to her sons, who are slow to avenge their brother, on an occasion when they complain that the meat she serves is not cut fine enough: 'Your brother was cut into pieces even larger than these, and yet you did not complain' (see p. 167) and this is enough to send them raging out. Gluckman's statement (1965, p. 22) that 'we must not take sagas and tales of feuding as evidence' that violent conflicts really occurred, 'for they may, like the Nuer "man of the earth's curse" stand as warnings', seems to me simply absurd.[8] There is plenty of historical and archaeological evidence as to the violent nature of Viking society, and the sagas are a body of literature which closely corresponds to this picture. Far from being warnings against violence, they are exemplary tales showing the greatness and virtue in acts of the most extreme aggression, which are inevitably seen as acts of heroism and the most honourable way for a man to behave.

There are, however, some good arguments against the real existence of a normative effect of fiction. The most convincing seem to me to be those which depend on the concept of 'selective perception'. It does seem to be true that the individual consumer of fiction, not excluding TV fiction, screens out and thus does not perceive whatever is presented to him which is outside his limits of tolerance. He thus avoids a potentially painful conflict with his own values. In the expressive English working-class phrase, 'he doesn't want to know'.

And yet, by what instant subliminal process is this accomplished? It is easy enough to switch off consciously a political talk by an opposing party, but in the case of fictional narrative or broadcast of news events an extraordinarily delicate and complex adjustment of perception of the content of what actually appears on the screen occurs, so that only a compatible portion of it is *experienced as seen*.

Apparently a censorious part of the psyche—the super-ego?— in a space of time which is minimal, nearly nil, scans what is shown and instantly selects and rejects, recording what is acceptable on the basis of the total life-conditioning of the viewer, and discarding what is unacceptable. All this happens with a continuous flow of images before the viewer sees what he consciously does see. John Whale (1969) has some interesting material on this process in cases of political bias. Viewers who saw live on TV the 'Police Riot' (so described by the Presidential Committee appointed to investigate it) at the Democratic Convention in Chicago in 1968 saw on their TV screens the savage attacks by police against student and other anti-war demonstrators, as ordered by Mayor Daley. Nevertheless (ibid., p. 105):

> the Federal Communications Commission asked the networks to reply to the 'hundreds of complaints' which the Commission had received about the unfairness of television reports from Chicago. Opinion polls showed the same thing. Great numbers of people found it possible to exonerate Mr Daley simply by disbelieving what they had seen.

Here the image was received, but discredited because of previously-held concepts about the police and Mayor Daley. Whale comments later about this particular consolidation of the value-system (ibid., p. 158):

> Rather than believe that they lived in a repressive society, great numbers of Americans at all levels of education were convinced that television pictures of police action in Chicago in August 1968 had been so selective as to be simply untruthful.

TV, then, does not have absolute powers of persuasion on a population which is a totally passive recipient of whatever appears on it, and thus infinitely malleable. Evidence is not evidence, much less proof, unless it is consonant with what is already believed—the 'domain assumptions' discussed by Alvin Gouldner in *The Coming Crisis of Western Sociology* (1971).[9] This does tend to show that the early critics of TV, like the eighteenth-century critics of the dangerous normative effects of the novel, were somewhat needlessly alarmed.

There are limits to the absolute normative powers of the mass media and because of this it has been claimed by Denis McQuail, in *Toward a Sociology of Mass Communications* (1969, pp. 42–3, 71–5, 77, 86–7, 90–1), among many others, notably spokesmen for the media but also a number of independent researchers, that the effect of such communications can never be innovating, only reinforcing. The mass media, according to this hypothesis, exist 'for the use and gratification of the consumer', who determines by selective perception what he actually sees, and chooses what he prefers to see. Ultimately, by preferential choice, he influences what programmes are actually shown. If the media cannot introduce unacceptable ideas, such as the legitimation of the use of violence, because people will reject it as morally repugnant, there can be no danger from this source.

This argument, however, assumes that there is in existence an absolute moral standard, incapable of modification by social influence; and it is thus in contradiction to all sociological thinking, which assumes that 'moral *is* social'. It also neglects the Freudian psychological truism which posits an unknown quantity of latent destructive impulses—held in check by socially developed inhibitions which continued exposure to the fictional presentation of violence as the normal solution to problems may destroy. The argument is somewhat like that which says that no one can ever be harmed by experiments in hypnotism, because no person will do anything under hypnosis which he really does not want to do.

According to this idea, if a hypnotised woman is told she is holding a loaded pistol, and is ordered to shoot her husband with it, she will come into a conflict between command and desire which will break the hypnotic spell. However, of X number of women with whom this game is played, an unknown number, N, will really 'point the gun' and 'pull the trigger'—a circumstance which makes this a most unsuitable party game. Selective perception may cause us to reject the evil we do not really want, but what of the evil we really do want?

The expectation of some such effect is the rational basis for the existence of censorship, and there seems no reason to suppose that those who impose censorship are not conscious of feeling this expectation. Since all authorities everywhere have a natural vested interest in preserving the allegiance of the population to the general body of postulates and customs which is the necessary condition of their own continued enjoyment of the legitimate exercise of power, they have reason enough to make some effort to control literature, and they do.

The most simple and direct of these efforts is of course simple censorship, which attempts to filter out, by forbidding its publication, whatever may cause disruption. We have seen in the previous chapter how the 1850 Decree of the Russian Governor-General of Finland specifically forbade the *publication of fiction in the Finnish language*, as anyone who read fiction in Finnish was uneducated (belonged to the lowest stratum of society), and fiction was apt to unsettle them. But undoubtedly the more effective control, and one which has historical precedence, is indirect influence by social pressure and the tacit encouragement of social reward.

Whoever creates fiction which is seen or expected to have a socially desirable effect—that is, supportive of the favoured values, is rewarded by the gift of those prizes which are available in that society. In 'heroic' (tribal, warrior) societies, these will be honour, prestige, the right to receive hospitality— 'Who', says Homer, 'would invite a stranger, unless perhaps a godlike poet. . . ?'—the protection of the great, and a limited amount of wealth in the form of gifts. What might be called negative prizes, not less valuable, are also to be obtained: Odysseus, when he came home and slaughtered his wife's suitors, also hanged the maid-servants who had been compelled to lie with them. However, he spared, for the sake of having his deeds recorded, the godlike poet who had been constrained to enliven their feasts. A similar restraint was shown towards Egil the Poet, when he fell into the hands of his enemy, Erik Blood-Axe, who happened to be King at York at the time. Although Egil had killed many of Erik's kinsmen, including one of his sons, his life was spared when he composed a twenty-seven-verse *drapa* in Erik's praise, and received the poet's reward, his own wolf-grey head. When this was promised him, he immediately made a little verse in thanks:[10]

> I am not sorry,
> King, to receive
> The hideous gift
> Which is my head.
> No one went forth
> With a better gift
> From the great-minded
> Son of a lord.

In our own time and culture, the reward may be more prosaically described in one word: money. Money is the natural common denominator of value in the bourgeois world, and it carries with it privilege and honour: the status of having created something for which a lot of money has been paid. Virginia Woolf in her essay 'The niece of an Earl' (1966) remarks that 'literary success invariably means a rise, never a fall . . . in the social scale'. The later novels of a successful writer depict ever higher levels of society, because he is invited and moves into their world. 'The rising novelist is never pestered to come to gin and winkles with the plumber and his wife.' The effect of prosperity and fame is never a sinking down through the social strata—on the contrary, the writer of acceptable and popular fiction is wafted up the social ladder,[11] and, besides acquiring the money which makes it possible to lead a more varied and attractive life, has access to a professional, sophisticated, international and pleasure-orientated social group which multiplies many times the value of the money itself in adding enjoyment to life. There are also such vanity-traps as the chance of appearing on the mass media as an expert of some sort, thus enjoying an additional sense of power and influence. 'Society', then, not conspiratorially or directly or officially, as with censorship, but casually and indirectly, without conscious planning, but through the operation of the market and a related series of causes and effects, reacts in a practical way to *fiction* as to a social force, and by the granting or withholding of very attractive rewards to its practitioners, has some success in channelising and controlling their product.

The 'socialising' (i.e. taming) effect of societal rewards also on writers of protest literature has often been noted. By income, and consequently by association, they become members of the ruling Establishment. Quite often they were born there[12] and their protests are the mere expression of annoyance at being excluded for lack of money. Fictional characters, as well as authors, are often floated back in, like the hero of *Hurry On Down*, by John Wain (1954). The Angry Young Men of the 1950s have not, on the whole, earned as much as Barbara Cartland, but they have earned quite enough to support the life-style and stances of insider élites. This of course is nothing new: Thackeray, for instance, a moderately severe castigator of the aristocracy in his youth, found that he liked dukes very well when he had become, as Charlotte Brontë said, 'the pet and darling of high society'. In a society open and flexible enough to allow and even generously reward protest and scathing criticism, protest and scathing criticism are rather easily de-fused and absorbed. Theatres of protest, such as the Berliner Ensemble and the Royal Court Theatre in London, find their respectful audience in the class they so furiously attack, and quite often become financially successful. American Negro novelists are a special case in point. A new wave of Negro intellectuals appeared in the post-First World War years of the Depression in the USA, and, as Robert Bone says in *The Negro Novel in America* (1958, p. 165):

> During the thirties the Communist party provided a broad arena of interracial contact for the Negro intellectual. But no sooner did he break out of his closed racial world into this new political milieu than he was directed . . . to 'rediscover' his Negro roots. As a writer he was expected to contribute to 'the Negro people's struggle for national liberation', that is, to write protest novels.

Bone goes on to say that the support of the war effort by the Communist Party militated against the protest novel, and he says on previous pages (163–4) that after the war increasing affluence, the 'G.I. Bill of Rights' which brought college and graduate education within reach of all ex-soldiers, and in some cases 'foundation grants, which in themselves reflect a new willingness to recognise and encourage Negro accomplishment in the arts', intensified this effect. He names a few recipients of grants (ibid., p. 164n):

> Ralph Ellison, Willard Motley, and Owen Dodson were Rosenwald Fellows; Ann Petry held a Houghton Mifflin Literary Fellowship; J. Saunders Redding held both a Guggenheim Fellowship and a Rockefeller Foundation Grant; and Willard Motley received a grant from the Newberry Library Fund.

Bone concludes that because of these factors (ibid., p. 165. My italics),

> In so far as the party's hold over an important group of Negro novelists has been broken, these novelists *have been free to join the revolt against protest* which has gathered momentum during the post-war years.

This last statement certainly seems very peculiar today. It is explainable, however, by the fact that this book was published by the Yale University Press in 1958; so closely does fashion in social theory follow the social situation.

Certainly, however, ways are opened to protesters which absorb them into the system. A cynic might even believe that the quickest way to the top is up the outside, shaking fists and shouting slogans, and then climbing comfortably in through a twenty-second-floor window, while the conformists are patiently slogging up the regular route indoors. This method is only for those with a good head for heights.

The above strictures do not, of course, apply to all writers of protest or revolutionary literature. Michael Gold, for instance, whose brilliant *Jews Without Money* (1930) made him famous, never cashed in on the opportunities which then became available. He spent his life in patient hackwork on the *Daily Worker*, the Communist newspaper, and never wrote another good book. Unlike writers such as Steinbeck and Dos Passos, he never compromised his revolutionary position, and never joined the Establishment.

For there is at any time in existence a large body of tendentious fiction, the literature of protest, of exposé and social change. It would be a mistake to suppose that it is only the rulers of society who assume that fiction is a normative influence. At least two experts

4

on revolution think so too. Thus Mao Tse-tung, in *Talks at the Yenan Forum on Literature and Art* (1942), gives it even an exaggerated importance: 'If we had no literature and art, even in the broadest and most ordinary sense, we could not carry on the revolutionary movement and win victory.' I think, but I may be wrong, that he here refers not only to the propaganda influence of art, but to its social function as a delineator of human values and aspirations. Previously Lenin had stated, in much more pragmatic and functional terms, that 'Proletarian literature and art are cogs and wheels in the whole revolutionary machine.'

The assumption here is that the fate of imaginary people, when *made known*, that is, when social interaction is *related as fictional narrative*, will have the power to mobilise public opinion, change the accepted values and norms, and force a change in social relations themselves. One outstanding success of this method is the passage of the Pure Food laws in the USA (1907), directly attributable to the effect of public opinion on the profits of the meat industry (sales plummeted) due to the exposé of packing methods and hygiene in *The Jungle* (1906) by Upton Sinclair. This was not exactly what Sinclair had in mind: he aimed to improve, by exposing how bad they were, the wretched social and industrial condition of immigrant workers in the industry; the public, however, were concerned with what directly affected them as consumers: the filthy and dangerous meat. Sinclair is said to have remarked, 'I aimed at America's heart and hit its stomach.' Other well-known examples of the direct effect of propaganda in the form of fiction are Chinese operas such as *The White-haired Girl*, and the change in public consciousness from indifference to indignation at the treatment of children in England, due to the influence of the novels of Dickens. Here again, however, selective perception is at work: Dickens was effective because he was popular, and he was popular not only because of his skill and vitality, but because what he had to say was acceptable: the brutality of the eighteenth century was giving way to the rudimentary social conscience of the nineteenth, also expressed in the work of Parliamentary Committees of Enquiry on poverty, child labour, prison reform, and the like.

It appears that the Tsarist bureaucracy, admittedly one of the most incompetent in recent history, while alert to the subversive potential of fiction, was unaware that it was also potentially supportive of the social status quo, and could be encouraged by the judicious application of positive sanctions to increase quietism through 'use and gratification'.

At the same time, while in more open societies rewards have certainly an effect on the content of what writers produce, I think it probable that a far more pervasive influence is exerted by the general amorphous but discernible power of public opinion. Even official censorship itself, in viable societies, is responsive to this 'public sense of morality', as the law is also. This can be seen in the fact that legal judgments in prosecutions for publishing pornography are given on the basis of what is accepted as tolerable in the society *at the time*, and legal codes in this area, such as the Television Code (1964) and the new Code of 1971, are purposely left unspecific as to the exact content of what is permissible. In the TV Code (1964), the VT Authority must satisfy itself (Section 3 (i) (a)):

> that nothing is included in the programmes which offends against good taste or decency or is likely to incite to crime or lead to disorder or be offensive to public feeling.

That formulation gives no description of the sort of thing which *would* offend public feeling: this must be tested at the time by public reaction.

In this the laws of censorship are no different from other laws: all of them are subject to change because of formal or informal public reaction to them. Laws are notoriously repealed by being broken: the Volstead (Prohibition) Act in the USA, the ban on marches and processions in Northern Ireland in 1971–2. If the public consistently and flagrantly refuses to obey them, they cannot be enforced. Similarly, when the public sense of justice turns against the prescribed penalties, it may be impossible to convict for the crime, as in the case of the death penalty for offences such as petty theft, which have come to seem minor. In this case the penalties must be modified, or there is in effect no law against such petty crimes. The fact that in 1971, no death sentence had been executed in the USA for four-and-a-half years makes it arguable that public sentiment had turned against the death penalty as such, to an extent which the Supreme Court might recognise by a Constitutional amendment.

The public sense of justice has thus a definite and measurable effect on the formal structure of the societal norms as expressed formally in laws. It is nevertheless 'fluid', ever-changing at various rates of speed, and the process and direction of change are to a great extent unknown and unpredictable. I would suggest that one factor in this process is the normative effect of fiction on people's vision of society and selection of values.

The limits of tolerance are constantly changing, and the change may of course be in either direction. Thus Jane Austen has one of her girl heroines, c. 1810, dip into the eighteenth-century *Spectator*, and 'she wondered at the taste of the age which could endure it'. Dickens, rather later in the nineteenth century, in the true Victorian age, speaking in his autobiography of his childhood love of books, says, 'I have been Tom Jones for a week together—a child's Tom Jones, a harmless creature.' By which he presumably means a sexless Tom Jones. Ian Watt rather biblically calls Tom Jones 'a fornicator' (1957, p. 11), but most modern scholars have no serious criticism of Mr Jones's conduct, unless it might be in the matter of his taking money from Lady Bellaston for sexual services, almost the only point which is seriously discussed.

There was no law which prevented Dickens and Austen, two authors of outstanding originality, great personal confidence, and independent judgment, from reading as much bawdy eighteenth-century literature as they chose. Yet they seem to feel the need to apologise, in a sort of disclaimer addressed to their public. In this I think they acknowledge the dictates of the moral climate of the age in which they write. This 'taste of the age', of which writers are at least as conscious as other people, has doubtless great influence in shaping what seems to be their private fantasy, as it appears to themselves, prior to the intentional shaping of it into a vision which may be presented to the public.

In all that has been said so far, while we see that there is general agreement that literature has a normative effect on society, as shown by the existence of such opposing institutions as censorship and protest literature, most of the evidence has been that of the contra-phenomenon, the effect of society on literature. This is of the highest importance, as by reading backward from fiction we are able to perceive the outlines of the society which produced it. However, our present purpose is different. We are trying to discover—if we can—why and how, by what actual means, fiction can so influence its consumers as to provoke the whole system of sanctions, both negative and positive, in an effort to control it.

What makes mere flimsy stories so powerful that books should be burned 'by the public hangman' or infuriated crowds?

How is it possible that the unreal world of fictional narrative should effectively intrude into the real, material, matter-of-fact world of ordinary life? Surely it is very strange that imaginary creatures, known moreover to be imaginary, should have any influence at all on the actions and relationships of real people?

Participation

Reading fiction includes a psychological sense of participation. The reader has an induced awareness of undergoing the experience he reads about—he feels that he is, for the time, living in the story; while at the same time (unless he is Don Quixote) knowing very well that he is not, and that the story is not *really* real. This is partly because he merges his personality in that of the protagonist who attracts him—he *is* 'Tom Jones for a week together' (or Emma or Long John Silver)—and partly because, as Cyril Connolly (1945, p. 60) says, 'Great writers create worlds which we are proud to inhabit.' The art of writing narrative fiction includes coaxing the reader into the story; it is not only a matter of 'making the characters live', but of persuading the reader that he is living with them—of making him proud to inhabit their world.

The pleasure of this participation, tantamount to living extra temporary lives, is surely one of the most intense to be got from literature. As to why it should be possible, one can only speculate. Ernst Fischer, in *The Necessity of Art*, puts it very plainly (1963, pp. 7–8):

> As a first step we must realize that we are inclined to take an astonishing phenomenon too much for granted. And it is certainly astonishing: countless millions read books, listen to music, watch the theatre, go to the cinema. Why? To say that they seek distraction, relaxation, entertainment, is to beg the question. Why is it distracting, relaxing, entertaining, to sink oneself in someone else's life and problems, to identify oneself with a painting or a piece of music or with the characters in a novel, play or film? Why do we respond to such 'unreality' as though it were reality intensified? . . . And if one answers that we want to escape from an unsatisfactory existence into a richer one, into experience without risk, then the next question arises: why is our own existence not enough? Why this desire to fulfil our unfulfilled lives through other figures, other forms,

to gaze from the darkness . . . at a lighted stage where something that is only play can so utterly absorb us?'

Fischer answers himself that 'man wants to be more than just himself. He wants to be a *whole* man. He is not satisfied with being a separate individual . . . he longs . . . to unite his limited "I" in art with a communal existence. . . .'

This I think is substantially correct. The individualistic nature of modern industrial society makes unwilling isolates of many millions of people who are not natural loners, and art and literature are one means of 'participating' in communal existence. That art and literature *are* communal, and give this sense of participation, I think is due to their origin as part of the necessary functional ritual of religion and justice in the small-scale societies which framed the life of the human race for most of the time the species has existed. For those small groups—clans, tribes, and villages—social solidarity was an evident necessity. If the people as a group were to survive, the group must come first, before personal aggrandisement or the survival of individuals. There are two ways to do this: sharing and elimination. There is nothing mutually exclusive about these policies; a viable society living on the borderline of subsistence will need to use both. Means of economic existence, especially food, will be shared; but in time of famine, non-producers of food, the old and the young, will be sacrificed. In good times, the product of successful hunting will be shared among the whole village, although it may be a catch of one hunter alone, and he may be consistently the most skilful and successful. His skill, however, must not make his family rich at the cost of hunger for others: all must survive, and so the meat is shared. Sharing is not a spontaneous act, but highly institutionalised; among the Eskimo, where starvation was a real danger, each family in a village had a traditional right to a certain part of the animal.

Peter Freuchen lived and traded among the Thule or Polar Eskimoes for more than fifty years.[13] He married a Thule woman, Navarana, who gave him much insight into the system of compulsory generosity; for example she inflicted a crushing punishment on a stingy hunter by loading his wife with presents, eventually forcing the couple to leave the settlement. Navarana also told Freuchen much about the principles of sharing and the sanctions of honour and shame which enforced these principles. Freuchen

THE TRANSMISSION OF NORMS IN FICTION 45

himself, as a hunter, participated in the claiming and sharing of meat and fur. For the hunter to share is both obligatory and honourable, his chief reward being high status for his skill, including his luck, and this high status is greatly valued.

These groups must not only eat, but maintain a certain social stability, and for this it was, and is, necessary to have other rules as well. Aggression to be directed only outward ('Let War be with the stranger, and at the stranger's gate')[14] and strictly limited within the group: no cannibalism, no incest, no shedding of kindred blood. In social units which were primary groups, with all members living in life-long continuous contact, there was on the one hand every opportunity for acts of violence, greed, and lust, and on the other hand every chance for the personally powerful to get away with it—with disastrous effect on survival of the group—unless they were deterred by some force so powerful as to be in fact irresistible. The State did not exist (and in any case has never been able to maintain such irresistible force), but the necessary sanctions did in fact evolve in the form of taboos, whose terrifying deterrent effect depended on the fact that their operation was as certain and as swift as the action of laws of nature. The criminal was automatically destroyed, regardless of his intent, his conscious guilt, or even his knowledge of the crime (as with Oedipus). This primitive norm of justice is expressed in the *Agamemnon* of Aeschylus: 'So long as Zeus holds sway, *the doer suffers.*'

Since the laws of taboo are not in fact laws of nature in the same way as the law of gravity (anyone who walks off the roof will fall, regardless of intent or knowledge of the condition—where the edge is, for instance—the act is enough: *the doer suffers*), it was necessary for them to be enforced by social means.

The most important of these, perhaps, is the one often noted: the internal effect on the criminal of the knowledge that he has broken taboo. The conscience with which his society has imprinted him destroys him from within—as often noted to this day by anthropologists—just as Orestes was instantly aware of the Furies hunting him down when he had killed his mother, though no one else could see them.

But failing this, or perhaps with his consent because he knows he is guilty, 'society', that is all its other members, turns on him and drives him out or destroys him, thus removing his dangerous presence from the group.

In this act of justice, all members participate. A good example of this is seen in Chinua Achebe's African novel, *Things Fall Apart* (1958), in which the protagonist, Okwonko, having killed a youth by accident, has polluted the village to such an extent that he and his family are driven into exile before the next dawn, and must return to his mother's village for seven years. Okwonko's dangerous uncleanness is not purely accidental, however, it is over-determined, as Freud would define it. He had previously killed a boy wilfully—'a child', moreover, 'who called him father', an act which verged on shedding kindred blood; he had also beaten his wife during the Week of Peace ('an act so offensive to the Earth Mother that whole villages have been destroyed for less')—and was thus plainly revealed as a social menace who must be removed.

In this act of justice, primitive society requires the participation of all members: Okwonko's friend comes to warn him: but he also helps to tear down and destroy his huts, so that no trace of him remains in the village.

As we see, personal affection does not permit exclusion of individuals from participation in the execution of justice, and no normal person would really want to be excluded. Exclusion, temporary or permanent, means social death. These are societies in which all economic, religious, and legal actions are part of the common life. Every value, protection, object and area belongs to the group. Everything outside is alien and dangerous, every outside person a potential enemy. These societies require participation for cohesion, they cannot tolerate bystanders, outsiders, or dissenters. The hatred and fear of witches, felt to this day by the type of close-knit community which believes in them, is due no doubt to the secret and solitary nature of their activities: they are permanent crypto-outsiders.[15]

Necessary social cohesion in this type of society is ultimately derived from ownership and work in common, and the sharing of defence against other such groups, but it is certainly reinforced and institutionalised by ritual. In economic life these are the rites of fertility, harvest festivals of thanks, dances and pictorial art to produce luck in hunting and so on. The rites of religion, with their communal participation; and the social drama of the enforcement of the law.

It is a commonplace that the Athenian drama developed from the rites of religion.[16] These rites, of course, are a socio-religious ritual:

part 'history'—the deeds of the god, his life, acts, miracles and death—this is narrative; and part communion: the participation of all in the rehearsal (in the sense of repetition) of these events, which binds the people together in the communion of having 'experienced' them in the ritual of acting them out.

Dr Johnson, in *A Journey to the Western Islands of Scotland* (1930 edn, p. 58), says of illiterate tribal societies:

> In nations, where there is hardly the use of letters, what is once out of sight is lost for ever. . . . Their only registers are stated observances and practical representations. For this reason an age of ignorance is an age of ceremony. Pageants, and processions, and commemorations, gradually shrink away, as better methods come into use of recording events, and preserving rights.

An interesting modern example of the conscious use of this method to develop communality of feeling, establish history, and create a work of art, is given by George A. Huaco in his discussion of the filming of Eisenstein's *October* (1965, pp. 117–18; my italics):

> Strictly speaking, *October* did not have a plot—it simply retold the legendary exploits by which 'the people' had defeated their evil enemies and moved to establish the earthly paradise. The religious undertone was not accidental. The capture of the Winter Palace was filmed at night in Leningrad with the participation of thousands from among the population. But in a sense, these thousands were not non-professional actors; they had had several years of training in these particular theatrical roles. Behind Eisenstein's *October* lay the so-called political mystery plays, *mass spectacles in which the sacred events of the new faith were re-enacted by the population at large.*

Huaco quotes his source (Huntley Carter, 1924), as follows (ibid.):

> Mass performances on a heroic and gigantic scale have been given from time to time since 1918; in which outstanding directors, decorators, actors and half the population of certain districts have taken part. In each of these performances many thousands of people have participated. For instance, in a 'mystery' played before the Bourse, 80,000 persons took part. . . . A characteristic example appears in the 'Storming of the

Winter Palace'. . . . At the start, 1,500 people were the actors
. . . pupils of the theatre schools, members of the Club for
Proletarian Culture, of the Theatre Societies, of the Red Army,
and the Baltic Fleet. But at the conclusion more than 100,000
people were participating, pouring out from the tribunes and
from the houses. The spectacle began at ten at night.

It seems unnecessary to call these secular historical re-enactments
'mysteries' or 'religious', unless we are speaking in Durkheimian
terms of religion as the essence of society. But certainly they were
an effort to develop communal historical consciousness by mass
participation in a ritual repetition of historical events, and are thus
similar to the communion of the Mass.
While religious ritual is essentially 'historical narrative' (the
deeds of the gods), what has perhaps not been sufficiently noted
before is that the Greek drama, by which we mean the classical
Athenian drama of the fifth century B.C., derived from religious
ritual though it may be, is essentially the ritual presentation of
crime and punishment, and more specifically, of the destruction of
the criminal who breaks taboo—'the doer suffers'. As Svend Ranulf
pointed out in his massive and brilliant study of Greek drama, *The
Jealousy of the Gods and Criminal Law at Athens* (1936) (now in-
explicably out of print in both Danish and English) the persistent
theme is the destruction of people who may have sinned unknowingly, at the direct instigation of the gods, or who may be even
completely innocent and whose whole clan, moreover, is innocent.
In many cases, their downfall seems extremely unjust from a
modern viewpoint, as modern ideas of guilt include elements of
intent, malice, and knowledge. However, these dramas were evidently regarded as exemplary tales, and satisfied the public conscience of the people of Athens. It is worth noting, however, that
the period of the classical drama is the same as the period of the
conflict of norms in real life embodied in the Laws of Solon, in
which a great and conscious effort was made to replace the authority
of the tribes who inhabited the Athenian state with the authority of
the city. This will be discussed further in chapter 5.
For our purpose, however, it is sufficient to note that St John
was not the first to say that 'It is necessary for one man to die for
the people.' This is a persistent element in the religious rites of
small-scale hunting, and particularly agricultural societies, echoing

right down to the corn-dollies, last sheaves, and Green Men of nineteenth-century Europe, including England. It was unlucky to bear in the last sheaf, and for good reason: for hundreds of years that person had been torn to pieces to ensure the fertility of the fields for next year. For a utilitarian purpose, a chosen one was sacrificed. There are literally thousands, or better say, innumerable variations on this theme, whether a nineteenth-century Danish peasant, as Evald Tang Kristensen tells us (1936, p. 341), buried a live calf under the barn door as a precaution against contagious abortion in the herd, or whether the King, as we are told in *The Elder Edda* (ninth century) is slaughtered to end a famine:

> It happened in old days that swordsmen made red the earth with blood of their own lord, when the Swedes in hope of a good year turned bloody weapons on Domaldi, hater of the Jutes.

This is from the *Ynglingatàl*, and the comment by Snorri Sturlason, who recorded it in the thirteenth century, was:

> Famine ruled the land after three years of bad crops, and when all other means of averting disaster failed, the Swedes sacrificed their King and killed him.

(The ruler of an area was responsible for the weather in it.)

In general, in these societies, disaster was seen as the result of evil-doing, and the miscreant must be found and punished for the sake of the continuance of the society. The group must cleanse itself of the evil influence by separating the villain from itself: he must be driven out, rejected, destroyed: for the survival of the people, one member must die.

Durkheim's sophisticated argument—(1969)—that not only the punishment of crime, but crime itself, is necessary for social cohesion, is apposite here. 'We do not punish it because it is a crime,' is what he implies, 'but it is a crime because we punish it.' By punishing it, society declares what is a crime, that is, defines the boundaries of permissible behaviour; and also by punishing it, and particularly by social participation in the punishment, social indignation is mobilised in defence of the norms.

There is a sense in which the two concepts, religious sacrifice and punishment, coincide. In the institution of the scapegoat, the animal or person who is guiltless (indeed if he is the God or the Son of God he cannot sin), is loaded with the crimes of the whole community and then destroyed. He is the innocent and perhaps willing sacrifice for the common good. In a climax of communal participation in mounting social tension and hysteria, he disappears into death or exile, taking all evil with him. Cleansed and relaxed, the survivors will then proceed with normal life until the next crisis or ritual occasion, when the same remedy will prove equally effective.

Social and psychological need to participate in these dramas of punishment must have been very great. It is easy enough, from the point of view of individualistic, self-aggrandising modern norms, to see the plain advantage attached to belonging to the majority which kills, rather than being the victim. This is the theme of Shirley Jackson's horrific story, 'The Lottery' (1948), which transposes the custom to modern suburban Connecticut—no one wants to be the chosen one. But I see no reason to suppose that the role of willing scapegoat and victim, or criminal transgressor, was (is?) not also passionately desired. Why should not those religions, as well as another, have martyrs? Archaeological evidence from bog-burials, found right across the north of Europe and dating from the Bronze Age, raises the point. An example is the noble and beatific face of the Bronze Age corpse known as the Tolland Man, taken from a Danish bog after two thousand years with the cord which strangled him still around his neck. Was he, and others like him, a punished criminal or a willing sacrificial victim, or both at once (Glob, 1969)?

In literature, classical tragedy is essentially devoted to the theme of the heroic individual who, by excess of virtue, becomes a breaker of norms and thus a criminal. Tragedy is by definition the destruction of a person of extraordinary merit through the excess of this, which leads to *hubris*, a pride which is an encroachment on the Gods. Their jealousy is aroused, and they strike down the guilty one. The heroes of sagas are in somewhat similar dilemmas, caught between conflicts of obligations. Heroic society requires the hero to excel, but not to excel to excess.

Since the roles overlap, the criminal also is seen as a hero. Furthermore, the criminal is evidently as necessary as the concept of crime and its punishment, for the maintenance of equilibrium in society. Although of course one can really only speculate as to the status and motivation of Bronze Age victims, there is no doubt that in more modern times the criminal-as-hero has had great powers of attraction, including sexual glamour. The cult of the highwayman in the eighteenth century and of the gangster in the twentieth are evidence of this. Dr Johnson felt that public hangings should not be abolished because 'The old method was most satisfactory to all parties; the public was gratified by a procession; the criminal was supported by it.' Fielding, on the other hand, consistent with his general effort to reduce crime by making it less attractive, was opposed to public executions, as 'The day appointed by law for the thief's shame is the day of glory in his opinion. His procession to Tyburn and his last moments are all triumphant' (Jones, 1933, p. 204). Certainly the procession through London on to Tyburn on the eight annual Hanging Days was a triumphal progress, and Hanging Days were unofficial public holidays. John Gay in *The Beggar's Opera* (1728) describes the adoration of the young criminal on his way to his hanging (Act I, Scene IV):

> Beneath the left Ear, so fit but a Cord,
> The Youth in his Cart hath the Air of a Lord,
> And we cry, There dies an Adonis!

Needless to say, there was no conscious intention of making crime and criminals attractive by means of public executions; on the contrary, the object was to frighten others away from a life of crime. Then, as now, there was a delusory idea that punishment was a deterrent, linked with the idea of the exemplary sacrifice of the criminal. Thus we have Henry Fielding, a most humane magistrate as well as a novelist of extraordinary sensibility, quoting the reply of 'the late excellent Judge Burnet' to a convicted felon, who said, 'It is very hard, my lord, to hang a poor man for stealing a horse,' ' "You are not to be hanged, sir," answered my ever-honoured and beloved friend, "for stealing a horse, but you are to be hanged that horses may not be stolen" ' (Jones, 1933, p. 222). Then as now however, the deterrent did not work. These well-attended spectacles ('In September 1849 John Gleeson, a murderer of some note, was hanged outside Kirksale Jail in Liverpool, before a gathering estimated at 100,000 strong' (Chesney, 1970, p. 302)—and Liverpool was nothing compared to London) were themselves the scene of crime—pickpockets and prostitutes were certainly busy at them—and cannot be said to have deterred potential criminals (ibid., p. 305):

A Bristol prison chaplain declared that out of 167 condemned criminals whom he had interviewed during his career, only three had not witnessed an execution.

The reasons generally offered by lawyers and criminologists for the lack of effective deterrence to crime in the large number of hanging offences in England in the eighteenth and beginning of the nineteenth centuries, coupled with the public spectacle of executions, are the low rate of detection and punishment, and the prevalent poverty and chaos incident to the urbanisation of rural people: the crowding into the cities, which forced people into a criminal life regardless of the risk. This is doubtless true, but it would be well to add that among those crowds were many courting danger, aware of the risks, but compulsively following a criminal course like gamblers who play to lose—because they are eager to fill the glamorous role of sacrificial victim and 'die game'. An example from *Covent Garden Journal*, 4 February 1792: 'The woman who was committed to Newgate on Thursday night for the murder of the girl in Noble Street, being asked why she did it, said she wanted to be hanged.'

This notion receives some support from the well-known charisma and sexual attractiveness of highwaymen, mentioned earlier. A wave of highway robbery was said to follow every run of performances of *The Beggar's Opera* (Jones, 1933, p. 89, n. 3: ref. to Schultz, 1923, p. 246), and Fielding wrote *Jonathan Wild* for the express purpose of de-glamourising crime. The linked notions of masculinity and death, sexual charm and danger, can be seen not only in the cult of the highwaymen, but in that of bandits (Hobsbawm, 1969), gangsters (including the Mafia),[17] bull-fighters, Hell's Angels (Thompson, 1966), guerrilla fighters, members of resistance movements, and to a lesser extent, soldiers. All of these people have a felt aura of sudden, violent, impending death, and all of them act out a kind of aggression against the norms and are death-guilty for it. This last is important: the police, who certainly have a dangerous job, are specifically employed in maintaining the norms, never in challenging them. They have absolutely no sexy image as so many doomed Adonises, the efforts of the mass media notwithstanding.

Real crime and real criminals engage the passions of the population. A good real-life crime is sure-fire front-page material, and a trial scene is a sure attention-getter in a play or novel. The public is still involved with crime and punishment, though it no longer tears the victim/criminal to pieces spontaneously, nor escorts him to the gallows in a sacrificial procession. Consequently fiction which revolves around crime and punishment is both popular and important; Julian Symons quotes Nicolas Freeling, who argues for the basic seriousness of the crime novel (1972, p. 82):

> Murder, and any other crime, is not a part of entertainment but an integral part of life. We are all murderers, we are all spies, we are all criminals and to choose a crime as the mainspring of a book's action is only to find one of the simplest ways of focusing eyes on our life and our world.

Real crime and real criminals continue to exist. But at some point in the past their crime and punishment was *ritualised*. Their real punishment was exemplary, and it was recorded and crystallised in symbolic re-enactment: the drama of pity and terror. This did not displace but accompanied the ritualisation of the drama of law, the establishment of procedures to determine guilt and fix punishment.

Something similar happened in religion, with the substitution of the ritual for the real death of the 'god'. Ritual, and subsequently literature, is essentially an act of substitution. If originally the religious rites demanded the real death of a member of the society (perhaps the most perfect member, involving a negative selection), the invention of the ritual *drama* of sacrifice instead was a social invention of inestimable value. To substitute a sacrificial animal for Isaac, the beloved child, was brilliant; to make wine and bread serve as blood and flesh in later religion was an act of genius. Small-scale societies, poor in members, animals, and wealth, could ill spare any of them. Once substitutions have been invented they are an obvious symbolic solution of the problem, and are freely used. Museums of pre-history, such as the National Museum in Copenhagen, are rich in examples of substitute sacrifices: the worn-out dagger as grave-goods instead of the precious bronze sword the scabbard leads one to expect; axe-heads and boats the size of toys, symbolically offered in place of the real ones.

Let me suggest that the drama was a similar invention, a substitution of a ritually represented event for a real one. It deals with crime, but not real crime; and punishment, but no one is really killed. The social and ritual real punishment of real criminals has no doubt a normative effect (although, as noted above, not always the one intended), but although it is socially necessary to expound and reinforce the norms, there is not always an appropriate criminal to hand. The classical drama at once represents, and limits the incidence of, crime. Crimes are described, but never committed; no scene of actual violence may appear on the stage—such matters are *obscene* (= 'off-stage', not to be shown). Actors are said to be killed, but survive the performance: the same happy arrangement as with the substitution of ritual sacrifice for real killing in religious rites. But at the same time, the emotion of the audience is engaged; the Chorus is their representative and interpreter: 'The Chorus occupied an area of its own between the actors and the audience' (Lloyd-Jones, 1970, p. 3), and the argument is directed to involve and convince the audience, as in the primitive and direct act of justice which the drama represents and replaces. The function of the drama, according to Aristotle, was to purge the audience of pity and terror. They have a surrogate participation in the crime and also in the punishment, identifying now with the criminal, now with the avenging power of society. They have the sensation of doing and suffering, but without committing any crime or executing or suffering any punishment. They see, and, what is more important, they feel, by emotional participation, what is crime and what the punishment must be, but they neither kill nor are they killed, in fact, no blood is shed. The invention of this didactic substitute for the exemplary cruelties of despotic justice must surely be counted as one more proof of the superiority of Greek civilisation.

That classical Greek tragedy is the drama of crime and punishment may be seen from the themes presented. That it was intended as a normative influence for the whole population, we may infer from the public nature of the drama. The plays were part of the annual city festivals: one play of a trilogy was acted on each of the three days of the festival. The rewards of playwrights and actors were rewards given by the city: mostly the ascription of honour, the laurel-wreath as bestowed on athletes who excelled in the Games (Havelock, 1970, p. xvi).

Three prizes were awarded for first, second and third places, and though special judges were selected for this purpose they made their decision in front of the audience, which did not hesitate to register its own preferences. Thus the plays were composed for the Athenian public, not for an esoteric minority.

The theatre itself was an important public building, paid for from the public funds (though doubtless a plain hillside served as a stage for hundreds of years before the social structure of the city was large and formal enough to demand a purpose-built theatre). Sometimes a rich citizen paid for the production of a Chorus or a whole play—but this was not an investment (except in increased status), it was a public service, and honoured as such. The Athenians paid for their theatre seats, but a subsidy of two obols was paid to the poorer citizens from a special fund, the 'theoric fund', said to have been established by Pericles in the fifth century. Any attempt to use this fund for any other purpose, even in time of war, met furious resistance: such was the importance of the theatre to the city.

If the theatre was normative, public and subsidised, it cannot have been the theatre of an élite, nor can theatre-going have been a high-status proof of a superior cultural discrimination. If it was effectively to influence the norms of the whole population, the widest possible participation in the drama was necessary, and this we see was the case. What proof we have is inferential—the size of Greek cities is reckoned from the size of the theatre, for it should accommodate the population. (I am told that the size of Aidone in Sicily will never be known, despite extensive archaeological investigation, because in the 1950s and 1960s all the stones of the theatre that were visible were taken away to make the tourist road around the coast.) There seems to have been something approaching 100 per cent attendance, including women and children: a surviving fragment complains that the Furies in the *Eumenides* of Aeschylus were so horrific in appearance that women miscarried and children were frightened into fits. They obviously would not have suffered these inconveniences had they not been present. And the experience of the drama was not confined to the cities: after the three days of playing at the city festivals plays were taken on a tour of the provinces.

The Greeks, as we know and as Kitto states in *The Greeks* (1967), were saturated with Homer. The evidence suggests they they were also saturated with classical Athenian drama.

Icelandic saga literature was, and to a surprisingly great extent still is, known to the whole population. The sagas were not, like the Athenian drama, the participatory 'enactment' of crime and punishment. They consist of 'histories' of the great clans and their most notable members, in which a claim is established for their high reputation. They maintain a cooler distance from the listener, and

5

make a demand rather for admiration than for entanglement. Nevertheless, their normative intentions are clear, they show right and wrong actions, what leads to high esteem and what deeds are to be despised. But since they are also concerned with a society in which the State effectively does not exist (the Icelandic settlers were fleeing the tyranny of Harald Fairhair and his basic feudalism in Norway), the same pre-State condition of justice prevails: the doer suffers (the consequences of his deeds which reveal his true nature, by which he is judged). The happy ending of the bourgeois novel is conspicuously absent—the best to be hoped for is the attainment of high reputation, otherwise there is nothing but old age, senility, and death.

These two bodies of popular didactic literature, from classical Greece and pre-feudal Scandinavia, together with the drama of Elizabethan England, rank by general consent among the very greatest literary art ever produced, certainly at the top of the Western cultural tradition. Their aesthetic and moral importance is never seriously questioned (except by Bernard Shaw, who preferred his own plays). And I would emphasise again that they were created for and were seen, heard, absorbed and internalised as moral directives by the whole population.

In the face of these undoubted facts, it is extraordinary that it is possible to argue, as Edward Shils does in 'Mass society and its culture', that 'In modern society, the number of consumers of superior culture has never been large; in pre-modern societies it was even smaller.'

Shils, blinded perhaps by life in America, and certainly blind to the normative functions of literature, describes three grades of culture, 'superior', 'mediocre', and 'brutal'. *Superior* culture is the province of an élite, those who possess enough wealth to have leisure and trained sensibilities. They alone are capable of understanding it, although there are of course persons of sensibility without wealth, who share to some extent in the appreciation of fine culture; this gives them a certain acquired élite status. *Mediocre* culture is imitative and essentially mass-produced. It apes the quality of superior culture, without, however, having originality or particular artistic merit. Nevertheless, it is not despicable, and may be shared by a larger portion of the population.

Then there is *brutal* culture, the culture of the masses or general population. This is greatly inferior in all ways, including the lack of writing. 'Superior' and 'mediocre' culture depend on the existence of writing, whereas one of the salient characteristics of brutal culture at all times is the lack of it: 'until recently there has been little professional production, machinery for preservation and transmission is lacking', and, in brutal culture, 'oral transmission plays a greater part in maintaining traditions of expression and performance than in the case of superior and mediocre cultures'. It has been noted before that even great Homer nods, but few, I think, before Shils, have ever called him 'brutal' (meaning, perhaps, 'brutish'). But because he is evidently infatuated with the idea of culture as exclusive and arcane, Dr Shils proposes categories which would lead to such absurdities as saying, for instance, that Verlaine was a greater poet than Aeschylus.

To sum up: the pleasure of participation in fiction, which gives the unreal lives presented there the fascination they hold for us, has its origin in the functional necessities of small-scale societies. The excitement of sharing in the enforcement of taboo, and in the repetition of the 'history' of the clan and of its godhead, were an essential part of the social bond, cementing ties of identity with the group and reinforcing self-identity.

The ritual of the law, where justice must be seen to be done, and the public execution of justice, which persisted until relatively modern times (the last public execution in England was in 1859), satisfied the need to share the actions of society. The continued fascination of the literature of crime and punishment, even now, is a substitute satisfaction. The cult of the criminal-as-hero, which even applies to such monsters as Manson, is evidence of a (perhaps frequently-occurring) wish to identify with the one who challenges society and becomes its victim.

It was a great leap of social invention when real legal and sacrificial processes were made symbolic, not only ritualised but performed in a fictional, substitute form. While the public was somewhat separated from the action—made spectators rather than actors, and separated by the intermediary Chorus—their emotions were still engaged, and the normative lessons of crime and punishment (but minus the actual killing) were imprinted on their consciences. For this to be possible, it had also to be possible that the mass of the population could be reached by means of poetry, song, dance, mime, and acting: the theatre arts, in fact. In the Greek cities, the drama was made possible by the existence of the audience, already collected in the city population. But it was a social decision which provided the technical and human resources necessary to develop ritual and stage it as drama. Most important, it is a simple fact that great art, the greatest literature ever known, can be absorbed and internalised by whole populations. Two examples, Greece and Iceland, are sufficient to prove that the highest form of literature is not the exclusive province of a few specially sensitised individuals, but that Vico was right when he called the poets the teachers of the people; to teach them they must reach them, and they can.

Personification

Not all literature is normative in the sense of being a warning account of crime and punishment. There is a substantial body of it which might be called the product of the praise-singer. The heroic epic or clan-saga (Slægtsaga) is of course the prototypical form of this. Epics and sagas consist of narrative accounts of the deeds of notable individuals, usually warrior chieftains. These persons are described, their lives and deeds recorded, primarily to proclaim and perpetuate their own reputations, based on excellent achievements, rather than as a model for the behaviour of others. But they are not considered simply as individuals, either: they are firmly fixed in the setting of their clan, which settles not only their social position by birth, but also indicates their probable personal physical and mental characteristics. The story begins characteristically two or three generations before the birth of the hero, for it is necessary to know the acts and nature of his ancestors; the genealogies, so irritating to modern readers, were a necessary part of character delineation.

The appearance of the heroic epic historically precedes the drama of retribution: the classical Athenian drama developed from incidents, some of them quite minor, in the Homeric poems. Aeschylus himself described his plays as 'slices from Homer's feast'.

Unlike the drama, the heroic epic holds the audience at a distance; they are being told of great deeds, but of the great deeds of heroes, which they are called on to admire, not share. It does not call for the emotional involvement, the sense of participation in crime and justice, which induces the *cathartic* effect of tragedy. Nevertheless, the heroic epic certainly shows who, by his acts, is deserving of praise and who of blame, and certainly in the saga at least gives the sanction of public opinion to make it unmistakable, in such phrases as 'Then all men said . . .' or 'Most agreed that . . .' such a deed was good or bad. On the whole, the auditor is kept at a little distance. Nevertheless, the *person* of the hero becomes a heroic type, and his personification of heroism may become internalised as a trigger for action.

A very apposite illustration of this, relative to what Dennis *et al.* (1956) call 'the heroic mythology of industry', was told me by a student, an ex-collier. His father and grandfather had been men of legendary strength and size, and there were many stories told in the pit of their heroic acts, coupled with the reminder to him that 'tha'll niver bi th' man thi feyther was'. He could not hope to match them in sheer physical prowess, but nevertheless got a reputation for fearing nothing, through right action in various crisis situations. One of them occurred at a time when the roof was coming down, slowly; he retreated coolly and slowly, placing pit-props under it as it sagged, until, with a flash, it occurred to him that he 'could have been running away like all the other buggers'. Not until later did he realise he had done automatically what his father had done in a similar case—it was one of the heroic stories about him. The right and heroic action was recorded in the story, and so internalised that the son reproduced the act without thinking. The pattern was set and did not need to be reinvented, it was coupled with the favourable (heroic) image, and inspired unconscious imitation. Without disparaging the deed, it seems probable that part of the favourable aura of the story was the happy ending—the father succeeded, and the son expected to do so, and did.

One should add that the mining community in England has many traits in common with 'heroic' warrior society: the high value on competitive excellence, which measures masculinity (another high value), and the strong sense of communal identity with the own group and exclusion of 'others'. This has been generally supposed to be based on long-standing local communities, but the 100 per cent solidarity of the 1972 Miners' Strike, at a time when for ten years the mining population had been redistributed throughout the country (as well as losing many members), seems to show that it is an occupational rather than a geographical phenomenon.

An example of *negative personification*, also taken from popular mythology, is the Ghost of the Dishonest Land-Surveyor, several accounts of which were collected by E. Tang Kristensen (1891, p. 115). This evil spectre was the personification of the impotent rage of the Danish peasants who felt (with reason) that they had been cheated in the distribution of the common land of the villages in the nineteenth-century Land Reforms. They found that the best land, and an unreasonably large amount of it, had gone to the richest and wiliest of their fellows, whom they suspected (correctly) of bribing the surveyor. For accepting these bribes and unjustly apportioning the land, the Dishonest Surveyor was condemned for a certain time to walk the earth, dragging his surveying chain behind him. A particular injustice is transformed from an action to a ghostly personification, and a safety-valve is found for resentment. The whole guilt and punishment is placed on the Surveyor, and we may say with Durkheim that they knew he was a criminal because they punished him. The Surveyor is relatively easy to punish in this wishful way—he was a stranger, perhaps not peasant-born (although if he was, it would be another grievance), and above all he had done all the evil he could do and gone away. The rich peasants who had bribed him, however, remain as powerful neighbours, against whom no wishful revenge is possible: we hear nothing of the Ghost of the Rich Peasant who Bribed the Surveyor.

Actions, good or bad, are related as examples of norms; and the actors are embodiments of the qualities represented. For the student who wishes to use literature as a key to the specific values of a period or cultural area, the point is to discover the author's intentions: what actions and persons are supposed to be admirable? One criterion is the distribution of reward: in heroic literature, he who gets the greatest reputation is the most admirable, though he may die miserably—not only in battle, but old and mad, like many a saga hero. And that is because reputation, *arete*, *eftermaal*, is the greatest value in that society. This differs markedly from the bourgeois novel, where the favourite is the one who gets the money and the mate—a point which will be discussed in the next chapter. Aside from the scoring of results, though, a measure of value may be seen in what counts as sexual attractiveness, particularly at times when standards are changing.

When we are told, for instance, as we frequently were, not too long ago, that the heroine's generously curved mouth and somewhat irregular features were too something-or-other to suit the require-ments of classical or perfect beauty, the author is staking a claim for a new standard of attractiveness which is different from, and more exciting than, that supposed to be accepted by society: normal taste requires a perfect oval face, regular features, decorum and submissive behaviour, whereas the author is presenting a competing norm of sexual attraction, based on a more active, adventurous and romantic norm: a Marianne, a Becky Sharp, an Iris March.

Changes in what is valued occur in literature as they do in society, when new social structures are in conflict with old ones which they strive to destroy and replace. Thus at the very beginning of the bourgeois period, we see a veritable fusillade against the ideals of feudal, heroic chivalry. Don Quixote, in a Spain for which the flood of gold from the New World, coinciding with the end of the Middle Ages, seemed to open unlimited possibilities for the future, personifies the uselessness and unreality of values which are no longer acceptable; and, lovable though he may be, we are left in no doubt that he is also an awful old fool. The poor and helpless fantastical knight, wandering in the chaos of the end of the Middle Ages, is a frequent figure in the picaresque which preceded the novel. Lazarillo de Tormes, the protagonist of a sixteenth-century Spanish picaresque, served such a man for a while—this penniless gentleman stalked about chewing a toothpick, to conceal that he had not dined for two days; he will not steal himself, but accepts the fruits of Lazarillo's thefts without enquiry: an easy satire on displaced aristocracy. Then Shakespeare attacks military honour—'to seek the bubble, Reputation, even in the cannon's mouth', and Falstaff asks, 'Who has it? He that died a' Wednesday.' Certainly honour was still an acclaimed value in Elizabethan England, and for long afterwards, but Elizabethan England was in that situation described by Goldmann, when the social processes were in an exceptionally rapid 'structuration and destrutcion'. Falstaff's cheerful rational self-aggrandising immorality was certainly punished—he is rejected and destroyed—but it is evident that he had the heart of his author and of all audiences since, for expressing sentiments which were inexpressible in truly 'heroic' society. Thersites was destroyed for far less. Falstaff rises to a bourgeois dignity, expressed, too, in typical bourgeois terms, when he turns away and says, 'Master Shallow, I owe you twenty pound.'

In general, it is astonishing what a seepage there is of the values of society into the depiction of the social, physical, and even sexual characteristics of persons in narrative fiction. The norms of sexual attraction are an indicator of what the society counts as desirable. We take it for granted that the literature of societies with aristocratic values describes the attraction of its heroes in terms of their aristocratic origin. Thus in chivalrous romance the protagonists are always of noble birth, even if this is concealed for the time. This is true also of courtly dance-ballads, a medieval form which, like TV, was actually in use up and down the social scale from castle to village green. Thus, 'Glasgerion was a king's owne sonne, And a harper he was good' (Child, 1883–98, Ballad no. 67).[18] Both men and women are routinely described as 'stately', 'proud', 'of high-born kin' and so on, and popular heroes such as Robin Hood are said to be displaced noblemen, who just happen to be living with peasant outlaws. Even in America in the nineteenth century there was enough belief in aristocracy, or disbelief in the common man, to create a myth about Abraham Lincoln, that he was not a simple frontiersman, but an illegitimate son of Alexander Hamilton or George Washington, typical upper-class and educated ideals.

Insistence on aristocratic origin in fiction argues a high value for this in society. In many cases, though, it is the key point to the story: in the ballad of Glasgerion cited above, he plays so well that 'ladies waxed wood' (mad), and one of them, the king's daughter as it happens, invites him to come to her at night. He asks his servant Jack to wake him for the assignation, but Jack puts on his master's clothes ('He seemed a gentleman') and goes himself, where his behaviour betrays his base origin:

> He did not take that lady gay
>   To boulster nor to bedd,
> But downe upon her chamber floor
>   Full soon he hath her layd.

> He did not kisse that lady gay,
>   When he came nor when he youd,
> And sore mistrusted that lady gay
>   He was of some churlës blood.

When the real Glasgerion turns up she lets him in, asking if he has forgotten anything, 'Or are you back returned again, To know more of my love?' She is prepared to overlook his behaviour, until the truth comes out, when she instantly 'pulld forth a litel pen-kniffe' and stabbed herself, saying:

> There shall never no churlës blood
>   Spring within my body.

This leaves Glasgerion nothing to do but go home and kill Jack and himself, and honour is, to some extent, avenged.

Dishonour is not sexual union outside marriage, but with a social inferior; rank equals sexual eligibility. It may also exclude or cancel out other factors. Stendhal, writing in the almost totally bourgeois but nevertheless quasi-aristocratic French nineteenth century, says in *On Love* of cross-class liaisons: 'A duchess is never over thirty to a bourgeois.'

This phenomenon is by no means confined to aristocratic society. In societies where bourgeois values are absolutely supreme, money replaces birth as the highest value, and money thus acquires valid sexual attraction. This has never been expressed better (though it lurks under the surface in all novels) than by Scott Fitzgerald in *The Great Gatsby*.

Gatsby, who is deeply and romantically in love with Daisy, is discussing her with the narrator, her cousin Nick. Nick says, 'And her voice is full of . . .' Gatsby interrupts to say, 'Her voice is full of money.' This is not cynical. Gatsby is not a fortune-hunter: he has plenty of (ill-gotten) money of his own, money he acquired in the hope of getting close to Daisy and carrying her off from her husband. He lives for Daisy, and in the event dies for her as well, and he states the simple fact that money is one of her traits, and part of the timbre and quality of her voice. Money = sexual attraction.

Randall Jarrell, the poet and critic, remarks of this scene, in his one brilliant satirical novel, *Pictures from an Institution* (1954), that (p.26):

> There was a part of Gatsby that his bank, the company that insured him, and other institutions knew—a part that was in love not with Daisy but with the bank.

But in this I think he is mistaken. Fitzgerald the artist and Gatsby the protagonist know what they are talking about. Daisy and the bank are one—the bank is as much a part of her sexual charm as her beauty, in a society where the (established and secure, as it turns out to Gatsby's cost) possession of money is the highest value.

Since dominant status = sexual attraction, there is a noticeable tendency, where fiction turns on the question of who marries whom, for attraction to be upward in the social scale. Tom Jones sighs for Sophia Western, Moll Flanders for the elder brother, Clarissa Harlowe for Lovelace. We feel that there is something flat about the marriage of Robinson Crusoe which, as has been pointed out quite often, he disposes of in half a sentence: he married 'not either to my disadvantage or dissatisfaction'. And the extremely suitable matches of Jane Austen's heroines, so likely to lead to rational happiness, are markedly unpassionate and unromantic.

On the whole, in life as in literature, the measure of attractiveness may be the degree of approximation to traits of the exemplary (usually upper) class. In life, if not in literature, this will usually have no further consequences than sexual ranking within a social group. But there are certainly situations, even in highly stratified societies like feudal Europe, where this (genuine) attraction causes an upward leap by the lover, in which the motivation is not simply the obvious one of getting the practical advantage of the match—certainly in warrior societies this is a risky business, quite likely to lead to the death of both partners—but the driving power of real sexual urgency. Gatsby is a modern example of this drive, and there is a massive body of trivial literature devoted to it: the whole body of Horatio Alger stories: daring-feat-faithful-service-and-marriage-to-the-boss's-daughter. The female version is the Cinderella motive, a staple of women's magazines for at least one hundred and fifty years. (Not to mention *Jane Eyre* and many others.) These are not, as Ian Watt and Leo Lowenthal would have it, merely the minimisation of personal relationships in obedience to the Protestant ethic: they represent a real attraction: rich = sexy, as money is the measure of all things. Aspiring upward was dangerous and often fatal in pre-bourgeois literature: in conformity with the Protestant ethic, however, it is a moral imperative, despite seeming incongruence within another imperative, that of the selfmade man: 'Thrive before you wive', says Benjamin Franklin, in *Poor Richard's Almanac*. The conflict of norms is resolved by thriving *through* wiving.

But it takes two to tango. Even if every marriage made were a marriage of upward mobility, it would still be the case that half the population married *down*. Coincident with the boss's-daughter syndrome, we have what might be described as the raggle-taggle-gipsy syndrome.

In terms of dominant social values, how can this choice be justified? For there is definitely an element of feminine choice of a man of inferior station:[19]

> But aye she loot the tears doon fa'
> For Jock o' Hazeldean.

Rejection of arranged marriage appears even in these pre-bourgeois ballads, individual passion is insisted on and damn the inconvenience to the family:

> Dame and knight are waitin' a',
> The Lady is na' seen,
> She's ower the border and awa'
> Wi' Jock o' Hazeldean.

Does she then really want to lie in a cold open field, along with the black-jack gipsy-O? This choice may perhaps be justified, even in terms of the highly stratified society. In warrior societies there has always been a chance for the most reckless as well as the most skilful to acquire rank through competitive excellence, and here the bold lover who captures an upper-class woman lays a claim, as Bothwell did with Mary Queen of Scots. If he can consolidate his position, he has won, and *by virtue of his success*, has become an eligible choice for her, as he has proved himself to have those qualities of aggression which have a high social value. Similarly, in bourgeois society, the poor boy who *makes good* ('good' here = wealth) shows himself to be a better match, through his personal ability to make money, than those who are born to it. Thus marrying up or down, they still aspire to the normative values of society which guide sexual attractiveness.

If literary characters personify social norms and values, they also set patterns for imitation which are very much wanted in times when society is being unmade and reassembled in new and strange ways. At the end of the Middle Ages, literature showed by example that one *ought not to be* like Don Quixote, but rather like Henry V; and also that it is right to exercise scepticism and common sense: Sancho Panza and Falstaff.

The new, and consequently unfamiliar roles appropriate to new classes and occupations want definition, and are susceptible to influence by fictional patterns. Svend Møller Kristensen, the Danish literary sociologist, remarks (1970)[20] that the fascination of Balzac is precisely that he supplies the felt need of a new class looking for an image of itself. It has been noticed that the generation of colonial administrators, soldiers, and civilian imperial servants immediately after Kipling's heyday behaved more like his characters than the generation from which he drew his models. A. Conan Doyle, too (Symons, 1972, p. 68),

> was a super-typical Victorian, a bluff Imperialist extrovert who congratulated himself on having 'the strongest influence over young men, especially young athletic sporting men, of anyone in England (bar Kipling)'.

The ability to predict and shape future patterns of behaviour and values is not due simply to that clairvoyant ability to foresee the future with which writers are all too ready to credit themselves. It is the result of the relief with which people seize any graspable definition of how they are supposed to act, when there are no normative instructions coming from the past which can cope with new situations. There is thus often a conscious effort, in a new society, to establish an appropriate literature, not only in the interests of nationalistic pride or dislike for the old patterns after a conflict, but for the very practical purpose of giving the people viable models of behaviour. Marcus Cunliffe (1954) described these efforts in the newly formed United States: the idea was to cast off the yoke of British culture, and there were even some hotheads who wanted to appropriate the English language and make the British speak Greek.

In the modern world and for most people, the principal source of fiction is the mass media, and of these there can be no doubt that TV is the most important. But is it normative? This seems indeterminably in doubt. The Pilkington Committee (1960, p. 15) stated:

> So far, there is little conclusive evidence on the effects of television (or other media) on values and moral attitudes. But those who work professionally in this sphere told us that what evidence there was showed us that there was *an* effect . . .
> Unless and until there is unmistakable proof to the contrary, the presumption must be that television (and other media) is and will be a main factor in influencing the values and moral standards of our society.

It cannot be proved, but they certainly feel that it is so. It has justly been noted, particularly with reference to American TV, that advertisers do not spend millions of dollars on it because it does not influence people, but because it does. And if TV commercials, which are fictional situations in which products are presented, can influence people to buy them, why not assume that fictional presentation of alternative patterns of behaviour can influence people to adopt the one presented as the best?

My students have consistently disputed the notion that fiction may be normative. They are quite ready to admit that it may *have* a normative effect, but cannot believe that this is intended and directed. I think it is deducible simply by observation of the content of TV, without any inside knowledge of decision-making, which is in any case hard to get, as the structure is so fluid, understated, and non-bureaucratic. There certainly is great topicality in inserting practical messages. One of these same sceptical students reported, at a time when a flu epidemic was imminent and the public was being urged to take flu shots, hearing a woman on a bus saying, 'We might as well go along and have those flu shots—the Newcomers are having them.' 'The Newcomers' was a fairly short-lived series which attempted to do for the middle class what 'Coronation Street' does for the working class. It was full of useful hints: arguments at the breakfast table about whether the boy could have a motor-bike: 'Look what happened to Jimmy!' 'He didn't wear his helmet.' 'Neither would you.' 'Yes I would', and so on—all perfectly credible family conversation, but the message Wear Your Helmet was very clear.

'The Archers', an immemorial BBC radio serial, is devoted to farming: it has also been called a lobby for farmers. When the annual price review (of agricultural products) appears in the spring, in real life, the programmes of 'The Archers' are full of discussions of it. The setting is a rural community, and it is full of practical hints to farmers about new techniques and methods. It is no great secret that these hints are conveyed to writers and producers by the Department of Agriculture, and that farmers are consulted by the Department, not only as to how they like the programme and if they are helped by the information given, but as to what other problems they would like to see taken up and solved by fictional example. So far, so value-free. However, one of the main problems of farmers is the cost and status of farm labourers, and particularly the possibility of their successfully demanding more money and better conditions. I am told that the desirable norm consistently depicted in 'The Archers' is that of the highly stratified, squirearchical rural village, with emphasis on an occasionally grumbling, but on the whole contented-with-their-lot, labouring class, and a responsible, competent, and attractive gentry.

Turning now to basic institutions, I think we may say that TV is pro-family. Wherever the family appears in a TV *series*, it is represented as desirable. Single-shot dramas, such as Ken Loach's *Family Life*, are exceptions to this—but they *are* exceptions, and controversial. As TV presents it in fiction, family life is the optimal social situation, and while its disruption may be necessary (Detective-Inspector Goss in 'Z-Cars') it is always unfortunate. Maybe this is accidental or sheer realism, but it appears to me that it happens because a function of the media is to be supportive of social institutions by influencing public attitudes in their favour. Certainly the family is an essential institution, even in modern industrial society, because of its remaining functions: emotional and sexual centre, child-rearing and socialising centre, rest and recreation for the industrial work-force—and, not least, consumer-unit. No series of programmes destructive of the family *as such* could possibly be broadcast.

This proposition may be tested by considering whether a TV serial based closely on Oscar Lewis's *The Children of Sanchez* (1962) could be broadcast. Evidently it could not, despite picturesque setting, sharp delineation of character, plenty of life, incident, drama, excitement, charm. But though Jésùs Sanchez is a sort of folk-hero, his domination stunts and destroys his children; he has several wives at once; mothers die, wives are abandoned, children are brutally beaten; brothers complain that they are not allowed to beat their sisters: 'I feel as if I have no sisters!'; no one works rationally and consistently except the father: the boys are aimless, one sister wants to 'better herself' but is prevented, the other is a deserted wife with several children. It is a world of violence, fatalism, suspicion, superstition, ignorance, intense emotion, unemployment and poverty. All this could never be presented as a picture of family life (unless, it were smoothed, soothed and changed out of all recognition), because Lewis does not present it as exceptional, or deviant, or comic, or the object of social work like the (multi-problem family in the TV series 'The Doctors'). On the contrary, he makes it clear that this pattern is about average for their neighbourhood, and substantially the family life of millions of people on every continent. No government, nor any other agency rich and powerful enough to sponsor TV, has any interest in publicising such a picture of family life as the natural scene of mutual destruction.

Lewis's picture of the situation of the family in Mexico is similar

to what Gorky says of life in his grandfather's house and family in
My Childhood (1969, p. 172):

> Long afterwards I understood that to Russians, through the
> poverty and squalor of their lives, suffering comes as a diversion,
> is turned into play and they play at it like children and seldom
> feel ashamed of their misfortune. In the monotony of everyday
> existence grief comes as a holiday, and a fire is an entertainment.
> A scratch embellishes an empty face.

The one condition, I suppose, under which 'Sanchez' could be a
TV serial would be falsification: if it were made sentimental in the
same spirit in which *The Forsyte Saga* was turned from a (rather
feeble, to be sure) piece of social criticism to an exercise in nostalgia
and a study of the accuracy of studio props—and the most successful
TV series ever made. With *Sanchez*, the warm, life-enhancing side
of poverty might be emphasised: the human importance of the
intense relationships, so stripped of middle-class inhibitions and
hypocrisy, and bourgeois thought for the morrow. This might be
done in the spirit of those who write about poverty in Appalachia
as a good thing, or in that of the later work of Oscar Lewis such as
La Vida (1966), where he writes about poverty like a doctor who has
fallen in love with the disease. But while there might be reasons,
such as the promotion of passive acceptance of the status quo, to
show that poverty is not so bad after all, there could never be
reasons to show that the Family is a Bad Thing; so we may safely
postulate that 'La Vecindad' will never replace 'Coronation Street'
as the standard of normality.

BBC has some programmes quite specifically designed to give information by fictional means. One of these in the winter of 1972 was
a series called 'The Befrienders', designed to popularise the real-life
volunteer organisation, the Samaritans, which offers desperate
people a chance to talk about their problems, originally with the
idea of providing a last defence against suicide. Certainly there are
valid 'pure TV' reasons for such a programme. Everyone is interested in case-histories, the problems are often dramatic, the Befrienders themselves present an interesting working group, with a
clinical interest similar to that of doctors, but with an everyman
appeal—they have no special education, just aptitude. Then there
is a public service element, also legitimate: informing the public
about the Samaritans and possibly recruiting new Samaritan

volunteers (there was advertising in the press for this, referring to the programme). Also, it is not unlikely that some people might be helped directly by being presented with at least one fictional solution to a common problem.

It was the more interesting, therefore, to see the attitude which was implicit in the treatment of one case. A middle-aged (49) executive construction engineer had been squeezed out of his firm in a consolidation. This man was suicidal because his self-esteem was tied absolutely to success, high earning power, and his role as protector of his family; his wife he reckoned was only capable of running the house ('mind you, she does that perfectly'). He was so full of shame and guilt that for months he desperately looked for work, without telling his wife that he was unemployed. The point was made, both by him and by the Befriender who talked to him, that there were 75,000 executives of his grade out of work in England, 2,000 of them in his own field; but the fact that it was not his fault that he was unemployed, but the ordinary operation of the economic system, *was never put forward as a reason* why he should not feel a burden of personal guilt. He was advised to confide in his wife and children; they proved to be sympathetic and mature, and he took a job at much less pay and status: good practical advice no doubt, but treating a serious social problem with a narrow personal solution, although the mere elucidation of the social situation would doubtless have saved him a lot of pain.

British TV is unique in that the most persistently normative, best written, best produced, best played and most enjoyable series are those devoted to the agencies of social control: first and foremost the police, but also 'Special Branch', 'Fraud Squad', the Treasury ('The Man from Haven'), and various anti-espionage efforts. The others have certainly elements of modish fantasy, but the police series at least make a conscientious effort to present a down-to-earth realistic image, certainly favourable to the police but maintaining credibility by various ploys. One is the realistic presentation of the working-class origin and orientation of most policemen, which corresponds to the factual situation, and contrasts to the classless Galahads who appear on American cops-and-robbers series. (I remember seeing a real-life petition in favour of a jailed London restaurateur, doing time for rape, in which an indignant lady complained that there would be no justice so long as the police came from the same class as criminals—but they do.) The police in British

TV personify law and order, or the effort to enforce the law, but they are well equipped with personal failings, complaints, fatigue, apt to be single or divorced or with shaky marriages, and often disgusted with the job. Quilley and Skinner both have a tendency to threaten to quit the Force because of this. All of this is trivial, of course: the image they project on the whole is of a protective, conscientious, honest, hard-working body of men, with plenty of bravery and ingenuity which they diffidently conceal and produce when necessary. According to T. A. Critchley in *Conquest of Violence* (1970) a great factor in the lack of violence in English political life—in demonstrations and the like—is the good image of the police as non-violent themselves, and as essentially working-class: 'citizens in uniform' rather than an arrogant and distant body who force the public into submission. Critchley fears a possible increase in general violence as a result of the increasing professionalism of the police and their consequent loss of contact with the public. At present foreigners, at least, have a good image, from the American tourist ('Your police are wonderful!') to the Polish Professor of Medieval History who said, 'This is the only country, East *or* West, where one could entertain for a moment the idea of a good image of the police.'

Not that other countries don't try. American TV police have been, certainly until very recently, completely incredible because the Galahad image was at the furthest possible remove from the public's experience of the police. A minimal brusque camaraderie, imperviousness to fear or bullets, 100 per cent correctitude, and that's about it, except for, recently, racial integration as in 'Hawaii-Five-O', and the clever and likeable 'Colombo'. The less amenable the projection is to corroboration, the fewer will be those who believe the image; on the other hand, those who do believe it (as in the case by John Whale, cited in the previous section) will cling to the belief despite contrary evidence.

The British police are concerned to maintain good relations with the public and take the TV police series very seriously. Advisers are supplied, to provide a standard of accuracy as to procedure and so on.[21] And either they, or someone else, are diligent in promoting special police interests: when the police were (really) negotiating for more pay in the winter of 1970-1, there was a lot of discussion among characters on 'Z-Cars' and 'Softly-Softly' about low wages and how they needed and deserved more; some talk of quitting

6

here, too. In the same period, when there were in the national press several well-publicised cases of police corruption, there was an unusually large number of stories involving the *suspicion* of police corruption, which always turned out be be unfounded. Either there was a misunderstanding about some really legal activity, or the villain was an ex-cop, dismissed years before, and his former colleagues were unusually eager to get him sent up—'Nothing a copper hates like a bent copper!'; or occasionally it was a frame-up, as when Hawkins in 'Softly-Softly' was falsely accused, by a long-haired hippy demonstrator, of making a homosexual advance.

The public is not invited in these series to *identify* with the police so much as to sympathise with them and help them (especially by supplying information, not least about their own family members, mates, or lovers). The police are consistently portrayed as unprivileged relative to the public, not as having very attractive work-relationships or friendship among themselves: these portrayals can hardly be recruiting posters. But they do above all personify the legitimate use of regulatory force in society, in these well-known inarticulate but virtuous figures. Because they represent in credible form exactly this legitimacy of the established order, they are able to have considerable normative influence on what is accepted as legitimate. If, according to Socrates, virtue is what a good man does, then legal is what the police do on 'Z-Cars' and 'Softly-Softly'; and this is capable of considerable topical importance.

For it is surprising how topical they manage to be, considering that there is a time-lag of months between start of production and broadcast on TV. 'Z-Cars' is said to be uniquely satisfying to writers because the gap is only about five weeks. But evidently the broadcasters must have a stock of material in readiness for various contingencies. This occurred to me when, on a Sunday, Welsh Nationalists blew up a water-main to Birmingham, and on the Wednesday that very thing happened on 'Softly-Softly'.

There is a certain amount of unintentional interaction: real incidents of shooting at passing cars on the motorway inspired a TV story, which was followed by another real and this time fatal shooting (1971). This is obviously not the intention of the series.

But topicality can be used, despite time lag, to give a normative message. For example, in 'Z-Cars' on 14 February 1972 (during the very effective Miners' Strike) in a story called *Promotion*, the general line of which was the unenviable lot of policemen, Inspector Goss has one of his rare evenings at home. His highly valued marriage is always in danger because he cannot give enough time and attention to it, but while he and Mrs Goss sat together there was a distinct flickering in the lighting and the following exchange:

Mrs Goss   What would happen if every copper in the world were to strike for higher wages and shorter hours?

Goss   They wouldn't. (Pause—then, thoughtfully) That's why they're policemen.

Then the lighting changed back to normal. I cannot prove it, but I think that while it was not possible to make a whole episode to order, those two actors were called in and a few moments of topical comment on strikers (bad) and policemen (good) were shot and spliced in.

The police are usually shown in their most flattering roles, not only catching ordinary villains but the engagé champions of the poor and helpless—they are particularly furious about petty swindlers who 'do old dears' out of their meagre savings. They also do a lot of informal social work—settling quarrels, helping the destitute once in a way from their own pockets. This image is straight PR work. The story very often leads to the situation in which it appears that villains want nothing more than to make a written statement in the interrogation room (those who do not are indeed naughty). Often, too, the point is made that their associates ought to inform on them. All this is, I suppose, a legitimate effort to combat the successful commission of crime. There are other aspects of the personification process in the police series which are rather more ominous, however.

One of these is the inspiration of contempt for dissident groups, especially of young people, and another is the apparent legitimation of police violence through use of it by those who personify an acceptable authority.

Doubtless both of these could be defended on the grounds of realism: it is probably perfectly true that the police *do* dislike long-haired dissident youth, and that the previously presented picture of a 100 per cent non-brutal police force had lost credibility.

In 1970, for instance, there had been an episode in 'Softly-Softly' in which a young policewoman had been savagely beaten-up—ribs broken and other damage—by a villain who was being interrogated by Barlow and Hawkins—('That girl will be in hospital for two months!')—who were having great difficulty restraining their anger,

especially as the man was extraordinarily insolent and provocative—
'You set that bird onto me!'. Barlow had to keep leaving the room
to keep himself enough in hand to refrain from assaulting the
prisoner.

This all seemed to me simply incredible, and I asked some senior
police officials about it at Bramshill Police College. Would they not,
in real life, simply have beaten him up, as they certainly would in
the United States? But this was vigorously denied—absolutely unthinkable that any policeman in England should lay a finger on a
prisoner, quite out of the question.

Yet see what a change in the image one short year can bring! On
3 November 1971, 'Softly-Softly' broadcast an episode called *Do
You Need Help?* which had so many interesting facets that it is
worth describing in some detail.

The crux of this story is that a very wicked group, resembling
Release or ADE or the Claimants' Union, has plastered the town
with posters and leaflets asking Do You Need Help? This not only
encroaches on the established welfare services, including the informal benevolence of the police, but it includes help for those
busted for drugs, in trouble with landlords, and—oh, horror!—
advice on contraception and abortion. At the police briefing a trendy
young cop remarks, 'The more you have of one, the less you need
of the other,' but he is quickly crushed. The police mount a campaign to drive these people out of town, mostly by leaning on them
at a café they frequent, vaguely threatening the homosexual bar-
tender (point against homosexuals here; they corrupt youth), and
trying to make girls go home and save themselves from the evil life
to which they are being introduced. Special indignation that one
girl comes from an upper-class part of town—where the houses have
names, not numbers—how vile that she of all people should be involved! This girl later turns out to have VD, and the leader of the
Help group refuses to help her—rotten to the core as he is—though
in fact all he would have to do would be to tell her to attend the VD
clinic at the local hospital, a message which would certainly be
prominently posted in the kind of loos she was frequenting, for that
matter. She, however, commits suicide in despair (and in a public
convenience).

. Having established the general detestability of these young rotters,
the leader, seized in a kind of opium-den with his mistress preparing
him a pipe, is given a punch by Sgt Evans, not from necessity in

arresting him, but from anger. He (Evans) quite properly admits this and is reprimanded.

The superb crafty invulnerability of these series is shown by the fact that while all this concentration of the police on the young people was going on, a real villain gets away with a big coup involving several thousand pounds. The story thus provides two sets of morals: prejudice against youth, hippie youth, dissident youth, and especially youth who want to interfere with life-style and normative control, is justified by showing that they have really no wish to help others but are destructive and cowardly; and while of course deplorable, it is understandable that the police occasionally wallop them. And at the same time, for a different section of the audience, the moral is presented that the police should get on with their job of catching crooks and not bother about these essentially harmless kids. It is not really surprising that it is difficult to establish the exact normative effects, never mind intentions, of the media!

However, the trend of legitimising police violence continued. On 1 December 1971, also on 'Softly-Softly', Barlow allows himself to be needled into a rage by an old acquaintance, a man who started his criminal career at the same time Barlow started his police career. At one point in the interrogation he is provoked to the extent of seizing this man by the throat and yelling, 'We're all sadists, we like it!' Nevertheless, enough nostalgia of old adversaryship develops that when this villain's young mate calls him an old fool (for confessing), Barlow punches him in the gut hard enough to double him up, in front of a nationwide audience at peak viewing time.

This, as I say, is a change, and a change in the direction of acceptance of more toughness and less correctness in authority personified by fictional police.

Other series featuring authority seem also to emphasise this. An interminable spy-story called 'Spy-Trap' (1972) quite regularly had persons who were wanted for questioning brought to a fairly mysterious, anonymous headquarters. They regularly said, 'But you can't keep me here!'—referring, no doubt, to the legal protection known as habeas corpus—but it always turned out that they could be so kept without being charged. (Example: 'Spy-Trap', 5 April 1972: 'I can keep you here for as long as I like. I can keep you here until you tell me what I want to know.') The Minister on 'Doomwatch' made the same kind of statement: 'I can't do what? What is it that I cannot do?' (about holding a suspect). On 24 August a high

Treasury official (in 'The Man from Haven') remarked (somewhat jocularly), 'What are telephones for, if not to be tapped in the public interest?' A series called 'Special Branch' made a point of the minute dossiers kept on student revolutionaries—'Is Chris still with the Trots? Three months is unusual for him', and the risks of getting a dossier kept on you: 'You'll never get a decent job.' This probably lacked a certain credibility, and had not much success in keeping young people conformist. But it was a crude effort compared with the really sophisticated, long-continued, and frequently broadcast (one every day, on an average) efforts of the police series.

Personification differs, as a normative medium, from the type of participation discussed in the previous section, and also from identification as it will be discussed in the next one. The norms are presented as the immutable established facts of society, and the public is invited to react in relation to them, not to be them.

Identification

In the consumption of literature and the transmission of norms through literature, *identification* has more in common with *participation* than it does with *personification*. Personification is the process by which norms and values are made visible by being represented as fictional characters, and when this is established (as we have seen with the police series), the actions of these characters validate the norms, thus making them acceptable. Participation, according to the hypothesis I offer in the introduction to this chapter, derives ultimately from the collective nature of justice and religion in primitive society, and literary forms such as tragic drama and thriller-fiction are a substitute for actual physical participation in both crime and punishment. They not only, however, provide a surrogate satisfaction, but there is reason to think that they also inspire imitation by the transmission of norms of violence, and this is the basis of many anxious pieces of research about the mass media, as well as, in general terms, being the rationale of censorship.

Identification is a well-known phenomenon, and has been thoroughly established as an attraction of literature. It is perhaps more natural to the individualistic novel form than to other forms of literature. The Athenian citizen could accept Agamemnon, King of Men, as a personification of kingship and legitimate political rule, without necessarily feeling any close personal identity with him, as the modern TV viewer can accept policemen or business tycoons on the same basis. But in the novel, which as Ian Watt (1957) says is the narrative of a particular individual,[22] the reader must find a character with which to feel the sympathy of kinship. It is not simply a coincidence that novels revolving around anti-heroes are described as 'anti-novels'. The hero is legitimised by acceptance of his atrocious behaviour (this has always happened, despite the intentions of the author: Richardson complained of moral ambiguity in a public which seriously asked, 'Who can decide between a Lovelace and a Clarissa?'; and there were readers, then as now, who quite liked Jonathan Wild)—or the writer cannot hold a sympathetic audience. Orwell, in his essay on Kipling, says that his literary excellence is underrated, because the sentiments he expresses must be revolting to every civilised person. William Faulkner suffers from the same disability. He is a superb writer, whose dark, elaborate baroque style elevates to high literature the kind of stories you hear in the country (in Mississippi). But at least one reader feels baffled by having no character with whom it is possible to identify. The sensation is that of a bird flying over a spectacularly destroyed countryside, and finding no place on which to alight.

Identification is unavoidably a transaction between writer and reader, a matter of choice (remembering that we are not entirely free to choose what to choose), and is consequently affected by changes in the social character of readers. When Jane Austen said of *Emma* that this time she was going to take a heroine that no one would much like except herself, she was probably speaking truly of the accepted norm of her day. But certainly modern readers find it easier to identify with bossy, independent, witty, mentally and physically active heroines like Emma and Lizzie Bennett, than with that boring Fanny, always dawdling in a sickly way about Mansfield Park. And Fanny was a pattern of a nineteenth-century English, middle-class virtuous young woman: mild, submissive, serviceable, intent on being good and letting who would be clever, priggishly avoiding occasions of enjoyment—and with a streak of Protestant conscience which gives her the necessary courage and obstinacy to stand up to the formidable Sir Thomas Bertram, on whom she is wholly dependent, and absolutely reject an advantageous proposal of marriage.

The appeal to the individual conscience as the final arbiter is, as Ian Watt demonstrates in the first chapter of *The Rise of the Novel*, an essential component of the bourgeois norms associated with philosophical realism, the Protestant ethic, the rise of capitalism, and the novel as a literary form associated with all these phenomena: and on this ground alone it is possible to admire Fanny to this day, unless the reader has become irritated beyond endurance with her creep-mousy life-style and rejected her long before even the amateur theatricals.

There must be a common ground to make identification possible, and this has a general cultural and a class-cultural element. It is impossible to identify with, or even understand, the action of literature which is so culturally alien that the norms presented are not understandable. Laura Bohannan (1966) showed this very convincingly in 'Shakespeare in the Bush', an exercise in the non-universality of great art. Despite what she had been told in England about *Hamlet* as a universally valid drama, she found it impossible to make it understandable to the African people she was living with and studying, who had a custom of story-telling and a considerable oral literature. The concepts underlying the action of *Hamlet* made little sense to them because their own concepts were different. They have, for instance, no idea of ghosts: King Hamlet must have been a zombie instead; they believe that widows should marry again immediately, preferably to the dead husband's brother; and they assumed that Laertes had sold his sister to the witches to be killed. Identification in European terms was impossible, and personification had to be modified to create a quite different version compatible with their own norms.

Even within the same national culture, a historical change in the class composition of the audience with accompanying change of dominant class-cultural norms can lead to a startling reversal in the interpretation of a classic masterpiece. This has happened with the Danish comedy, Ludvig Holberg's *Jeppe paa Bjerget* (1723).

The comic action centres on the drunken peasant Jeppe, who, besides being poor, is bullied by his wife Nelle, who commands him, beats him, and has been more or less openly sleeping for years with the deacon (a shady character in Danish peasant culture: see Hans Andersen's *Little Claus and Big Claus*). Jeppe, lying drunk in the road, is found by the Baron and his friends and put, asleep, into the Baron's bed and nightgown. They bamboozle him into believing that he really is the Baron, and that his whole peasant life was an hallucination, a dream while he was temporarily mad.

When this comedy was written, in 1723, the audience was substantially composed of the Baron and his friends: the sophisticated Copenhagen élite. This point is made absurdly explicit in a theatre poster of the time, which begs gentlefolk, who are pleased to honour the theatre by their presence, to leave their liveried servants outside. These were the grandsons of the new nobility who had been imported from Germany with the Oldenburg line at the Reformation (1526), and who surrounded the autocratic monarchy with a bureaucratic class of administrators, strengthened by the recruitment of gifted sons of the bourgeoisie to whom advancement was made very open. Some top posts were specifically reserved for men of bourgeois origin, 'while the old Danish landed nobility ebbed out like the tide and seemed about to perish' (Kristensen, 1970).[23] The new class, climbers and aspirants to titles (Holberg himself became a Baron), was eager to put the greatest possible social distance between the common people and itself. As Sir Walter Elliot discovered in *Persuasion*, to follow and flatter others, without being followed and flattered in turn, is but a half enjoyment. These new men found the confusion and humiliation of the gross peasant irresistibly funny, and were no doubt entirely on the Baron's side when in the Epilogue, addressing his friends and the audience as 'Children' he explains how important it is for everyone to keep in his social place. This was certainly a leading theme with Holberg, especially in *The Political Candlestick-Maker*, which 'proves' that artisans should not read newspapers and concern themselves with politics to the detriment of their trade.

Now, however, the Danish audience is composed essentially of people of peasant origin—Danish names ending with -sen, -gaard, and trade names such as Møller, Smed, etc., are peasant within four generations at most—the descendants of Jeppe, in short; and it would be impossible to play the comedy without directing all the sympathy to him. Jeppe now emerges as the only truly human character in the play, a sort of folk-hero, ill-treated and with a lifetime of suffering behind him, but shrewd, humorous and humane for all that, while the Baron and his friends shrink to the scale of nasty-minded, spoiled and malicious brats.

At one point in the comedy, Jeppe is made to believe that he is to be hanged, and according to peasant custom says farewell and thanks for good service to all his dependants; but Jeppe is so miserably poor that these are only his daughter (who unlike his other children was born before the Deacon came to the village) and his farm animals. This was good for a hearty, brutal laugh in the eighteenth century, but now his speech, 'Farewell, my spotted horse . . .' must be played with genuine pathos, and is genuinely moving.

To be thus adaptable to identification by members of two opposing systems of cultural norms argues a certain ambivalence in the literary work, and this is certainly true both of Jeppe and of Holberg himself. Jeppe at crucial moments reacts as a peasant to the wrongs of the peasantry, even while thinking himself to be the Baron. When the Baron's overseer of the estate introduces himself, he straightway orders him to be hanged, and when the man, astonished, asks why, Jeppe says, 'What, you are an overseer and you don't know why you should be hanged? You who oppress and squeeze the peasant, and cut the very silver buttons off his coat?' Jeppe apologises, and says, 'That [imaginary] peasant keeps coming up in me', and it is not too fanciful to say that the peasant keeps coming up in Holberg as well. Perhaps he became a Baron because he had Jeppe in his bed. Not that Holberg was peasant-born. He was of bourgeois origin, claimed to have a bourgeois point of view, and certainly in his *Moralske Tanker* (1744) expressed a bourgeois philosophy. But he had nevertheless considerable sympathy with the common people, which led him to the realistic innovation of putting them on the stage in his comedies in their ordinary working clothes and language. This made his plays seem old-fashioned and disagreeable for a long time while the Danish theatre in the nineteenth century was going through a genteel period of stupefying mediocrity, mysteriously known to them as the Golden Age, and Holberg gets his grand recognition and revival in modern times with the triumph of social democracy and the common man.

The basis for identity must exist in factors which lie outside literature itself: there must be enough cultural similarity to make sympathy and understanding possible. We may be fascinated by, but we can never identify with, what is totally strange. But if the reader or watcher of drama can recognise enough of himself in a fictional character to make identification possible, identification with a literary character may be quite decisive in transmitting norms and influencing personal behaviour. Montaigne said mockingly that 'If no one had ever learned to read, very few people would be in love', and he was certainly right about the enormous legitimising effect literature has had since the Renaissance—or perhaps since what Auden (1967) calls 'the discovery of *amor* in the 13th century' —on the idea of 'being in love' as a desirable, indeed the most desirable state. This effect occurs because readers are able to identify with the hero or heroine, who is not (and especially since the appearance of the bourgeois novel) markedly different from themselves.

Fiction not only legitimises emotions and aspirations, it also, again particularly since the appearance of the novel with its devotion to the minutiæ of personal relationships, gives models and patterns of acceptable and unacceptable behaviour. I have certainly noticed that those who never read, or never have read, fiction, tend to be obtuse and insensitive in personal relationships. It does really seem as if the consumption of fiction is a part of the necessary education of modern people in the fine points of human relationships: so many examples are given of how people are, how they may be expected to react, and what the harvest is likely to be.

Notes

1 At the same time, we must not forget the ancient policy of rulers to court popularity by providing pure entertainment. This has sometimes taken the form of spectacles, public games, music, pageants, fireworks, and similar insubstantial pleasures. These give no benefit except sheer enjoyment: and yet to offer them partakes of the nature of hospitality, and puts the public in a mood of goodwill toward the giver.

2 The Icelandic scribe who recorded and thus preserved *Thidrek's Saga*, probably in the thirteenth century. Cited by Magnus Magnusson in the Introduction to his translation of *Njal's Saga* (1970).

3 See the annotated bibliography (a model for all bibliographies!) in McQuail (1969). Especially: Himmelweit *et al.* (1958), Musgrave (1969) and Whale (1969). Also the BBC report (1970). A great deal of research is now being done, in various areas of mass communications, at the University of Leicester in the Centre for Mass Communication Research and at the University of Birmingham at the Centre for Contemporary Cultural Studies, to give only two academic examples.

4 See also news story: *South Africa to have segregated television*, by Dan van der Vat from Cape Town, *The Times* (London) 28 April 1971.

5 In the trial of Lieutenant Calley (1970–1) for the My Lai killings in 1968, the US Army was evidently concerned to dissociate the image of the Army from the idea of mass murder by a vigorous prosecution in which justice was done and seen to be done. In the event, they need not have bothered, as the image of mass-murderer of civilian women and small children was quite acceptable to the American public. A typical letter in *Time* magazine (3 May 1971): 'It does not matter whether Lieut. Calley was guilty or not. When we send our boys to fight and die for us, we should stand behind them come hell

or high water.' Answers to polls frequently suggested that 'that's the sort of thing that happens in wartime'. There seemed a basic indifference to the atrocity of the actions, and much public sentiment was expressed to Free Calley!

6 Essay on 'Fenimore Cooper's Leatherstocking Novels':

> And Natty, what sort of a white man is he? Why, he is a man with a gun. He is a killer, a slayer. . . . The essential American soul is hard, isolate, stoic, and a killer. It has never yet melted.

7 Fiedler (1966) uses 603 pages to enlarge upon the following words of Lawrence (1923).

> And again, this perpetual blood-brother theme of the Leatherstocking novels, Natty and Chingachook, the Great Serpent. . . . What did Cooper dream beyond democracy? Why, in his immortal friendship of Chingachook and Natty Bumppo he dreamed the nucleus of a new society. That is, he dreamed a new human relationship. A stark, stripped, human relationship of two men, deeper than the deeps of sex. Deeper than property, deeper than fatherhood, deeper than marriage, deeper than love.

8 It really is not possible to have it both ways. *Njal's Saga*, the longest and best known of the Icelandic sagas, written if not composed in the thirteenth century, is certainly a massive piece of propaganda against the blood-feud, on the ground of their senseless, interminable destructiveness. But it attacks them because they existed, not because they did not. Also, it contains a good portion of description of the feud and its norms, especially in the pre-Christian first half, glorifying the heroic virtues and strict obligations necessary to it.

9 Gouldner (1971, p. 31):

> Background assumptions of more limited application, for example about man and society, are what I shall call 'domain assumptions'. Domain assumptions are the background assumptions applied only to a single domain; they are, in effect, the metaphysics of the domain. Domain assumptions about man and society might include, for example, dispositions to believe that men are rational or irrational; that society is precarious or fundamentally stable; that social problems will correct themselves without intervention; that human behaviour is unpredictable; that man's true humanity resides in his feelings and sentiments.

While I agree that 'domain assumptions' is an extremely useful concept, in fact indispensable for problems of normative influence, I cannot help observing that Gouldner himself had already given a pretty example of his own 'domain assumption' that sociological theory is a male prerogative (p. 8):

> Theory is commonly transmitted by *older men* to *younger men* who are in some way dependent on them. The theoretical apathy of a young radical is thus sometimes an expression of *his* vigorous striving toward individuality and autonomy, and of *his* need to become and live as a *man*, and, if possible, as a better *man* than *his* elders have been.

> Somewhere in the young radical's thoughts is the suspicion that not only are received, traditional theories wrong or irrelevant, but that they are also *unmanly*; he sees them as the timidity-generating creations of timid *men*.

The italics used for *unmanly* are, significantly, Gouldner's. The rest are mine.

10 *Egil's Saga*, from the *Elder Edda*, as recorded in the thirteenth century by (probably) Snorri Sturlasson. Egil died *c.* 910. My translation from Olaf Hansen's verse translation in N. M. Petersen's Danish version, 1969.

11 People with no capital to invest have nevertheless found it possible to become rich through a literary career. Writing fiction has also been a means of *regaining* a lost social status and influence. There is an extraordinarily high correlation between fathers who have failed, through death or financial disaster because of shiftlessness or disinclination, to maintain the social and economic position of their children, and the efforts of these to regain their status through a literary career. This class includes Henry Fielding, Mary Russell Mitford, Dickens, Thackeray, Melville, Mark Twain, Hemingway, F. Scott Fitzgerald, and many others.

12 See note 11.

13 See Freuchen (1961). See particularly ch. 6, 'Polar justice: crime and punishment among the Eskimo', and ch. 8, 'The Eskimo mind'. A recent discussion of institutionalised sharing is in 'Sharing by hunters' by Dowling (1968), p. 502.

14 Description of the sanctions of the Furies against the shedding of kindred blood (*Eumenides*, ll. 355-9):

> when violence
> nurtured in the home strikes a dear one down,
> after it in pursuit we go,
> and mighty though the killer be
> we put him in darkness through the fresh blood on his hands.

15 Witchcraft is secret. Witches are unknown, unlike priests or other public officials. Some modern students emphasise the autistic nature of witchcraft: 'Azande believe that some people are witches and can injure them in virtue of an inherent quality. A witch performs no rite, utters no spell, and possesses no medicine. An act of witchcraft is a psychic act.' E. E. Evans-Pritchard, *Witchcraft, Oracles and Spells among the Azande*, 1937. (Cited by Parrinder 1963, p. 133.) The rites, ceremonies, invocations and incantations which witches lack belong to public and communally practised religion, and serve to strengthen the social bond by shared experience in acting out the narrative of religion. The witch is not only secret, but solitary; and is feared for the power of a malevolence which is unsanctified by the group and which the group cannot control.

16 See Durkheim (1912); Pickard-Cambridge (1953); Thomson (1941); Harrison (1962). Goodlad's valuable work (1971) has in ch. 2, 'The association of drama with ritual', a great deal of illuminating insight.

17 Not only Mario Puzo's super-best-selling novel (and film) *The Godfather*, but the whole series of gangster movies of the 1930s.

18 Glasgerion . . . is recorded to have been an eminent poet of distinguished birth, son of Owain, Prince of Glamorgan.

19 *Jock o' Hazeldean*, one of Scott's successful bits of epigony—the other in verse is *Proud Maisry*—is derived from the first stanza of version E of Child Ballad No. 293. The situation remains emotionally valid well into the nineteenth-century bourgeois period.

20 He cites (1970, p. 45) the statement of St Beuve, that Paris quickly began to resemble the fantastic picture of Paris created by Balzac.

21 The British Army, it seems, would like to have a similar arrangement. A student reports being at 'Operation New Look', a seminar at the Staff College, Camberley, on one of the arranged visits and seminars of the Department of Sociology of the University of Reading, when the point came up, together with the remark that, funnily enough, there were several TV directors present who worked on police series. These were invited to give their views as to how the police got the excellent image they have, and answered, 'We put in what the Police ask us to.' There was some speculative discussion as to whether such programmes would be possible for the benefit of the Army image.

22 Watt (1957), ch. 1, 'Realism and the novel form': 'the plot had to be acted out by particular people in particular circumstances' (p. 15).

23 Kristensen (1970), 'Holberg, forudsœtninger og virkninger'. I am greatly indebted to this essay.

Chapter 3

The so-called 'realism' of the novel

I

If all the novels ever written were read, collated, and analysed for content, which I have no intention of doing, it would be found by quantitative analysis that the overwhelming majority of them deal with situations leading to a solution which could conveniently be expressed in some such formula as 'and then they lived happily ever after'.

By 'happily ever after' is meant marrying the person one wants to marry, the establishment of a new family unit, and the acquisition of enough money.

The novel is capable of infinite variations on this formula: sometimes the social unit founded on the emotional bond is reaffirmed by a 'return'—as in Joyce's *Ulysses*, Virginia Woolf's *Mrs Dalloway* and *Between the Acts*; there are occasional reversals of the happy ending: Madame Bovary pursued love and money in a way which did not lead to rational happiness; change of partners is allowed in modern novels; marriage is not always insisted on; but in general the theme of novels is the discovery of a love-object, the crystallisation, as Stendhal described it, of the emotion, and the acquisition of the loved one and at the same time of enough money to make the new family unit plausible.

The theme of money invariably accompanies the theme of love— whether they have it or have it not, how to get it, and what difference it makes in their lives. In the eighteenth and early nineteenth centuries this meant not only the elopement of the lovers, but their return and reconciliation with their parents, and receiving by gift or inheritance 'a fortune'. Kipling, in his anonymous 'Epitaph' (in the *Saturday Review*) of the old-fashioned three-volume novel, which he likens to a three-decker ship, sums up the typical ending:

All's well, all's well aboard her, there's dancing on her decks,
I left the lovers loving, and the parents signing cheques.

In the eighteenth century, Tom Jones prototypically proves to be the rightful heir to a fortune; in the twentieth, Lucky Jim, by an accident of personality, gets not just the girl but a good job and prospects.

Lukács in *The Historical Novel* (1960, p. 122) cites Manzoni's complaint of the 'immoderate preponderance of the love motif' in the French classical drama (Corneille and Racine), which, he argues, is due to the 'formal problems and their distorting effect', the supposed classical necessity to compress the action to twenty-four hours. The novel, however, has no such restrictions, it can ramble indefinitely, and is often said to be 'about' anything at all. Nevertheless, the novel typically is 'about' love and money, and the narrative is concerned with how to get them.

Usually, the events which lead to the happy ending are the adventures and development of a young person, sometimes from childhood, through various obstacles; overcoming these demonstrates some particular interesting superiority. The person moves, typically, from a position of relative ignorance and social impotence, to success and knowledge and full membership in adult society. The hero/heroine has moved upward in the social scale, and also acquired a life-partner. The novel of development and success is so familiar that it is sometimes assumed to be the only kind there is, but here again there are exceptions: *The Warden* by Trollope is about an old man's conscience, but his increase in knowledge is a social disaster. But it is possible to say that the novel in general deals with a few years in youth, which is after all a small period of life, and with a highly selected part of the experience even of this segment. Galling though it must be to agree with Kingsley Amis, he is certainly in the right when he speaks in *The Green Man* (1969) of 'the endemic unreality of all fiction', and says of novelists (1971, p. 71), 'theirs [is] a puny and a piffling art, one that, even at its best, can render truthfully no more than a few minor parts of the total world it pretends to take as its field of reference'.

When one considers how not just some people, but all people, spend their time between getting up in the morning and going to sleep at night, it becomes evident that the novel is remarkably selective for emotional, rather than emotionally neutral events. It is human relationships which count in the novel, and this distorts the concept of *work*—to take only one major human activity—almost out of existence. We see Mr Morell as a family man, but never follow him to the coal-face, or C. P. Snow's academics into the classroom. We do see Robinson Crusoe at work, and Swiss Family Robinson as well, but he is alone and they are also shipwrecked: the theme is 'success in extreme situations'. We will never know just what it is that Mr Wilcox does in the City: his role there is important in the novel *(Howards End)* because it shapes his human relationships outside of it.

Some effort has been made by consciously 'proletarian' novelists to bring in work as subject matter: Arthur Seaton in *Saturday Night and Sunday Morning* (1958) is seen standing at his machine, but all his thoughts are away from what he does, he is certainly alienated from his work except as a source of money; the Joads in *The Grapes of Wrath* (1939) strip down an engine in a way which was acceptable to a real-life mechanic ('You *could* do it that way—I'd do it another way, but that way would be all right.'). But these are indeed exceptional. The novel selects for personal rather than impersonal relationships in a way which is markedly distorting, especially in modern industrial society, where such a very high proportion of time is spent in secondary, rather than primary, relationships and institutions. This would seem to detract from the novel's claim to realism.

For the novel has a reputation for realism, and has been defined as realistic; specifically, not only more realistic than other fiction, but the first fiction which presents life as it is, and individual unique persons as themselves, in contrast to other literature which deals in values and social types. Ian Watt makes this distinction very clearly (1957, p. 13):

> Previous literary forms had reflected the general tendency of their cultures to make conformity to traditional practice the major test of truth: the plots of classical and renaissance epic, for example, were based on past history or fable, and the merits of the author's treatment were judged largely according to a view of literary decorum derived from the accepted models in the genre. This literary traditionalism was first and most fully challenged by the novel, whose primary criterion was truth to individual experience—individual experience which is always unique and therefore new.

7

This definition makes the novel a sort of case-history; and it is interesting that the first novelists, Defoe and Richardson, went to some pains to give the appearance of presenting a true account of actual lives, forming their fictions as letters or autobiographical reminiscence, indignantly denying that they were engaged in fictional invention. Nevertheless, the novel does not in fact simply record what happens to a unique individual, excluding nothing, imposing no pattern. 'Stream of consciousness' writing has attempted to reproduce 'real life' in this way, but found it is impossible. The novel is an art form; it has a pattern, it selects themes and characters which are suitable or possible for novelistic use, and these are different at different times. The shortest discussion of the themes of novels, such as that recorded above, shows that 'truth to individual experience' certainly does not mean 'the whole truth' about any individual, or individual as opposed to typical persons.

What is the novel's claim to tell the truth? Edmund Gosse in 1911[1] defined it as 'A sustained story which is not historically true but might very easily be so', and George Saintsbury in 1916 (Spearman, 1966) said that it dealt with 'ordinary life and incident, with character, with a great deal of conversation, and—in story, in talk, in comment and everywhere—with all sorts of miscellaneous matters'. Mary McCarthy (1961) in a fairly recent definition claims for it above all a realistic treatment of life, and specifically excludes the supernatural as an active agency:

> If a criterion is wanted for telling a novel from a fable or a
> tale or a romance (or a drama), a simple rule of thumb would
> be the absence of the supernatural.

This is rather awkward, as it unfortunately excludes from the category a number of what can only be called novels, by Graham Greene and Muriel Spark, in which divine intervention is essential to the plot. Either one must admit the Catholic version of the supernatural to the category of reality, or say that the novel depicts, not the reality of the real world, but the reality of the beliefs of the author: his norms and values.

All of these modern definitions, and many others like them, seem to be a development of the statement by Dr Johnson in *The Rambler* (no. 4, Saturday, 31 March 1750), in the first great period of the novel:

The works of fiction, with which the present generation seems more particularly delighted, are such as exhibit life in its true state, diversified only by accidents that daily happen in the world, and influenced by passions and qualities which are really to be found in conversing with mankind.

He makes it clear, however, that he is specifically comparing the novel with the trivial 'heroic romances' which had been the favoured light reading of the previous generation, when he says of the novel:

Its province is to bring about natural events by easy means, and keep up curiosity without the help of wonder: it is therefore precluded from the machines and expedients of the heroic romance, and can neither employ giants to snatch away a lady from the nuptial rites, nor knights to bring her back from captivity; it can neither bewilder its personages in deserts, nor lodge them in imaginary castles.

But once the novel is committed to the notion of realism, it must stand the test of credibility. No one can rationally dispute the facts about giants and imaginary castles, but

The task of our present writers is very different; it requires, together with the learning which is to be gained from books, that experience which can never be attained by solitary diligence, but must arise from general converse and accurate observation of the living world. Their performances have, as Horace expresses it, *plus oneris quantum veniae minus*, little indulgence, and therefore more difficulty. They are engaged in portraits of which everyone knows the original, and can detect any deviation from exactness of resemblance. Other writings are safe, except from the malice of learning, but these are in danger from every common reader; as the slipper ill-executed was censured by a shoemaker who happened to stop in his way at the Venus of Appelles.

The expertise of the public in matters of factual knowledge about the society in which they and the novel live, and in expectations of how fictional people may be expected to behave, is certainly one of the great checks on the exuberance of writers. There must be enough contact with the expectations of readers to sustain credibility, and it is a legitimate criticism of a work of fiction to say

'Nonsense, people don't act like that!'—a remark made often enough about the works of Iris Murdoch in the present, and about those of Charlotte M. Yonge (but for a different reason) in the past. Since these writers are both indisputably novelists, there must be another dimension to novel-writing than the simple delineation of recognisable character and event.

Then again, the claim is made for the novel that it is realistic because of the very particular descriptions of objects and actions in it—Defoe is masterly at this, also Richardson—think of the famous scene in *Clarissa Harlowe*, where the heroine's sister is handling the wedding finery. Dickens pauses in the story to give the solid detail— ('roast shoulder of lamb with potatoes under')—and so do many others, including Hemingway. Novelists do set the scene and maintain their people among these solid-seeming properties, but this can only be considered exclusive to the novel if one compares it solely with the romances which immediately preceded it. Epic poetry has also this characteristic of solid detail. Homer, with all his gods, kings and heroes, at the very dawn of European literature, is famous for this same particularity. Auerbach devotes the first chapter of his *Mimesis* (1953) to a brilliant discourse on just this kind of preoccupation with factual detail in the *Odyssey*, respecting a wound of Odysseus. The appearance of this wound, its history and the occasion in his childhood when he got it—a mass of factual material is presented, and the story is brought to a complete stop while all this is recounted. Thoreau (1854), too, in praising Homer for his clearness and particularity, says, 'If he do but send his messenger to Achilles, he does not leave us to wonder how he got there, but we go with him, step by step, beside the resounding sea.'[2] The novel does use realistic detail, but it is not the only literary form which does so.

The discrepancy between the real length of human life, and the small section of it customarily treated in the novel, has already been mentioned. The novel's prescriptive territory is that part of human activity which is devoted to getting established and settled in life. Novelists who have daringly varied the prescription by taking up the story after marriage usually soon reveal themselves to be doing nothing more original than arranging a settling with a different partner. In any case, the story is substantially that of attraction-pursuit-success, and concomitant upward mobility, either symbolic or real.

I would like to offer the hypothesis that the novel adopts this particular set of patterns, not because they correspond to the whole reality of human life—it does not in fact include an unlimited number of 'miscellaneous matters'—but because the themes of individual success, individual choice of marriage partner, pursuit of money and social mobility, correspond to the ideal norms of bourgeois society, and the novel is as much an expression of bourgeois norms—it is the prototypical bourgeois art-form—as epic poetry is of heroic warrior society and the tragic drama of crime and punishment of the city-state. In so far as the novel is realistic in detail, it is so because it was made for and by the bourgeoisie, a class of practical and pragmatic, down-to-earth people who were themselves interested in the price and appearance of everything, in downright speech, and in recognisable manners.

Dr Johnson certainly recognised the didactic function of literature, and in particular the fact that novels were chiefly read by 'the young, the ignorant, and the idle', who would use them as models of behaviour in their own first ventures into the world. For this reason, having in mind Lovelace in *Clarissa Harlowe*, published in 1748, and *Tom Jones*, which first appeared in 1749, in his same *Rambler* essay of 1750 he denounced *too much* realism in the portrayal of character:

> But when an adventurer is levelled with the rest of the world, and acts in such scenes of the universal drama, as may be the lot of any other man; young spectators fix their eyes upon him with closer attention and hope, by observing his behaviour and success, to regulate their own practices, when they shall be engaged in the like part.

And, because of this use made of novels, he calls for a restriction of realism in the depiction of character which would certainly have had an enthusiastic nod of recognition in the Soviet Union (my italics):

> If the world be promiscuously described, I cannot see *of what use* it can be to read the account; or why it may not be *as safe* to turn the eye upon mankind as upon a mirror which shows all that presents itself without discrimination.
>
> It is therefore not a sufficient vindication of a character, that it is drawn as it appears; for many characters ought never to be drawn: . . . *The purpose of these writings is surely . . . to initiate youth by mock encounters* in the art of necessary defence, *and to increase prudence without impairing virtue.*

... In narratives where historical veracity has no place, I cannot discover why there should not be exhibited the most perfect idea of virtue; of virtue not angelical, nor above probability, *for what we cannot credit, we shall never imitate*, but the highest and purest that humanity can reach, which, exercised in such trials as the various revolutions of things shall bring upon it, may, by conquering some calamities and enduring others, teach us what we may hope, and what we can perform. *Vice, for vice is necessary to be shown, should always disgust*; nor should the graces of gaiety, or the dignity of courage, be so united with it, as to reconcile it to the mind. Wherever it appears, it should raise hatred by the malignity of its practices, and contempt by the sameness of its stratagems: for while it is supported by either parts or spirit, it will be seldom heartily abhorred. ... It is to be steadily inculcated, that virtue is the highest proof of understanding, and the only solid basis of greatness; and that vice is the natural consequence of narrow thoughts; that it begins in mistake, and ends in ignominy.

Since these strictures were directed against two of the very greatest English novelists, it is plain that the programme they propose cannot be essential to the existence of the novel. The novel is not didactic in the simplistic sense desired by Dr Johnson (although great efforts were made in the nineteenth century to make it so),[3] but it is didactic on a much deeper level of correspondence to the expectations and norms of bourgeois society. Success, not virtue, is the attraction. So much so that virtue itself is rewarded with success.

The preoccupation of the novel with the period of settling in life, I suggest, is due to the fact that with the new sets of behavioural patterns associated with the breakdown of traditional society and the gradual establishment of one far more open, mercantile, and mobile, it became an ever more strict social imperative that young people find their own way in life. It was no longer enough, for a significant section of the population, to stay at home and be settled on a farm or in a shop—young people must bustle about, make their livings, get out into the world and manage their own affairs. Similarly with marriage: the right to freedom of personal choice is a major theme in European literature from the beginning of the bourgeois period (say, *Romeo and Juliet*). And the requirement of the individual falling in love as the only legitimate basis for marriage is a battle which was fought, ever more successfully, against parents and guardians in literature (not only the novel—most comedies revolve round this theme), for two hundred years; this was the same period in which arranged marriage was giving way in real life to marriage by individual selection.

The requirement of *success* in the novel—the hero or heroine must move upwards in society and in wealth—corresponds also with the moral imperatives of the Protestant ethic: Work! Venture! Succeed! It is to be noted that the success in question is an *individual* success, not the rise to power of a clan or class. Even where the protagonist starts as a representative of a class and the book contains an exposé of social conditions (Jack London's *Valley of the Moon* (1914) is a good example—the book begins in the mood of Upton Sinclair's *Jungle* (1906), as an exposé of the conditions of working-class people in San Francisco; but the moral is the same as that of H. G. Wells: 'The main thing about the working class is to get out of it'; starting as a teamster and part-time boxer, the hero ends up as a rich landowner), the novel plot moves inexorably upward. Again, this is not because everyone succeeds in real life, but because the real bourgeois norms require it as an ideal.

Both the norm of success and the norm of individualism, as Ian Watt demonstrates conclusively in *The Rise of the Novel*, are related to philosophical realism as it developed in the seventeenth and eighteenth centuries, with its emphasis on scientific truth, and the legitimisation of individual sense-impressions as the final arbiter of fact. This philosophy, so suited to a pragmatic, hard-headed businessman's mentality, is also that which lies behind the rationale of the novel. In fact one might almost without alteration say of the novel what Marx and Engels in *The Communist Manifesto* said about the bourgeoisie as such (1951 edn, p. 35):

> The bourgeoisie, wherever it has got the upper hand, has put an end to all feudal, patriarchal, idyllic relations. It has pitilessly torn asunder the motley feudal ties that bound man to his 'natural superiors', and has left remaining no other nexus between man and man than callous 'cash payment'. It has drowned the most heavenly ecstasies of religious fervour, of chivalrous enthusiasm, of philistine sentimentalism, in the icy water of egotistical calculation. It has resolved personal worth into exchange value.

It is not necessary to take the simile so far as to speculate upon Free Trade, but certainly the requirements of individualism in the novel make the love theme a continual destruction of all feudal patriarchal ties and arrangements, and the requirement of personal success in the realistic world of bourgeois society, make the acquisition of money the natural accompaniment of love.

The question must arise, if bourgeois norms reduce all relationships to exchange value, then personal relationships must be devalued, and indeed we have seen this persuasively argued by Ian Watt and also by Leo Lowenthal in his essay on 'Robinson Crusoe' (1960). It is a large component in Galsworthy's description of the Forsytes in *The Man of Property* (1906), and of E. M. Forster's description of the Wilcoxes, 'the world of telegrams and anger', in *Howards End* (1910). If, then, personal relationships are so devalued in the bourgeois norms, so much so that many novels take just this devaluation as their theme, how is it possible to contend that love, or falling in love, that quintessential personal relationship, is a necessary theme, one of the triad of necessary themes, with success and money, in the novel?

There is no necessity to assume that contradictions cannot exist in literature, as well as in life. The supreme importance of the idea of the individual as the judge and centre of everything is basic to bourgeois morality. All feudal ties are really torn asunder, all obligations to family, clan and class dissolved. The only loyalty larger than self-interest is the patriotic devotion to the nation-state, certainly frequently called into play in the political and military life of the bourgeois period, but these are seldom the themes of novels,[4] except, significantly, in war time.

Passionate and romantic love certainly appeared in literature before the novel—Greek pastoral romances are full of it, troubadourial poetry and 'heroic romance' is infested with it, pastiches of epic poetry such as Ariosto and the like pay a great deal of attention to it as a spring of action and motivation of attitudes and behaviour. But in all these cases, love is treated as a catastrophe, a disaster which disturbs the normal order of things, and leads to trouble of many kinds, usually including bloodshed. It remains for the novel to present love as the normal preliminary to marriage, the one ingredient without which no marriage or coupling can be said to be tolerable. This is really a radical break with the social system which had obtained for hundreds of years, in which marriages were arranged between families and the young persons involved were simply the representatives of each side, chosen to continue the economic life of the group. Love, of course, was an unpredictable result of personal choice: but it went *against* not *with* the tide. To demand that the disposition of property, the future of the family, the construction of the basic unit of society, should depend on an exclusive sexual and social attraction which transcends in importance all other considerations, is really to make an extraordinary claim.

This claim is only possible on the basis of the supreme importance of the individual which is implicit in the Protestant ethic and bourgeois norms. It is also only possible in literature when in life the ties of family were loosening, children were more free to dispose of their lives, and in fact were under the necessity of doing so, in a society where traditional stability was superseded by activity and mobility.

Love does, as I say, appear in pre-bourgeois literature, but in a different sense. Auden in the opening sentences of *The Enchafèd Flood* (1951) calls attention to one of the nodal points at which it was recognised as important (p. 15):

> Revolutionary changes in sensibility or style are rare. The most famous is, perhaps, the conception of '*amor*' which appeared in Europe in the twelfth century.

But the essence of the Provençal poetry he refers to is the unattainability of the desired fair one, usually a married woman and securely locked up. Disastrous amorous encounters are quite frequent in ballads, both courtly and common, of the Middle Ages, but the emphasis is on the disastrous outcome, not any possible 'happy ending'. In *Njal's Saga* there are two love-matches, both disastrous. In one, Unn, a woman who has divorced her husband for good reason, marries again without consulting her kinsmen—for love, in fact—and this is one of the ultimate causes of the feud which destroys them all. Also Gunnar, the hero of absolutely perfect virtue, marries the ill-reputed Hallgerd—a woman who has got her first two husbands killed—in spite of everything he is told about her character; she, as it turns out, is the major contestant in the feud, thus leading indirectly to his death, and also is the direct cause of it when she refuses to give him two locks of her hair to string his bow when he is besieged by his enemies. The message is clear: infatuation is the worst possible basis for marriage. And this is typical of pre-novelistic literature.

Tribal society does not expect romantic love to be associated with marriage (Gluckman, 1965, p. 76):

> There is no expectation of intensive emotional attachment between spouses. Dr. Audrey Richards, writing about marriage among the Bemba of Northern Rhodesia, says: 'I once amazed a group of elderly Bemba by telling them an English folk-tale about the difficulties experienced by a prince in winning the hand of his bride—glassy mountains, chasms, dragons, giants and the like. An old chief present was genuinely astonished: "Why not take another girl?" he said.' A similar attitude was expressed by some Fingo elders who were discussing the problem of increasing runaway marriages and illegitimate births with the 1883 Commission on Native Law and Custom in South Africa. One of them complained: 'It is all this thing called love. We do not understand it at all. This thing called love has been introduced.' If husband and wife are so devoted to each other, or jealous of one another, that they insist against convention on spending their time together, then it is commonly thought that the woman has used magic to win her husband's love.

The most notable example in classical literature of the disastrous effect of romantic love is of course the Trojan War. And here Vico is insistent on the absence of any legitimate romantic passion in Homer (1744, Book II, 5. 708):

> gallant heroism is a creation of post-Homeric poets, who either made up fables of a new cast or took the old fables, originally grave and severe as becoming the founders of nations, and altered and corrupted them to suit the growing effeminacy of later times. We have a great proof of this . . . in the example of Achilles. On account of Briseis, taken from him by Agamemnon, he makes such an outcry as to fill heaven and earth and provide matters for the whole *Iliad*, yet nowhere in that entire epic does he give the faintest indication of amorous passion at being deprived of the girl. Similarly Meneleus, though on Helen's account he stirs all Greece to war against Troy, does not show throughout that whole long and great war,

the slightest sign of amorous distress or jealousy of Paris, who has robbed him of her and is enjoying her.

In both cases, though sexual passion is present, it is expressed in terms of pride and anger at being robbed of property—Achilles' complaint was that every other hero had his prize, he only had been deprived of his, and he raged against the loss of status—and not because of the pain of bereavement on losing someone beloved.

From about the time of the Renaissance the concept of the nature of love is drastically changed in the novel, away from the notion, current in the pre-bourgeois period, of a disastrous visitation quite often caused by the gods. It is felt (in *Romeo and Juliet*, for instance) to be not only powerful but normal, and that though the consequences *may* be tragic, they *ought not* to be: the young people do in fact marry, and it is only bad luck and the intransigence of their parents which destroys them, not the natural course of events from such a bad beginning as falling in love, as with previous fiction. From that time on, although in fiction there were innumerable obstacles, because in real life most marriages were in fact still arranged, the moral weight shifts more and more in favour of the young people in these contests, until, from about the middle of the nineteenth century, the plot which revolved on outwitting those who would enforce an arranged marriage was no longer viable as a theme for fiction, as it was no longer a live issue in life. The principle of individual choice of partner had now triumphed, and any parents who seriously insisted on arranging their children's marriages would have to be presented as perverse and atypical. I speak only of England, the United States, and Europe, of course: the literature and even the films of countries like Japan and India still have this as a living theme.

Love, then, became established with the novel because of the change in social norms and values at the beginning of the bourgeois period. In the first part of this era, it was very directly and openly intertwined with the money theme, and even now when love and money are often seen as contradictory elements, the separation is not a dismissal of the importance of money, but a statement of the superior importance of personal values or human relationships in general. Money has not disappeared from the novel, but it is less openly embraced.

The morality of Richardson's *Pamela* has often been derided: she escapes seduction and rape by her employer, but is willing to marry him and thus get an honourable establishment, nasty though he is. Since this book was commissioned and written specifically as a series of letters giving advice to young women going out to service,[5] it certainly conveys a clear commercial message: no fooling around, but bargain for marriage or nothing. The sub-title, 'Virtue Rewarded', condenses into the smallest possible number of words the values of the bourgeois norms: abstinence, chastity, postponement of pleasure, refusal of self-indulgence, defence of one's own self—all while maintaining a respectful carriage towards Authority. All this, however, is not for the sake of virtue as its own reward, but in the expectation of substantial financial and social advantages: a 'good' (rich) marriage, great establishment, respectability, the opportunity for display and the achievement of high status. Fielding, like practically all modern readers, despised the mean calculation of this type of negative virtue; but the bourgeois novel, dedicated to bourgeois norms, *cannot fail to reward with money* those protagonists who carry forward the ideals of the author: and so Tom Jones and Sophia, who personify Fielding's rather more attractive ideals of great physical health and beauty, good nature, generosity, capability of passion, activity, courage, and the rest, are also rewarded, not only with each other but also with a fortune quite capable of making them (and Moll Seagrim) happy.

Why should the novel be supposed to be particularly bourgeois? Diana Spearman in *The Novel and Society* (1966) challenges this supposition, saying that, at the time of the 'rise of the novel', far from being the dominant class in society and the class which set the normative trends, the bourgeoisie was relatively insignificant, power in the eighteenth century, as in previous centuries, being in the hands of the great landowners ('the Great'), who controlled not only agriculture but politics and trade as well. She gives herself a great deal of trouble presenting evidence of aristocratic investment in trade, in building speculation and manufacture, but in my opinion simply demonstrates the *bourgeoisification of the aristocracy*. Trade, speculation and manufacture were the ways to make money, from the seventeenth century onward, and the aristocracy, having money to invest because of their transformation of agriculture through three hundred years of Enclosure Acts from a feudal-subsistence to a mercantile economy, invested it. But though the

titled nobility might be at the top of the social pyramid, the transformation of society in the bourgeois era meant the creation of a vast
population of city-based, literate people, eager for entertainment
and instruction about the secular world. Virginia Woolf describes
them (1966, p. 69):

> A middle class had come into existence, able to read and
> anxious to read not only about the loves of princes and
> princesses, but about themselves and the details of their
> humdrum lives. Stretched upon a thousand pens, prose had
> accommodated itself to the demand; it had fitted itself to
> express the facts of life rather than the poetry.

It is of no use for Spearman to object that novels were read by the
lower orders, which they were ('Down in the kitchen, honest Dick
and Doll / Are studying Colonel Jack and Flanders Moll'), that
Fielding had aristocratic connections and a gentleman's education,
or that Defoe was not a bourgeois man (Spearman, op. cit., p. 29):

> From constant references by literary critics to the optimism of
> a rising middle class and Puritan commercial morality, it
> might be supposed that Defoe was the pattern of a successful
> and upright tradesman. In reality, not only was he a failure in
> business but his life was so unusual as to make it impossible
> to regard him as a representative of any class.

It is an extraordinary confusion of ideas which regards a failed
businessman as a non-businessman, and her tentative acceptance of
Richardson as bourgeois is no better (ibid., p. 32):

> Richardson was a prosperous tradesman and thus fits the middle-
> class theory, but he too, seems to have been led to writing
> Pamela by experiences peculiar to himself rather than by those
> he shared with his class or his period.

While we must admit that not every middle-class man in the
eighteenth century wrote Pamela, Richardson had stated explicitly
the circumstances in which he did so,[5] and nothing could be more
evident than that it was an essentially commercial venture, written
as ordered for the market, and to promote an explicitly bourgeois
mercantile morality. I would also be glad to know where Richardson
was when he was having experiences outside his class or his period?
It sounds like pure science-fiction. What makes a person, and particularly a writer, bourgeois, is not necessarily having a little shop,

but having a bourgeois soul; being fitted out with bourgeois ideals, attitudes, norms, values and expectations, which, because he cannot help it, seep into his delineation of his fictional characters and what he sets them to doing.

Moll Flanders, to take an obvious example, will never win any prize as Mrs Average Suburban Housewife. She is nevertheless a *bourgeoise* to the bottom of her calculating, adventurous, triumphant, mercenary soul. She is even true to the English bourgeois norms to the extent of having aristocratic hankerings and aspirations; in one of her marital ventures she states her idea of a suitable candidate: 'I was not averse to a tradesman; but then I would have a tradesman, forsooth, that was something of a gentleman too; that when my husband had a mind to carry me to the court or to the play, he might become a sword, and look as like a gentleman as another man.'

She embodies, with or without the consent of her author, the values, social habits, and point of view of the trading class, to no less an extent than her merchant 'brother' Robinson Crusoe, and, in spite of being a thief and a whore, to no less an extent than Pamela (Virtue-Rewarded) Andrews. The Protestant ethic finds one of its most explicit representatives in her, and her story is a rare allegory of the triumph of perseverance, foresight, and acquisitiveness over outward circumstances: leading, of course, to a happy ending, with plenty of money and the man she likes best (except her first lover, who is dead). Defoe is fond of putting his protagonists absolutely alone in the world to fend for themselves, and Moll is no exception. The notion of the discrete individual, an economic unit from the tenderest age, is part of the ideology of the Industrial Revolution, and Defoe was highly approving when he found during his Tour of the textile manufacturing district of Norfolk that (1927 edn, vol. 1, p. 62) 'as I passed this way in 1723, the manufacturers assured me, that there was not in all the eastern and middle part of Norfolk, any hand, unemploy'd, if they would work'; and that

> the very children after four or five Years of Age, could every one earn their own bread.

Moll was even younger; she thinks she was not above three years of age when she hid from some gipsies who were carrying her with them, and began her independent life as a parish ward.

From an early age, with true bourgeois enthusiasm, she aspires to be a 'gentlewoman', without knowing what that is exactly, but the essential part, from her (then) point of view, is not being sent out as a servant to do manual labour. This is the fate to which she would normally be destined, as a child cared for by the parish, but her prettiness and charm, and artless ambition, made her into a sort of pet with the mayor's wife and other bourgeois ladies of the town. She says she was very 'womanish' in her behaviour—always neatly dressed, and 'would be clean, and would dabble [her] clothes in water' herself if necessary. She thus from early childhood began to present the bourgeois image of respectability: there is nothing of the bohemian about Moll; even when she was a professional whore, and then a professional thief, she 'kept herself to herself', refused to associate with those in the same occupation except professionally: the 'she-comrade' who teaches her to steal never knows her real name, none of her associates know where she lives. She is always engaged in building up a respectable middle-class existence. As a child, her first ambition is only not to do housework, then to be respectably dressed and to live among gentlewomen. She is encouraged in this by Mrs Mayoress and the ladies who patronise her: ' "Nay, she may come to be a gentlewoman", says she, "for aught I know; she has a lady's hand, I assure you." ' Moll as a child is quite willing to do needlework or any genteel occupation; when very young she helps her good foster-mother, who keeps a small school, to teach the children, and also does sewing for the ladies who befriend her. Later in life she goes back to needlework for a while, in the period when she is 'past the age to be courted for a mistress' and has not yet begun her second career as a thief. Her great aim was never to be a master-criminal or great demi-mondaine, but always to be respectably settled in matrimony: 'I kept true to this notion that a woman should never be kept for a mistress that had money to make herself a wife.' But she certainly has bad luck with her husbands: they die, go bankrupt, prove to be penniless highwaymen, ruin her by speculation, and, worst of all, one turned out to be her own half-brother and she felt compelled to leave him. Over and over, she is left without money and alone, or maybe with a couple of children to dispose of, and with the world to begin again. As she rightly says (rightly, that is, in bourgeois society, not in tribal or aristocratic cultures), 'But I knew that with money in the pocket one is at home anywhere,' and she immediately sets about acquiring it in the best way possible to her.

She is certainly capable of passionate attachments, but money is well to the fore in them, and nowhere more so than in her original seduction in Colchester, by a man with whom she was passionately in love. He 'told me it was all an honest affection and that he meant no ill to me, and with that put five guineas into my hand and went downstairs. I was more confounded with the money than I was before with the love.' She was very attracted to him—'I struggled to get away, and yet did it but faintly neither'—and in her later recollections she bitterly reflects on the lack of ordinary commercial prudence displayed by both sides when he indulged in sexual passion, and she in love. For his part, 'if he had known me and how easy the trifle he aimed at was to be had, he would have troubled his head no further, but have given me four or five guineas and have lain with me the next time he had come at me'. On the other hand, she could have made a much better bargain: 'I might have made my own terms, and if I had not capitulated for an immediate marriage, I might have for a maintenance till marriage and might have had what I would; for he was rich to excess, besides what he had in expectation; but I had wholly abandoned all such thoughts . . . As for the gold, I spent whole hours in looking upon it; I told the guineas over a thousand times a day.' At the actual scene of bedding, he gives her a purse with a hundred guineas in it, and 'My colour came and went at the sight of the purse and with the fire of his proposal together, so that I could not say a word, and he easily perceived it; so, putting the purse into my bosom, I made no more resistance to him, but let him do just what he pleased.' It must have been damnably uncomfortable, but it certainly sets the pattern for the consistent confusion of passion and money throughout the book. She and her highwayman husband are passionately devoted, although they have each married the other for a delusory fortune: ' "But, my dear", said I, "what can we do now? We are both undone; and what better are we for being reconciled, seeing we have nothing to live on?" ' and so they must part, only to meet again, however, for the happy and wealthy ending.

But lest the reader object that money is so prominent in the affairs of Moll because she is a prostitute, and not because she is a bourgeoise, let us consider other novels. In *Vanity Fair*, not only does Becky Sharp reckon that it would take £5,000 a year to keep her honest and respectable, but old Mr Osborne, musing on the bankruptcy and ruin of his lifelong friend Sedley with some satisfaction, reflects 'And yet he was a better man than me, this time twenty years, by, I should say, ten thousand pounds'. George Osborne treats money with aristocratic disdain, thereby convincing his father's clerks that he will soon be ruined—and so he would have been if he had not died at Waterloo. E. M. Forster is very conscious of the importance of money as the background to everything in bourgeois life. His idealistic Schlegel girls are no less bourgeois than the practical, stirring businessmen of the Wilcox family, the driving folk who kept things going and built the Empire. The Schlegels specialise in sensibility, artistic appreciation and personal relation-ships (which in the long run, true to the novelistic obligation to reward virtue and the mercantile terminology of the bourgeois class, turn out to 'pay best'), but Margaret speaks of the little piles of golden guineas on which they stand—for other people, the water is up to their lips, but because of these stacks of guineas she and her brother and sister have their heads above water, they have five hundred pounds a year, and think the thoughts and have the feel-ings of five-hundred-pounders. The romantic and idealistic Helen, too, tries to make reparation to Leonard Bast by giving him money: money is *the* medium, to her as much as to the Wilcoxes. And he reveals his essential decency by refusing it—money is the test. The house, Howards End, seems to represent an earlier, pre-bourgeois England, with other values and understandings, but it has been taken over by the Wilcox-principle, conquered by marriage with the first and then the second Mrs Wilcox—Margaret Schlegel. There is an element of sex warfare here too, contained within the specialisation of function of different sections of the bourgeoisie. The women do not work, do not speculate: unlike Moll Flanders, they are not economically active. Their function is to 'do' the culture, the sensibility, the human relations, as well as being showcases for their husbands' wealth and proof of status. When Mrs Wilcox leaves the house to Margaret Schlegel, her ally in sensibility, this is felt as treachery by the Wilcox family, who suppress her Will—property should never be alienated; but because the virtues which Forster believes in are just those virtues of communication and human value represented by the Schlegels, and because in the bourgeois novel the good are rewarded with money, Margaret gets the house anyway. Poor Dolly, who has been snubbed and insulted into resembling her name ('It was an understood thing that everyone chaffed Dolly') still testifies as a sort of subversive witness— 'then

8

Margaret gets the house after all', in almost the last words of the book. Virtue Rewarded, yet once again.

It is not my intention to give a catalogue of the money motif in all novels, but to state that it is normally present, and since novels are committed to a bourgeois norm of financial success, the bestowal of money by the author is the usual reward for adherence to the code of right behaviour. Here the limited arc of the life-span dealt within the novel is important. It is primarily in the novel that rewards such as marriage for love, acquisition of money, and success, are achieved in this short span. When we compare the novel to the epic saga dealing with the whole life of a heroic warrior, it is clear that to get a secure title in the rewards valued by his society, primarily honour and status, he dies young after glorious deeds which secure his reputation, or, if he live long, he lives to decline in status, becoming foolish or madly senile, like Njal or Egil the Poet.

The insistence of the novel that everyone who obeys the norms grows rich and happy is of course not consistent with what can be observed in ordinary life, which is another count against the realism of the novel; it is real to norms, but not to life.

But another, more interesting, question is, if love and money are inseparably associated in novels, how do we explain the frequency with which novelistic protagonists reject their own advantage? The refusal of the pecuniarily advantageous marriage,[6] the insistence on following one's insecure vocation (*Portrait of the Artist as a Young Man* and many similar works), the rejection of the crooked deal, the noble lack of calculation concerning money in penniless heroines such as those of Edith Wharton, not to mention the Byronic or daemonic rejection of fortune and life itself by the heir of Redclyffe. Often this was only a temporary loss: Fanny marries Edmund Bertram *and* gets a suitable establishment. The pursuit of love and the pursuit of money no longer seem to go hand in hand as a matter of course, as in the innocent days of Moll Flanders and Pamela Andrews. Some personal integrity independent of, even contradictory to, the pursuit of money seems to be required in the later novel: but the result is the same, the hero maintains his integrity against all temptations and is rewarded by the accomplishment of his will, AND by money! To challenge the norms and still be rewarded with all the prizes contained in the system is certainly to make a very good bargain with fate. From the viewpoint of 'the sociology of literature' it is substantially the same bargain, discussed in the previous chapter, which literary challengers of society make when their attacks become commercial successes; it is not surprising that writers incorporate this element of their life experience in their work, as H. G. Wells did in *Ann Veronica* (1909), Galsworthy in *The Forsyte Saga* (first book, *The Man of Property*, 1906), and, more recently, Alan Sillitoe in *A Start in Life* (1970). When we consider the matter in terms of bourgeois norms, we find money firmly established as the measure of all things, not least when the collective values of society are to be challenged. To renounce money and position is, in terms of the bourgeois norms, to make the greatest possible sacrifice, and it is thus perfectly possible to choose love rather than mere dross and yet remain strictly within a morality which makes dross the highest value, and this is of course reinforced when, according to the normative principle of literature which rewards heroes with the highest available value, the hero also gets his share of dross, here to be understood as money.

II

One of Ian Watt's arguments for the realism of the novel, its 'truth to individual experience', is based on the style of names used in novelistic fiction, in contrast to those used in previous literature. In novels, he says, the names are ordinary real names, with no particular symbolic meaning, unlike the Everyman and Death of medieval morality plays, or the Mr Horner, Mr Pinchwife, Count Bellair, Squire Sullen, Lord Rake, Sir John Bruto, Colonel Bully, Lady Fanciful, and waiting-women called Mincing and Foible, of Restoration comedy. *The Pilgrim's Progress*, being a tract, does not count, so he discounts characters called Christian, Faithful, Giant Despair, and Mr Badman.

In *The Rise of the Novel* (1957) Ian Watt relates the use of nonsignificant proper names of characters to philosophical realism and the demands of individualism arising from it (pp. 18, 19, 20):

> Logically the problem of individual identity is closely related
> to the epistemological status of proper names; for, in the words
> of Hobbes, 'Proper names bring to mind one thing only;
> universals recall any one of many'. Proper names have exactly
> the same function in social life: they are the verbal expression

of the particular identity of each individual person. In literature, however, this function of proper names was first fully established in the novel.

Characters in previous forms of literature, of course, were usually given proper names; but the kind of names actually used showed that the author was not trying to establish his characters as completely individualised entities. The precepts of classical and renaissance criticism agreed with the practice of their literature in preferring either historical names or type names. In either case, the names set the characters in the context of a large body of expectations . . .

The early novelists, however, made an extremely significant break with tradition, and named their characters in such a way as to suggest that they were to be regarded as particular individuals in the contemporary social environment.

Not, as we have seen in Richardson's case, that there is no place in the novel for proper names that are in some way appropriate to the character concerned: but that this appropriateness must not be such as to impair the primary function of the name, which is to symbolise the fact that the character is to be regarded as though he were a particular person and not a type. Fielding, indeed, seems to have realised this by the time he came to write his last novel, *Amelia*: there his neo-classical preference for type-names finds expression only in such minor characters as Justice Thrasher and Bondum the bailiff; and all the main characters—the Booths, Miss Matthews, Dr. Harrison, Colonel James, Sergeant Atkinson, Captain Trent and Mrs. Bennet, for example—have ordinary and contemporary names. There is, indeed, some evidence that Fielding, like some modern novelists, took these names somewhat at random from a printed list of contemporary persons—all the surnames given above are in the list of subscribers to the 1724 folio edition of Gilbert Burney's *History of his Own Time*, an edition which Fielding is known to have owned.

But it is not really true that characteristic names disappear from literature with the novel. Certainly the first novelists in English, Defoe, Richardson and Fielding, use them freely. Watt himself notes in *Tom Jones*, the pedagogues Thwackum and Square, Mr

Allworthy, Heartfree, and Squire Western. He might have added that the name Sophia is not devoid of meaning, and that the name of Tom Jones itself is a common name to be sure, but a symbolically common name: it stands for natural man, a sort of Everyman of natural human virtues. Then Richardson, in *Clarissa Harlowe* certainly chose his names with care. The name of Lovelace has been noted by Dorothy van Ghent (1967, p. 45), Arnold Kettle (1953, vol. 2, p. 74), and others, for its hidden meaning of Loveless, a man incapable of loving; to this might be added the connotation of Lovelace (e.g., aristocratic finery—a comment on vanity from Richardson's essentially bourgeois-Puritan point of view) and Clarissa, of course, can hardly mean anything but 'the purest', culminating in what Kettle, in *An Introduction to the English Novel*, rightly calls 'that sublime cry of Clarissa's . . . that assertion of a woman's dignity within the moral jungle of arranged marriage and hypocritical prostitution. *"The man who has been the villain to me that you have been, shall never make me his wife."* ' At the same time, remembering the savage moral standards of the eighteenth century, we may as well face the fact that 'Harlowe' is pretty close to 'harlot', and that Clarissa herself and everyone else as well assumed she was a lost and degraded woman for having been raped while drugged and unconscious. It is also true that she had eloped with Lovelace, expecting of course to be married immediately, which makes his treachery more intolerable, but shows her to have put herself outside the normal protection of society. (It is of no use for Spearman to object, in the work mentioned, that Clarissa had only to appeal to the nearest constable or respectable citizen. Until the rape, she expected her elopement to be justified by marriage. But in the meantime she was in an anomic situation, with no status. And after the rape, she refused to accept the status of mistress (harlot), which Lovelace had planned, and so died.) She is thus described after her death as 'The finest young creature that ever went astray', a judgment which is nearly incomprehensible by modern standards, but not by contemporary ones.

Perhaps John Gay ought not to count in this exercise, but surely a name like MacHeath is as symbolic of a highwayman (on the heath) as Brecht's modern version of it, Mackie Messer, or, in English, Mack-the-Knife; and the same play contains characters called Peachum and Lockit. Fielding's *Jonathan Wild* was written with a didactic purpose—to de-glamourise crime, and as an antidote to *The Beggar's Opera*, so that one might have thought the title character's name was chosen on purpose, and perhaps it was; but in real life there was a real Jonathan Wild, a London king of crime. Nevertheless the comedy contains criminals with names such as Fierce, Snap, Sly, and a Miss Straddle, to take a few at random: these can hardly be called simple, neutral names with no symbolic content.

Moving forward into the nineteenth century, we find that Jane Austen is really full of neutral names: Janes, Elizabeths and Annes abound. But she does not restrict herself to them entirely: the names of Mr Darcy (D'Arcy) and the two Mr Knightleys have certainly an aristocratic ring; Mr Weston might be said to have the same hearty good-fellow aura as Squire Western in a more modern person without, of course, any squirearchical airs about him. Jane Austen has one cold-hearted scheming female named Lucy Steele, and another, common as dirt, called Mrs Clay. Mrs Clay is a 'poor and plausible' widow, whose father, a lawyer, is called Mr John Shepherd. This points not only to his function of protecting Sir Walter Elliot, but to his humble origins, perhaps two or three generations previous. Significantly, Admiral *Croft* in the same book (*Persuasion*) is specifically mentioned as representing all that Sir Walter detests: the tendency of the Navy to bring upward men of lowly origin to honours and wealth merely because of talent. Then Mr Elliot has married a woman of wealth, whose father was a butcher, and whose grandfather was a grazier—it seems as if the question of rank is here specifically declared to be the rise to élite status of the descendants of agricultural labourers!

Dickens, of course, is famous for names: Mr Murdstone, for instance, a murderer with a heart of stone, or what of Mr Gradgrind, Bounderby, and the Cheeryble Brothers, Scrooge (screw, squeeze, wring), and Newcomes and place-names like Dotheboys Hall? Thackeray as well, delineates Becky Sharp in her name, before we know anything else about her, and what of his Veneerings?

Henry James, too, is profligate in his use of characterising names. Take only one example, *The Golden Bowl*, with its insistent preoccupation with the money theme. The Prince who is destined to marry an American millionairess is named Amerigo (and thinks continually in golden images, especially when he thinks of women). Maggie, his bride, is the daughter of Adam Verver, a man who is described as having a face like a small, well-swept room (an elemental man: Adam) and who must have quite a lot of drive to make himself a multi-millionaire. Charlotte Stant may be significantly named: Stant suggests many things, such as *stint* (for lack of money, and also the obligation to do her stint as Mrs Verver), *stunt* (her stunted moral development, and the stunt of living among the rich without being one of them); also *stagnation*, *status*, *station* (in life). The house from which Charlotte and the Prince start their actual love affair is called Matcham, and is known for this sort of arrangement. James, meticulous and hypersensitive to nuances of meaning, can hardly have distributed these names by chance.

Then again, his famous ghost story, *The Turn of the Screw*, has been repeatedly analysed for meaning, and the names of the participants scrutinised for a possible clue as to what really is going on. Thus the children, Miles and Flora, are categorised by their names in male and female roles: a little soldier, a little flower. Mrs Grose, the housekeeper, is a simple soul, and illiterate, as her name suggests. Peter Quint is a name with harsh consonants, and also a clutching name: it can be said through clenched teeth. But more than this, it is hard not to give it sexual overtones, whether or not James was consciously aware of this. Peter is plain enough, and Quint as well. Quint also means five: which brings to mind a slip reported by Freud, which had the form of a joke: a woman patient complained that, to marry, a woman must needs have beauty, youth, wealth and manners, whereas a man need only have five straight limbs. Probably, however, James's conscious intention was closer to the social pretensions of Shakespeare's Peter Quince, that hempen homespun in *A Midsummer Night's Dream*, swaggering as a courtly actor and disguised as a lion.

Much is made in *The Turn of the Screw* of Quint's masquerade: having the power in the house 'over us all' and wearing 'somebody's clothes' (his master's), but being unmistakably —'no, never!'—not a gentleman. But the terrifying thing about the story is that one never knows really what is happening; it is impossible to decide whether the ghosts are real, or whether the governess has conjured them up, or imagined them, and what her character is really like. What makes it impossible to identify her and classify her with any certainty, is the fact that *she has no name*, and this means that we can never understand her, or know what James meant her character to be: *this* is the insoluble mystery. Names are not neutral labels, but definitions.

Names, then, are important as a part of characterisation in the novel as in all other fiction. If 'neutral' or common names are used, it is because a character is to be identified as a neutral or average person, not because he is not to be identified at all.

There are more modern examples of significant naming: one of them is in the work of F. Scott Fitzgerald: Gatsby is a man who is a *go-getter*, he has *got* a lot of money, and it is not unlikely that this involved the use of *gats*. And Dick Diver, the psychoanalyst in *Tender is the Night, dives* as an analyst into the subconscious of his patients, also into the Mediterranean in the beach-life world he has created; and the end of the book is his slow downward spiral into obscurity, when the rich have no further use for him.

An up-to-date example is *The Godfather*, Mario Puzo's super-best-seller about the Mafia. It starts with an undertaker named Bonasera (= 'goodnight' in Italian, not a bad name for an under-taker), contains a vicious killer named Clemenza ('mercy'), and the central family is named Corleone, meaning lion-hearted. Corleone really is a town in Sicily, and a Mafia-dominated town at that; still, it is a significant name. The father and founder of the dynasty is called Vito (= 'life'), the two sons Santino (= 'little saint'), and the triumphant one with the flaming sword, the new Godfather, is modestly entitled Michael—after the archangel?

Ian Watt (1957, p. 20) tells us that comedy is more apt to have type-names than serious literature is. Puzo, to be sure, rather depre-cates *The Godfather*, and says he was 'writing under his ability' in it. Much of the writing is really atrocious, but this does not detract from the realistic impact of this excursus into the norms of the Mafia clan-system of crime and blood-feud. It may very well be true that the significant naming of characters in a joking or ironical way is due to the author's lack of serious regard for his work: he probably thinks of it as a comedy. Still, the names have significance.

But there can be no lack of serious intention in Galsworthy, when he named the Forsytes after the prime bourgeois virtue, Foresight. Late in life he made a disclaimer of any intention to give social meaning in *The Forsyte Saga*, saying that he merely intended to show, through Irene, what effect a beautiful woman can have on the actions of men. The description of the species Forsyte, in *The Man of Property*, however, tells a different story (1963 edn, pp. 171–3):

'A Forsyte', replied young Jolyon, 'is a not uncommon animal. There are hundreds among the members of this Club. Hundreds out there on the streets; you meet them wherever you go.'

'And how do you tell them, may I ask?' said Bosinney.

'By their sense of property. A Forsyte takes a practical— one might say a common-sense—view of things, and a practical view of things is based primarily on a sense of property. A Forstye, you will notice, never gives himself away. . . . We are all, of course, all of us the slaves of property, and I admit that it's a question of degree, but what I call a "Forsyte" is a man who is decidedly more than less a slave of property. He knows a good thing, he knows a safe thing, and his grip on property—it doesn't matter whether it be wives, houses, money or reputation—is his hallmark.' . . .

'You talk of them', said Bosinney, 'as if they were half England.'

'They are,' repeated young Jolyon, 'half England, and the better half too, the safe half, the three per cent half, the half that counts. . . . But I'm not laughing. It is dangerous to go against the majority—and what a majority!' He fixed his eyes on Bosinney: 'It's dangerous to let anything carry you away— a house, a picture, a—woman.'

Nevertheless, implicit in the bourgeois norm of the supremacy of property is the possibility of challenging it by being 'carried away' by something else—claiming supremacy as a value for love, aesthetic passion, scientific or intellectual curiosity, or political integrity. The Forsytes are named as they are, not because it is an ordinary name casually selected as plausible for identifying the 'always unique and always new' history of any one family, but specifically to identify them as bourgeois, walking bundles of Protestant ethic virtues and vices, of which Foresight is obviously a chief component. They have their subjective characters, but all within the value-system of the trading, speculating, money-manipulating class whose value-system they represent as surely and as openly as *Karrig Niding*[7] in the Danish Morality Play or *Everyman* in the English one, represents medieval values.

Galsworthy intends to 'go against the majority' in the name of art and love: and Young Jolyon and Bosinney who have the conversation about the real nature of Forsytes both challenge the norms, giving up everything for love. Since Galsworthy, like every other writer, is really bound by the norms of his time, even in attacking them, he rewards his heroes with the regular bourgeois rewards, as described above: Bosinney gets the woman (love) and builds the house, though punished by accidental death; and Young Jolyon gets love, male children, and finally reconciliation and money.

The novel, then, like all other fiction, is concerned with social reality in a special sense. It describes and defines norms and values, and presents its characters as actors in the demonstration of them. In so far as the novel is realistic, that is, exhibiting 'life in its true state, diversified only by accidents that daily happen in the world', this is because the norms of bourgeois society and the Protestant ethic are in fact pragmatic, down-to-earth, materialistic. When there is sustained interest and credibility in the supernatural in the reading public, these appear readily enough in the novel. An example of this is Kingsley Amis's *The Green Man* (1969), which contains two ghosts, relics of paganism such as a prehistoric (working) charm; and a malevolent spirit conjured up out of 'much Verdure and Timber sufficient'; the exorcism of these by a priest according to the appropriate ritual of the Church of England; and a visit from, presumably, the Devil, with the anti-realistic accompaniment of stopping all earthly activity for a short time. All this besides the usual sexual and social complications—and, to do him justice, Amis does in fact show his hero at work, running an inn.

If I quarrel with that part of Ian Watt's argument which claims realism for the novel on the basis of the use of neutral, non-significant names, which seems to me simply not true, it is not because I wish to detract from the importance of *The Rise of the Novel*. It is and remains the most significant contribution in this field, and the classic chapter on '*Robinson Crusoe*, Individualism and the Novel' is a marvellous exposition of exactly the point I am making, that the novel is true to the norms of the class which created it, read it, and reads it and creates it anew, over and over again. It is no more and no less true to 'life' than other fiction, but can give us facts and fancies mixed; and it, above all, is not free to produce at random any values whatever, but is bound to the values of the bourgeois period which are clearly definable, elastic and seemingly various though they may be.

'Realism' itself is a convention, it is no more and no less 'true' than the conventions of romanticism or the heroic epic. There is a splendid example of this in film, where, since the invention of colour-film, the intention to be 'realistic' is often signified by the use of black-and-white or sepia, although the natural world is coloured. The novel has the equivalent effects in naturalistic dialogue, specific material descriptions, and the use of ordinary or mediocre characters. But these, as I have been labouring to show, are the projections of the norms of what the bourgeois mind considers the world to be really like.

Notes

1 Edmund Gosse, 1946 edition of the *Encyclopaedia Britannica*; this sentence 'slightly modified' from his article in the 1911 edition, as Diana Spearman says in *The Novel and Society* (1966).

2 This sentence is as typically American as it is possible to be: with a nod to the grandeur of Homer's grave style, the clause 'he does not leave us to wonder how he got there' could just as easily have been written by Mark Twain.

3 Internal and external censorship was certainly the rule in the nineteenth century—Scott, Trollope, Dickens, Thackeray and George Eliot all felt their responsibility in this matter. Trollope for instance 'noted with approval that no immodest girl is made alluring in all the novels of his contemporary' (Dickens), while Thackeray, when editor of the *Cornhill*, in a *Letter from the Editor to a Friend and Contributor*, explained that he expected its writers to 'have good manners, a good education, and write in good English', adding that 'we shall suppose the ladies and children always present'. Cit. Guinevere L. Griest (1970).

4 The historical novel, Lukács notwithstanding, is a bastard and an exceptional form, and of little importance in consideration of the novel as such, for reasons which will be mentioned in the next chapter.

5 'Two booksellers, my particular friends, entreated me to write for them a little volume of letters, in a common style, on such subjects as might be of use to those country readers, who were unable to indite for themselves. Will it be any harm, said I, in a piece you want to be written so low, if we should instruct them how they should think and act in common cases, as well as indite? They were the more urgent with me to begin the little volume for this hint. I set about it; and, in the progress of it, writing two or three letters to instruct handsome girls, who were obliged to go out to service, as we phrase it, how to avoid the snares that might be laid against their virtue. . . . Hence sprung *Pamela*.' Cited by Spearman (1966), from A. L. Barbauld (1804), *Correspondence of Samuel Richardson with an Introductory Memoir*.

6 Kettle (1957, vol. 1, p. 71): 'The conflict of *Clarissa* is the conflict of love (i.e. human dignity, sympathy, independence) versus money (i.e. property, position, "respectability", prejudice), which lies at the heart of almost all the novels of Fielding, Jane Austen, the Brontës, Thackeray, unalike as they are

the limitations of bourgeois norms, and novelistic rewards are distributed according to the dominant system, i.e. money = the highest value, therefore the appropriate reward for virtue.

7 *Karrig Niding*, a Danish morality play of the sixteenth century, praising the pre-bourgeois (e.g. peasant, tribal and feudal) virtues of hospitality and generosity with food. A man who is so stingy he starves his wife and servants and locks up the food when he goes from home is outwitted by a stranger who impersonates him and finally triumphantly ousts him from his possession of wife and farm.

Part II

Some attempts at 'sociology through literature'

Chapter 4

Fact in fiction: the use of fiction in the deduction of facts about society

Social fact may be revealed by fiction, even fiction of the most wildly improbable kind. There are two general categories of fact which may be obtained through fiction (see chapter 1, pp. 2–3): one is specific information about whether a social institution or custom exists or existed in the society which produced the fiction: the state of technology, the laws, the proscriptions of religion and so on. The other, and more important, is the information about values, norms and expectations in the society which may be *inferred* from the attitudes of the characters in fiction and their behaviour.

The warrant for the first type of deduction is the necessary coincidence of knowledge of the society between the creator and the consumer of fiction at any one time, as described by Dr Johnson in the *Rambler* essay mentioned previously. This enforces plausibility, which will be more noticeable when the fact or custom, whatever it is, is casually produced as a background to the action, than when it is the central interest. Specific events which are in fact exceptional or fantastic, might be presented as normal; but the background which is to make them plausible must be recognisable as factual by the contemporary reader.

An example of this: an Icelandic saga in which a new-born child has been rejected by his father—he will not be named or raised, but on the contrary exposed to perish outside the door. He is taken from his mother and laid on the floor, and screams out, 'Put me back in my mother's bed, I'm freezing on the floor—the place for a boy is by his father's hearth!' This utterance is of course impossible (though the piercing cry of the new-born conveys much the same message) and we immediately recognise it as fantastic; but the custom of rejecting and exposing infants is not at all impossible, and we legitimately wonder if this was a custom in Iceland in the saga period. We find, in fact, that quite a few other sagas use this event as the starting-point of a life-story, and evidence accumulates which suggests that this was really a custom; and our guess is confirmed when we discover that the first law-codes introduced in the Christian period in Scandinavia (from 1000 in Iceland, eleventh and twelfth centuries in Norway and Denmark, thirteenth century in Sweden) specifically forbid the exposure of children: 'every child born must be christened and raised'. At first there was an exception to this in Norway in cases of deformity or great poverty, but this is soon abolished (*Grey Goose Codex*: cit. Rosenberg, 1878–85, vol. II, p. 154), and it seems clear that there was such a custom, though it was rarely used, in the pre-Christian period.

Perhaps it will be claimed that the information from fiction is only credible because it is supported by legal evidence, presumably unbiased. But we ought to consider that a new code of morality may easily contain libels on the code which it intends to suppress and replace, whereas the author of a narrative merely refers to a body of experience which he possesses in common with his audience. If we are ignorant of the practice it is because we are strangers to the norms of a society which is so different from our own.

Another example of fiction—acknowledged to be based on impossibilities of fact and abnormalities of psychology—which nevertheless reveals a good deal about the norms of the society in which it appeared is the work of Edgar Allan Poe. Certainly his plots, his assumptions, and his characters are as far from being 'realistic' as it is possible to be. His obsession with death, including necrophilia, with isolation, with the physical rotting of the body, with the dead returned, with incest, with aristocratic Gothic horrors in deserted castles, tombs and decaying woods, may seem simply idiosyncratic neuroses. They have been traced to his personal psychological traumas, the shock and tragedy of the early death of his mother while he was an infant, the adoption of the Poe children separately in an alien and unsympathetic culture, and so on. Certainly there is a great subjective element in Poe's writings, not explainable entirely by his environment: not every adopted orphan of a beautiful actress becomes an alcoholic, a necrophile, and a poet. But aside from the use he made of literary traditions of romantic melancholy and Gothic death-obsession, there is something in his preoccupation with death which is not exactly alien from the cultural milieu of the time.

Poe was married, as we know, to a thirteen-year-old girl and lived with her and her mother in great poverty and misery. She died young, was buried, later exhumed, and her bones kept in a cardboard box under someone's bed. When Poe was dead and famous, they were discovered and exhibited: the public, on payment of a small sum, could see what was advertised as 'The Bones of Annabel Lee'.

Our own time has certainly plenty of moral evils: more obsessed with violence, with the exploitation of sex, with material consumption, than the first half of the nineteenth century in rural Southern America. Nevertheless, I do not think such an exhibition would be a paying proposition at the present time. We lack the developed appetite for the macabre, which Poe had certainly to a very high degree, but which was in some sort an echo and an exaggeration of his own society. There are passages in Mark Twain which show obsession with death, and it is not surprising when one considers that in rural nineteenth-century America disease, accident, doctoring, dying, laying-out and burying were all events within the family. Many an isolated farm had its own family burying-ground: perhaps the rule rather than the exception.

To say that writers necessarily reflect their own time, which I must repeat is the justification for using their fictions to study the facts of their society, is to say that they are bound to do so, and cannot choose to do otherwise. Thus Lukács says in *The Historical Novel* (1960, p. 32):

> The 'hero' of a Scott novel is always a more or less mediocre, average English gentleman. He generally possesses a certain, though never outstanding, degree of practical intelligence, a certain moral fortitude and decency which even rises to a capacity for self-sacrifice, but which never grows into a sweeping human passion, is never the enraptured devotion to a great cause. Not only are the Waverleys, Mortons, Osbaldistons and so on correct, decent, average representatives of the English petty aristocracy of this kind, but so, too, is Ivanhoe, the 'romantic' knight of the Middle Ages.

He further goes on to quote Balzac on the women in Scott's books (ibid., p. 34):

He says, for example, that with very few exceptions all of
Scott's heroines represent the same type of philistinely correct,
normal English women.

Both of these statements are of course perfectly correct: Scott's
heroes were restricted to his own moral universe, which, like all
other writers, he could not transcend. What is not so easy to understand is how then Lukács, a leading Marxist critic and a theoretician
of culture, can say of these characters, replications of mediocre
nineteenth-century English gentlefolk, that (ibid.):

> Scott's greatness lies in his capacity to give living human
> embodiment to historical-social types.

That (ibid., p. 35):

> In the entire history of the novel there are scarcely any works
> —except perhaps those of Cooper and Tolstoy—which come so
> near to the character of the old epos. This, as we shall see, is
> very closely linked with the nature of Scott's subject matter
> . . . with his selection of those periods and those strata of
> society which embody the old epic self-activity of man, the
> old epic directness of social life. This it is that makes Scott a
> great epic portrayer of 'the age of heroes', the age in and from
> which the true epic grows, in the sense of Vico and Hegel.

It will take more than the unity of opposites to reconcile the two
first statements with the last two. Lukács is quite right, in my
opinion, when he says that Scott cannot choose but create heroes in
his own image, or the image of his internalised values and norms,
derived from nineteenth-century middle-class life. All his romantic,
nineteenth-century Highland Gothicism cannot make his characters, intended by him to represent the wild warrior clan-based
society of the Middle Ages, anything but mediocre English petty
gentry. How, then, is it possible, if Lukács sees this so clearly, that
he can also imagine that Scott recreates the epic, in the sense that
Vico understands it? Is it possible to imagine anyone less like a
mediocre English gentleman, incapable of raw passion, than
Achilles? or Agamemnon, King of Men? Or the wise Odysseus,
that man of many devices? There cannot have been many 'correct,
normal' English gentlewomen of the nineteenth century who re-
sembled Clytemnestra or Helen of Troy, surely? Egil the Poet, an
epic hero, was considered pretty rough even by the Vikings—his

deeds included the time he bit his adversary's throat out, for instance, and the boy he killed, when he was about nine years old, and the occasion when in anger at his father, he, at the age of eleven, killed his father's favourite thrall. Very little English gentlemanly behaviour to be seen here; or in Gunnar of Hlidarendan, the pattern of virtue, who wondered if he was more unmanly than other men because he was rather sorry about having just killed eight men. These people are typically the heroes of epics. They live in another world in every sense, and can only be written about to any purpose in their own time, by people who understand their norms. Scott, in other words, did not 're-create the epic' as Lukács for some reason supposes in *The Historical Novel*. Lukács was far more in the right when he said in his youthful work, *The Theory of the Novel* (1971, p. 30):

> And if no one has ever equalled Homer, nor even approached him—for strictly speaking, his works alone are epics.

If it is objected that he claims only that Scott's works are more like epics *than any other novels* (except those of Cooper and Tolstoy), I can only say that this is irrelevant. None of them are epics, because the epic, as Vico pointed out over two hundred years ago, is rooted in the type of society we call 'heroic', and the novel is *par excellence* the product of bourgeois society. To pretend to write epics in novel-form is merely to write a kind of falsification of history, in which the real past is distorted into the pattern of the norms of the present. This may not be much more false than the ordinary writing of history, and it may be (which I suspect is its attraction for Lukács) didactic: a kind of massive comic-strip; the one thing it cannot be, however, is true epic.

If, then, writers are compelled witnesses for the truth of *their own sets of norms*, what are we to say of social fact when the witnesses disagree? When there are two or more sides to a massive clash of interests, when *all* the writing on a social institution or type of behaviour is motivated by passionate bias, and these biases are contradictory, how can fiction help us to any information at all?

I would maintain that it does, in many ways.

For one thing, as was said earlier, the bias is part of the information. If we know what the writer's bias is, we can place him in relation to the theme he has chosen, whatever he himself claims, because bias is involuntarily revealed in the work.

Also, despite the bias, a series of accounts of the same thing can give us a great deal of factual information about it, simply by collation of the total body of facts presented. We must grant at once that a *single* fictional account of an institution cannot be taken as proof, but accumulation of concurring statements by many witnesses must be allowed as evidence, as with any other phenomenon. The assumption in fiction that a given institution exists may be supported by other evidence (as with the exposure of infants in pre-Christian Scandinavia), but the deductions may justifiably be made even in the absence of this support; and this is where fiction is very useful in the collection of facts which might not otherwise be available.

Consider the institution of Negro slavery in America. How do we know it ever existed? If we had no other evidence than the following group of fictional and personal accounts: the *Life and Times of Frederick Douglass*; *Uncle Tom's Cabin*; *Huckleberry Finn*; various works of William Faulkner; *Gone with the Wind*; and the recent *Confessions of Nat Turner*, we would be in possession of a considerable body of factual information, despite the fact that these accounts are *all* biased one way or another and differ in origin in that they were written over a period of a hundred years by writers, black and white, male and female, living up and down the eastern seaboard from Maine to Mississippi. Ignoring the biases for the moment, and considering only the statements on which they all agree, we would be justified in deducing the following facts about the USA in the first half of the nineteenth century:

1   Negro chattel-slavery existed.
2   It existed within a certain area, the Southern states from Maryland and Kentucky to Louisiana, and was prohibited in the North and West, where runaway slaves might expect to find asylum.
3   The economic basis of the system was agricultural: fundamentally, but not exclusively, large-scale plantation production.
4   The economic structure corresponded to the racial stratification: owners were white and slaves black (although at one time there had been a fairly large group of white indentured servants working as temporary slaves—but there is little mention of this, if any, in the novels).
5   The owners were, in general, resident on the plantations; there was a particular and general system of social stratification on the

plantation for both blacks and whites, considered separately or together.

6 Among owners there was a recognised 'aristocratic' set of norms. These included a high value on a 'graceful' life-style, the most conspicuous elements of which were: the obligation of hospitality; elaborate and courtly manners, especially to (equal status) women; skill in various accomplishments such as dancing, riding, shooting, drinking; personal courage; a strong sense of honour with overtones of blood-feud; aversion to work, and a conspicuous lack of business competence, as a mark of gentility which also included an effortless assumption of wealth and socially acceptable constant debt with frequent bankruptcy.

7 There was a class of relatively poor white independent farmers, existing outside the slavery system except for providing overseers to the plantations. General agreement as to the norms and behaviour of this class: Simon Legree is the archetype, but Douglass has his Covey, Gore and others; Faulkner his Snopeses; Styron his Eppes, MacBride and More.

8 Importance of religion in the area, and its ambivalent effect on the slave-system.

9 Intimate and ambivalent social and sexual relationship between owners and house-servants; frequent self-identification of house-servants with owners.

10 Violence always latent, and frequently visible.

11 Shaky economic base of the slave-system, with ever-present danger of bankruptcy leading to sale of slaves: in fiction this is often the catalyst of action, such as running away.

This outline of characteristics of the slave-system, which could be almost indefinitely developed in detail from the novels, would give an invaluable and quite accurate mass of material to a researcher who knew nothing of the institution from any other source, even if all other information were extinguished.

What we may reasonably call facts, then, are the sum of what is left, agreed upon, when individual bias is cancelled out. What, then, shall we say of factual material on which sources disagree, the 'facts' presented as evidence to support value judgments on the institution of slavery? The arena of disagreement is above all what is presented as the moral and social behaviour and character of the two main classes on which slavery depends: the slaves on the one hand and the masters on the other.

All the authors cited agree that the slave-owning class had, or aspired to have, certain traits which, in European societies derived from feudalism, are, or were, associated with aristocratic norms: an obsession with honour, both personal and also the protection of the honour of the whole family, particularly the womenfolk; this includes the obligations, if not always of the blood-feud, at least of duelling in defence of honour. Associated with this, chivalrous 'old-fashioned' elaborate courtesy of manners, especially to women; some anti-Protestant-ethic norms: disinclination for work, especially of course manual labour; disinclination for business, and ineptitude in it, with a tendency to be cheated; hospitality: a virtue and an obligation, besides being a confirmation of status. And, if there is any education, a formalised Latin style of speech. The bias of the writers can be seen very clearly in the attitude they take to these norms. The bias, in short, is in itself very revelatory, and varies in exact correlation to the social, racial, and regional origin of the writer.

Mrs Stowe, who intentionally wrote a polemical book to stir the American conscience against slavery ('The little woman who started this great war', as Abraham Lincoln said, with a good deal of exaggeration) finds the owners superficially charming and well-mannered, but dissolute (given to drinking and gaming), incompetent in business affairs and consequently neglecting their duties to their inferiors. Through negligence they allow Legree full control without being aware (as it was their duty to be) of what he actually does. They are incapable of believing that blacks are human, and are thus guilty of inhuman and un-Christian callousness. If they are good—or saintly, like Little Eva—they die. Uncle Tom, another saintly character, also dies: it does seem that for Mrs Stowe the wages of Virtue is Death, in which her opinion coincides with that great bourgeois writer, Richardson, in his treatment of Clarissa. Slavery is so inherently evil that no good person can profit from it and prosper. It would not be hard to deduce that Mrs Stowe's real social situation is that of a Northern (her husband a professor at Bowdoin College in Maine), white, middle-class, religious, and highly moralistic woman. She had a 'concern', as Quakers say, about slavery, and spoke out.

Frederick Douglass, her contemporary, who was black, an

escaped slave, actively religious and prominent in the Northern Abolitionist Movement, finds the white masters generous in their hospitality to each other, but extremely stingy in their provision of food and clothing for slaves, even those doing hard physical work. He says that, far from taking on, as they and their apologists claimed, as a feudal duty the obligation of responsibility for sick or aged slaves, they 'free' them or otherwise get rid of them to avoid even the small expense involved in caring for those who cannot labour. He speaks of an old woman 'freed' to live alone in a hut in the woods, after a lifetime of hard labour, and mentions cripples who cannot work turned out to beg. He says that slavery itself, the requirements of the role of owning slaves, spoil even originally sweet natures, like that of his first mistress who taught him to read. He sees nothing of the glamour of the aristocratic manner, but finds the owners both grasping and incompetent.

Mark Twain presented several types of slave-owners on Huck's journey through the South. Despite his detestation of the idiotic brutality of the blood-feud ('a right smart chance of funerals') he is charmed almost against his will by the 'style' of the Grangerfords: their formal manners, their courage, their good looks, high spirits, and hospitality—even Huck is provided with a body-servant and counts for the time being as a young gentleman (which does not mean that he and his friend, the son of the house, do not go barefoot as usual). The modest material basis of this aristocratic norm is shown in the description of the parlour of the house as seen through Huck's admiring eyes: the most glorious thing about it is that there is no sign of a bed, 'and I've seen plenty of parlours in town with beds in them'. Otherwise it is a very modern Victorian parlour, contents itemised in true novel style, made gloomy by the death-obsessed crayon drawings by the dead daughter. Twain is the only one of the writers who shows any charity to the class of small farmers and townspeople of middling condition, and it is no coincidence at all that this is the class from which he came himself. These are people struggling on a small farm with one or two servants and no aristocratic pretensions. Silas Phelps, a small farmer and lay-preacher in the countryside, is sympathetically depicted in his kindness and helpless goodness in ordinary life, although he is rightly reported as quite ready to give Jim up to life-long slavery, no more troubled by doubts than if he had been a runaway horse or dog.

Margaret Mitchell, a modern writer (d. 1936), has only admiration for the class of owners—their beauty, their gaiety, their courage —a bit incompetent perhaps (at least the men are rather useless in practical matters) but flawless in courage, honourable, great fighters, surviving the destruction of their world by the Northern victory in the Civil War with good grace. The master–slave relationship to her is a good one, responsibility on one side, childlike trust and faithfulness on the other. The mistress of the plantation, in particular, works tirelessly at her great responsibilities of caring for the sick and in general administering the economy of the plantation; after the war these ladies were magnificent in courage and resourcefulness. One can only regret, according to *Gone with the Wind*, that such an admirable human type has been deprived of its rightful social rewards. And one can hardly be surprised to learn that Mrs Mitchell is from Atlanta, descendant of slave-owners, a social stratum of 'ruined aristocrats' which traditionally, as with their counterparts after the French and Russian revolutions, had an emotional investment in the glories of the past.

Faulkner, a Mississippian, on the whole believes in the slave-owner as an honourable and natural superior. For him they have, even to a magical degree, great style, great courage and moral superiority, and before the War (the 'Civil War' in the North: the 'War between the States' in the South) great vitality and superior physical and social attractiveness. Many of his stories turn on a presumption of natural superiority, gone to seed and degenerated in various ways because of lost grandeur: ruined plantations, no money, no hope for the future: result of the lost war. Faulkner, in *Intruder in the Dust*, says every Southerner has a romantic dream beginning with a different result in the Second Battle of Bull Run. His definition of 'every Southerner' is obviously rather limited, by class and race. But Faulkner differs from other Southern, pro-slavery writers in seeing also moral superiority of a different kind in the Negro: his aptitude for patient endurance, which is complementary to the slavery situation in which (Faulkner admits) he has a lot to endure. The type of moral superiority seen is certainly of a kind pleasing to white Southerners. He sees the two classes together as forming a natural unit 'the Nigger acting like a Nigger and the white folk acting like white folk, and no real hard feelings on either side', defending the South against the threatening outside world, especially 'the scum of the North and Europe'.

Styron's attitude, in *The Confessions of Nat Turner*, the most recent (1966) of these books on Negro slavery, is ambivalent as regards the owners: he seems to see them as kindly on the whole, but inefficient and misguided. Some indeed are unrealistically too kind—as the white owners who taught Nat to read and thus laid the foundations for his discontent, his insurrection, and many deaths including his own.

This is one key to understanding the bias of the writers; another is their attitude towards the slaves themselves. And here we are forced to conclude that though from two biased accounts of the same thing we cannot tell the truth of the thing described, still we may deduce from the bias the real social position of the writer describing it, whether he is conscious of it or not, and even against his will. Styron's *Nat Turner* and Douglass's (own) *Life and Times* are strictly comparable, as they deal with two men who in real historic life were in much the same situation: clever little black boys, made pets of and taught to read by their mistresses, destined to a life as house-servants—except that both resisted slavery: first by teaching others to read and uniting in religious studies, second by, in Nat's case (1831) leading a bloody insurrection which caused the death of fifty-five persons, in Douglass's case (1842) escaping to the North to become a journalist, lecturer and leading Abolitionist. Douglass no doubt intended to, and did, give a favourable account of himself and of his life; and Styron I believe also intended a sympathetic treatment. And yet compare their statements on various key points!

Styron, speaking as Nat Turner, gives as his most distinct memory of his mother that she allows herself to be raped by the white overseer and when he hears her singing and sweeping the kitchen afterwards, he hears (ibid., p. 150),

> her voice again, gentle, lonesome, unperturbed and serene as before

while his own reaction at his next sight of the rapist is to feel (ibid.),

> a sense of my weakness, my smallness, my defencelessness, my *niggerness* invading me like a wind to the marrow of my bones.

Of his mother, on the contrary, Douglass speaks in entirely different terms (1882, p. 39):

I have since learned that she was the only one of all the colored people in Tuckahoe who could read. How she acquired this knowledge I know not, for Tuckahoe was the last place in the world where she would have been likely to find facilities for learning. I can therefor proudly ascribe to her an earnest love of knowledge. That a field-hand should have learned to read in any slave state is remarkable, but the achievement of my mother, considering the place and circumstances, is very extraordinary. In view of this fact, I am happy to attribute any love of letters I may have, not to my presumed Anglo-Saxon ancestry, but to the native genius of my sable, unprotected, and uncultivated mother—a woman who belonged to a race whose mental endowments are still disparaged and despised.

This matter of learning, or even barely learning to read, is a key question in attitudes. Both Nat and Douglass were illegally taught to read, as stated above, but their reflections on this accomplishment are illustrative of their attitudes: Nat reflects, in prison (Styron, op. cit., p. 155):

Suppose then that I had been considerably less avid in my thirst for knowledge, so that it would not have occurred to me to steal that book. Or suppose, even more simply, that Samuel Turner—however decent and just an owner he might have remained anyway—had been less affected with that feverish and idealistic conviction that slaves were capable of intellectual enlightenment and enrichment of the spirit and had not, in his passion to prove this to himself and all who would bear witness, fastened on *me* as an experiment. (No, I am not being quite fair, for surely when I recollect the man with all the honesty I can muster I know that we were joined by strong ties of emotion.

He speculates on what his life would have been, had he remained an illiterate, loved, and adoring house-servant (ibid., p. 155-6):

It would not have been, to be sure, much of an existence, but how can I honestly say that I would not have been happier?

For the Preacher was right: *He that increaseth knowledge increases sorrow*. And Samuel Turner (whom I shall call Marse

> Samuel from now on, for that is how he was known to me)
> could not have known, in his innocence and decency, in his
> awesome goodness and softness of heart, what sorrow he was
> guilty of creating by feeding me that half-loaf of learning:
> far more bearable no loaf at all.

Frederick Douglass sees the matter entirely differently: it is possible
to maintain that he naturally would, writing his memoirs at the
height of his reputation in 1880 or so, whereas Turner is supposed
to be so speculating while in a prison cell waiting to be hanged.
Nevertheless it is worth noting how similar the thoughts ascribed
to Nat are to those sentiments which Douglass puts into the mouth
of Mr Auld, his owner. While it is true that Douglass's *Life and
Times* has served as a quarry for people writing about the period
(Howard Fast in the first American edition of *Freedom Road* takes a
scene with John Brown and uses it word for word), it is not necessary
to impute any intentional plagiarism here, as Styron puts into the
mind of a black insurrectionist the thoughts of his enemy, the
owner. It is rather, I suggest, the effect of the involuntary pressure
of Styron's own norms, due to his own real relationship to the
slave-system: he is, after all, a white Southerner from Virginia,
who grew up near to where Nat Turner's rebellion took place.

Douglass, writing about himself, sees the matter of education
quite differently from Styron writing about Nat Turner: he seizes
every crumb of learning he can get near, and has been taught to
read by his kind mistress, whose husband discovers that she has
committed this illegal act (Douglass, op. cit., p. 101. My italics).

> Of course he forbade her to give me any further instruction,
> telling her that in the first place it was unlawful, as it was also
> unsafe: 'For,' said he, 'if you give a nigger an inch he will take
> an ell. If he learns to read the Bible it will forever unfit him to
> be a slave. He should know nothing but the will of his master,
> and learn to obey it. *As to himself, learning will do him no good
> and a great deal of harm, making him disconsolate and unhappy.*
> If you teach him how to read, he'll want to know how to
> write, and this accomplished he'll be running away with
> himself.' Such was the tenor of Master Hugh's oracular
> exposition; and it must be confessed that he very clearly
> comprehended the nature and the requirements of master and
> slave. His discourse was the first decidedly anti-slavery lecture

to which it had been my lot to listen . . . 'Very well,' thought
I, 'Knowledge unfits a child to be a slave.' I instinctively
assented to the proposition and from that moment I understood
the direct pathway from slavery to freedom . . . Wise as Mr.
Auld was, he underestimated my comprehension, and had little
idea of the impressive use to which I was capable of putting
the impressive lesson he was giving his wife. He wanted me
to be a slave; I had already voted against that on the home
plantation . . . That which he most loved I most hated . . .
In learning to read, therefor, I am not sure that I do not owe
quite as much to the opposition of my master as to the kindly
assistance of my amiable mistress. I acknowledge the benefit
rendered to me by the one and by the other.

Styron's Nat echoes the opinions of the slave-owner on learning.
Let us take a sounding on the opinions of the two protagonists on
their friends, another crucial point at which values come into play.

Nat made a friend named Willis, 'Save for Wash and my mother
and house servants like Little Morning, Willis was the first Negro
I was ever close to'. Nat was attracted by him 'as soon as I saw him
at work' (Styron, op. cit., 202).

Willis was skilful and neat, a quick learner . . . He could not
read or write of course, but he had a sunny, generous,
obliging nature and was full of laughter; despite my early
suspicion of him—a hangover from my lifelong contempt of
all black people who dwelt down the slope—I found something
irresistible about his gaiety and his innocent, open disposition
and we became fast friends. Considering my habitual scorn, I
do not know how this happened . . . His only faith, like most
of the Negroes', was in omens and conjurs . . . His talk was
childish and guileless and obscene. I was very fond of him.

Of his other friend, Hark, he says (ibid., p. 57):

Loving him as I did, I often reproved myself for my outbursts
and the misery they caused him, but in certain ways he was
like a splendid dog, a young, beautiful, heedless, spirited dog
who had, nevertheless, to be trained to behave with dignity.

Compare this with the way Douglass speaks of his friends, who are
every bit as black, as unlettered, and as enslaved as Nat's (Douglass,
op. cit., pp. 193, 197–8):

Toward Henry and John Harris I felt a friendship as strong
as one man can feel for another, for I would have died with
and for them. . . . I had succeeded in winning to my scheme
a company of five young men, the very flower of the
neighbourhood, each one of whom would have commanded
one thousand dollars in the home market. At New Orleans
they would have brought fifteen hundred dollars apiece, and
perhaps more . . . I was the youngest but one of the party. I
had however the advantage of them all in experience, and in
knowledge of letters. This gave me a great influence over
them . . . Like men of sense, we counted the cost of the
enterprise to which we were committing ourselves . . . We
were plotting against our (so-called) lawful rulers, with this
difference—we sought our own good, and not the harm of our
enemies. We did not seek to overthrow them, but to escape
from them. As for Mr. Freeland, we all liked him, and would
gladly have remained with him, *as free men. Liberty* was our
aim, and we had now come to think we had a right to it
against every obstacle, even against the lives of our enslavers.

Nat, we are told, on the other hand, wanted to train Hark out of his
dog-like servility and into a frame of mind where he could 'gut a
white man and gut him without a blink or a qualm'. Freedom is
thus associated for Nat (according to Styron) with maniacal blood-
lust.

Then again, while Styron's Nat regards his friends as little more
than animals, he reacts with 'ingratitude, panic and self-concern'
to the offer of freedom in the future: because (Styron, op. cit.,
p. 194. My italics):

To part from a man like Marse Samuel, whom I regarded with
as much devotion as it was possible to contain, was loss
enough; it seemed almost insupportable to say goodbye to a
sunny and generous household which, *black though I was, had
cherished me* as a child and despite all—*despite the unrelenting
fact of my niggerness, the eternal subservience of my manner* and
the leftovers I ate . . . To be shut away from this was more
that I thought I could bear.

It is impossible to quote both books *in extenso*, but perhaps one
more instance of Nat's attitude, as represented by Styron, ought to

be given, a significant paragraph in which he describes the indifference of slaves when being sold away from home. All other writers, including defenders of slavery like Margaret Mitchell, emphasise as a virtue the strong emotional ties which bind the primary groups on the plantation together, whether in the Big House or in the 'Quarters', and the consequent tragic shock of a separation caused by the sale of slaves—the mere hint of which is enough to make Miss Watson's Jim, in *Huckleberry Finn,* run away from home. But as Styron's Nat recalls it (ibid., pp. 223–4):[1]

So George and Peter would go, or Sam and Andrew, or Lucy and her two young boys, packed off in a wagon which I myself would often drive to deliver them in Jerusalem, and always I was haunted and perplexed by the docile equanimity and good cheer with which these simple black people, irrevocably uprooted, would set out to encounter a strange and unknown destiny. Although they might cast backward what appeared to be the faintest glimmer of a wistful glance, this painful parting from a place which had been their entire universe for years caused them no more regret than did the future cast over them worry or foreboding: Missouri or Georgia were as far away as the stars, or as near as the next plantation, it was all the same to them, and with despair I marked how seldom they seemed to bother even bidding farewell to their friends. Only the rupture of some family tie I felt could grieve them, and such calamities did not happen here. Twittering and giggling, they mounted the wagon poised to carry them to an impossible fate at the uttermost end of the earth, and they could speak only of an aching knee, the potency of a hairball from a mule's stomach as against witches, the proper way to train a dog to tree a possum, and mumble incessantly about eating. Slumbrous in broad daylight, they would flop asleep against the side boards of the wagon, pink lips wet and apart, nodding off into oblivion even before they were carried past the bounds of that land which had composed the entire smell and substance of their lives and whose fields and meadows and woodland now dwindled away behind them, unseen and unremarked forever. They cared nothing about where they came from or where they were going, and so snored loudly or, abruptly waking, skylarked about, laughing and slapping each other,

and trying to catch at the overhead leaves. Like animals they
relinquished the past with as much dumb composure as they
accepted the present, and were unaware of any future at all.
Such creatures deserve to be sold, I thought bitterly, and I
was torn between detestation of them and regret that it was
too late for me to save them through the power of the Word.

The key words in this particular passage are *Such creatures deserve
to be sold*, a sentiment which must derive, however unwillingly or
unconsciously, from the norms of the slave-holding class. Styron,
with the best will in the world (presumably), asks us to believe in an
insurrectionary leader who loves his masters, regrets his education
because it has made him discontented and therefore unhappy,
despises his friends whom he thinks of as sub-human—and in
general hates Negroes ('I was torn between detestation of them')—is
panic-stricken at the thought of freedom, and yet is capable of
organising a campaign of murderous hatred against the people he
loves for the freedom of those he detests and despises. When we add
to the representation of his character that he is full of lustful
imaginings about white women, triggered off apparently whenever
he comes across them, and centring on the idea of *defilement*, it is
evident that the Nat Turner in this book is a stereotype of the feared
and hated Negro in the mind of the white southern slave-owner
class. This does no more in this case than indicate that this is
Styron's personal normative derivation, which we knew already
from other sources; but it does support the idea that it is impossible
for a writer to transcend his own initial socialisation by an act of
will, in this case to transport himself sympathetically inside the skin
of a black insurrectionist. And if the writer is bound to reveal in his
writings what are his real norms, regardless of any intention he may
have to the contrary, and if norms are not mere personal attitudes
but social values, given by the grouping or society to which he
belongs, it is possible to read the norms of the society back from
the norms of the writer, whether expressed intentionally or not.
    Virginia Woolf, in her brilliant short essay 'The Niece of an Earl'
(1966 edn.) on the importance of social stratification in English fiction,
says that we never get out of the glass box of class into which we
are born, and which gives the data by which we judge everything
else. There are numerous examples of writers trying to transcend
their class and failing: Tolstoy on his knees, begging the pardon of

his peasant mistress when he wants to marry the little countess, does not cease to be Count Tolstoy. Orwell made great efforts to get into the working class, but without success; and Styron played, but not very hard, at being a black insurrectionist.

It is not only the creators of imaginative literature who are bound by the norms of their social grouping: Erich Fromm in *Sigmund Freud's Mission* (1963) and Gunnar Brandell in *Freud och Sekelsluttet* (1963) have shown how this limitation applies even to a scientist whose talent amounted to genius and whose research into the psychological effects of norms changed the normative map of his society.

Note

1 It seems to me evident beyond the need for discussion, that Styron's attitude and values, plainly readable from the text, are those of upper-class (or aspiring to be) white, Southern, formerly slave-holding strata; emotionally rooted in racism; incorporating in the conceptual picture of blacks every available stereotype of this group, with special emphasis on sexual inflammability and putative self-disgust (projected by the white racist). The text seems so open that it seems to me extraordinary that there could have been a lengthy and acrimonious debate on the merits of this book as a truthful record of black attitudes.

Chapter 5

Some speculations on the possible existence of a matriarchal society in Greece, based on the *Oresteia* of Aeschylus

Some distinctions must be made, in the expression of norms in fiction, between what might be called 'private' literature and what might be called 'social' literature. Novels are *par excellence* 'private', in the sense that the actual reading of them is a communication between one writer and one reader—I say this fully aware that novels are only distributed because there is a collective process of printing and selling which makes their extensive readership possible, and a commercial publishing industry which decides what is to be printed and sold. These factors have been often identified, by Virginia Woolf and Ian Watt especially, with capitalism and the bourgeois period, and it is perfectly true that they are social phenomena and essential to understanding the sociology of literature. But my argument is not of the sociology of literature, but rather the use of literature as an instrument of sociological investigation.

The content of all literature is influenced to some extent by the mode and place of consumption and the official norms of the society, but probably the modern novel is least affected of all fictional forms, because of the privacy of consumption.

The present situation is in the greatest contrast to that of the nineteenth century, when novels were in very general use as family reading in the home circle. Furthermore, the reading was usually done by Papa, or failing that one of the sons of the house, while the women were modestly engaged in needlework. This, combined with the conscious moral censorship of Victorian fiction, with its supposition that the ladies and children are always present (see chapter 3, p. 113n), naturally produced a limitation on the presentation in fiction of Papa himself, amounting to a social control of the supposedly private vision of the writer: fiction to be consumed in the atmosphere of the patriarchal Victorian home must be supportive of that institution and the norms which it required of its members. One will search in vain for downright wicked fathers in Victorian fiction, and there are not many silly ones either (Mr Micawber and Mr Mantolini perhaps excepted). Papa would naturally refuse the sanction of his voice to attacks on fathers of families, when reading to his own little flock. On the other hand, there are plenty of silly mothers and foolish young girls, and a few downright wicked young men. Some fictional Victorian fathers are testy, and some tyrannical—but it is not unpleasing to be depicted as all-powerful. Ivy Compton-Burnett's reverse-Victorian novels, which appeared when the Victorian period was safely dead, derive a lot of their shock-value from the depiction of thoroughly nasty, tyrannical, stupid, petty and immoral fathers.

Certain areas of discussion were of course taboo in the family circle, the most noticeable to our eyes being any discussion of sexual matters, although romantic love was a favourite theme. Dickens, who passionately attacked social evils and especially the ill-treatment of children, projects these themes in workhouses, various employments, schools—there are no good schools in Dickens—prisons, gangs of thieves and in the family—but never once mentioned the child-prostitution which he of course was perfectly aware was a feature of London life.

The popularity or even the admitted distribution of literature depends on it remaining within the general area of tolerable acceptability in the society, and as these boundaries change in real life they also change in fiction. We have seen this happen in England from the bawdy Elizabethan period to the Puritan restrictions of the Commonwealth, the license of the Restoration period giving way to the humanitarian Age of Reason and this again fading away to the restrictions of the Victorian period, which we seem at the moment decisively to have left behind. But part of the permissiveness towards pornography of the present period is due to the removal of the consumption of fiction from the family circle to the isolated individual: the act of reading is now, as Virginia Woolf says, a piece of strictly private business between writer and reader. This means that the limits of tolerance are greatly extended: it is hard to believe that there are many family circles, even today, in which Selby's *Last Exit to Brooklyn* or *The Story of 'O'* by Reage could be read aloud.

Social participation in the consumption of fiction, then, limits its content to what the group as a whole, and/or its leader if it is a markedly hieratic group, will admit to conscious recognition.

Social participation also increases the normative influence of whatever fiction is tolerated: what is seen to be accepted is legitimised. This is one reason for the presumed great normative effect of TV. Like classical Athenian drama: *everyone* sees it; but it is unique in that it is delivered into the home, the scene of primary socialisation. McDougall (1920) and Zweig (1965) were neither the first nor the last to observe that individuals are easily influenced to accept the norms of their groups.

It is nevertheless not immediately apparent to us, in our society, where the highest value is the acquisition of wealth and power, and in which prestige follows the possession of these, to understand why stories and myths should have such a high normative effect: reading does not usually make people richer. Part of the answer doubtless is 'cultural lag' of the effect of social consumption of fiction before the invention of printing (one of Marshall McLuhan's *good* ideas, as distinct from the rubbish in which they are embedded, is that with the availability of print the social consumption of literature was ended and each consumed it privately and separately).

In 'heroic' societies, where literature was 'consumed' socially, the didactic effect would certainly be reinforced by the group, in the well-researched and well-known process of emotional reinforcement. But part of the effect is doubtless due to the very great importance of *words*, in societies in which the highest value is *reputation*: honour, or the recognition of competitive excellence.

For pre-bourgeois people in general, but most particularly in what are called 'heroic' societies—e.g. societies of the limited democracy of tribal warriors, in which each adult armed man has rights of discussion and participation in decisions, and there is no coercion except by persuasion—reputation is necessarily the great basis of distinction, and decisions must be taken in public debate. This gives the use of language a much higher status than it has with us.

It is hard to over-estimate the importance of reputation, rather than material gain, in tribal society. Those who suppose that wars would cease if all top statesmen and generals were put on an island together to fight it out, forget that for most of human history wars were in fact fought in person by top-élites, in the hope of adding to their reputation.

Good reputation is gained by excelling in fulfilling the normative obligations, at whatever risk or loss, and this is, in 'heroic' society, the motive of all honourable action. Honourable action not only gains honourable repute, but is undertaken for the purpose of gaining it. The importance of literature, or praise-singing, to these people lies in the fact that reputation is *what is said by others*, and honour consists of this reputation, and not by any means what the individual protagonist *knows internally* is honourable behaviour. This is in the strongest possible contrast with the bourgeois-Protestant norm of individualism, in which the final arbiter of trust is not the opinion of others, but the conviction of the individual conscience. The hero of the bourgeois novel is right *in spite of everybody else's opinion*. In 'heroic' or epic fiction, the appearances *are* the right or wrong, and the person is judged by them. We have this on the highest authority: Odin the All-wise says in the (ninth century) *Elder Edda*, in the Havamál ('words of the Highest'):

> Kinsmen will die, cattle will die,
> You yourself will also die.
> One thing only will stay alive—
> What is said of you when you are dead.

While as for the Greeks, Kitto discusses the same attitude in the scale of Greek values, 'the influence of the Greek sense of honour' (1967, p. 245).

> The Greek was very sensitive to his standing among his fellows: he was zealous, and expected to be zealous, in claiming what was due to him . . . the reward of virtue (*arete*, outstanding excellence) is the praise of one's fellows and posterity. This runs right through Greek life and history, from the singular touchiness of the Homeric hero about his 'prize'. Here is a typical remark:
> 'If you were to look at the ambitiousness of men, you would be surprised at how irrational it is, unless you understood their passionate thirst for fame, "to leave behind them", as the poet says, "a name for all succeeding ages". For this they are ready to face any danger—even more than for their own children: to spend their substance, to endure any physical hardship, to give their lives for it. Why, do you imagine that Alcestis would have given her life for Admetus, or Achilles

given his to defend Patroclus, if they had not thought their own arete would be immortal—as indeed it is? No, the nobler a man is, the more is undying fame and immortal arete the spring of his every action.'

This is the wise Diotima, instructing Socrates in Plato's *Symposium*. It is normal Greek doctrine: we find it in philosophers, poets, and political orators.

The fact that reputation is only words, what is said of one by others, and nevertheless is the best reward and *lasts for ever*, explains the importance of the poet or praise-singer in tribal society, and the didactic value of the examples of behaviour set forth in the poems.

Members of this type of society are bound to the opinion of the group; the individualistic Judaeo-Christian conscience, dealing directly with God alone, was not for them. Socrates, wisest of the Greeks, knew that the judgment against him was one that the Athenians were wrong in making and that they would bitterly repent. Nevertheless he drank the hemlock, refusing to flee the city as he easily could have done, because there was no life worth living for him if he evaded the sanctions of the group to which he was bound.

The group for him was the City. But in clan-based societies the members are even more 'members one of another'; the clan is self-renewing. Lacking a belief in personal immortality the Greeks and the pre-Christian Scandinavians could hope for immortality in reputation. Also, deceased members are reborn into the clan by having their names given to the new-born ('Our kinsman Ketil has come back to us'). The new-born does not exist as a human being until it is formally welcomed into the clan by *being given a name*.[1] Names are compulsively binding, and so are promises. In many religions, as George Thomson points out (1949, vol. 1), *creating* the universe is identical with *naming* its elements; he also states that small children, when drawing figures, leave out those parts they cannot name: unnamed equals non-existent.

Rumpelstiltskin, and the trolls who built so many Danish village churches (Kristensen, 1931, pp. 129–39), have to abandon their prey, according to promise, when their names are discovered and they are called by them; name-taboos and the carefully kept secrecy of *real* names, as knowledge of them would be dangerous in unfriendly hands, are among the most common taboos reported by anthropologists, and the Opies (1969, pp. 156–60) report the same of children in modern industrial England.

Names, then, like reputation, are attached to individuals and honour is personally achieved. But prior to individual efforts was the collective reputation of the family or clan: it matters to whom one is born, and we see epic and saga poetry tracing two or three generations before we get to the individual protagonist. Clan-members partake of the good or ill fortune of all members, collectively paying or receiving payment for crimes done by a single member, and bound to defend each one. It is not unreasonable under this system for a curse to rest on a family even unto the third or the fourth generation, or for a feud to be continued as long, since killing one clan-member is tantamount to killing any of his kinsmen. Obligations are collective—but reputation is unique. Heroic poetry, saga, and myth are the vehicles for the transmission of reputation, and thus of norms. Far from being merely 'serious entertainment', they are the medium through which actions are recorded and assessed, and examples set to influence behaviour by imitation.

Associated with the power of words is the idea that what is said is true. The celebrated guile of the Greeks was chiefly the ability to tell lies, for good or ill, in the same spirit in which Huckleberry Finn practised on the credulity of the barbarians he met on his journey. To lie is unexpected, but nevertheless frequent among the Greeks of classical literature. It is a profitable deviation where the truth is expected: Agamemnon, Odysseus, Clytemnestra and Orestes all tell significant lies in the Oresteian trilogy. In *Njal's Saga*, Mord Valgardson is able to work great havoc by lying, as the truth is expected of a go-between. In the same saga, when strange news is brought to Njal, he asks to have it repeated; when it is repeated three times he must believe it. The devaluation of the credibility of words in our society is well illustrated by the use of this as a comic device by Lewis Carroll: 'What I tell you three times is true!' says the Bellman.

Finally, magic spells are always cast in words, whatever other elements may be present. Runes are a well-known form of magic, their power evidently resting in their secret meaning. Non-Scandi-navian illiterate societies apparently attributed great power to them, perhaps not realising that they were merely the written form of a kind of basic Scandinavian language; it was in any case the *written* message which provoked the awe. Most rune-stones are really only memorial stones with rather dull messages: 'This stone was raised to Hedin—few are now better born than he' is a fair example. Some, but by no means all, contain curses on anyone who would move the stone to use it for another. The Latin letters which came to Scandinavia in the tenth, eleventh and twelfth centuries with the introduction of Christianity superseded runes and few could then read the runes, which became even more secret and mysterious. Perhaps more important, runic letters were associated with the pre-Christian religion, now down-graded to magic and superstition; and runes, especially outside of Scandinavia, acquired an aura of magic in themselves. M. R. James's story 'Casting the Runes' plays on this as a felt influence, even in modern times. It is perhaps significant that hundreds of rune-stones are left standing in the Nordic countries, quite often to the inconvenience of agriculture; and hundreds more have been de-contaminated, as it were, or de-fused, by being used at the entrance to churchyards.

In some tribal societies, besides the power of words in themselves, there is the very practical element in tribal democracy mentioned above, that there is no hierarchical order of command: the decision-making body is *all* the (armed) adult males, in council. Where none has the power to command, decisions must be made by agreement, reached through debate and argument. This gives a very high functional value to rhetoric, as indeed we see repeatedly and normally throughout Greek political history. And when the economic life of the society was some form of communal agrarian village, or communal hunting and fishing, the same was true of economic activity; perhaps this was more frequently delegated to a head man, although often on a temporary basis (revolving once a year, for example: common in the Danish agrarian village from the Middle Ages until well into the early nineteenth century).

These elements acting in combination: *reputation* as the highest value in the society; the magic power of words (including the assumption that they are true); and the customary conduct of affairs by debate, are highly productive of the creation of narrative fiction as a regular means by which the norms of the society are expressed. Greece and Scandinavia, and also the Teutonic tribes in Germany and England, had tribal democracy; the high value of reputation; and parts of Scandinavia also had the communal agrarian village: and here epic poetry appeared. Africa, with traditions of hundreds of years of tribal debate and an oral tradition of tales,

proverbs and dance-songs, and very often also communal agriculture and co-operative hunting, produced, as soon as there was
access to written language, a large body of novelistic literature: and
this in the first generation of education, and even though the written
language was a foreign one: French or English.

Religious ritual contributed to social literature not only a body of
myths, but the rituals themselves, from which it is generally agreed
that the Greek drama, that most social of social literature, emerged.
In religious ritual, the 'rational' content is the symbolic narrative of
the deeds of the gods; but the rituals had many other sensuous in-
gredients, through which the communication of the sacred nature
of the event was made: song, dance, other more or less musical
effects, intoxication by fumes or by drinking holy substances or
tasting hallucinogenic matter; the effect of darkness and sudden
light; and, most important, the sense of participation, of becoming
part of the body of the occasion at least by assent, in the whole
people assembled. The rituals embody and unify the whole tribe
or clan, and the Athenian drama in a more sophisticated way did
the same for the people of the polis. The ritual element is still
present in the Greek drama: what is suffered, is suffered for the
people. The ritual acts—the slayings—take place off-stage, but the
audience participates by sympathy; the chorus explains things to
the audience, but also represents and embodies them. The chorus
still, as in the former rituals, performs both song and dance as
accompaniment to the essential action. The subject matter of the
drama, moreover, was the myths and epic poetry which was the
cultural ambience of the Greeks, in terms of which the whole
population had for centuries been normatively socialised.

As discussed in chapter 2, pp. 53–7, it is impossible for any
literature to be more 'social' than the Athenian drama of the fifth
century B.C., which was mass culture of 100 per cent saturation,
since all residents were habitually in attendance, including women,
children, resident aliens, and slaves. It is not unreasonable to suppose that as the public financed the theatre, voted on the quality of
the dramas (through chosen experts to be sure, but the ordinary
public made their preference known by vocal demonstrations), it
was extraordinarily close to the values and ideal norms of the
society. The Danish sociologist Svend Ranulf has this to say (1936,
vol. 1, p. 5):

But in the work of Aeschylus, Sophocles and Herodotus the popular, traditional Athenian mentality found such direct expression as to enable a late posterity to become acquainted with it. We shall here leave unanswered the question, interesting in itself, why popular thought and feeling in the Athens of the 5th century should be expressed in works which are reckoned among the foremost in the literature of all times, while in most other communities evidence of such thought and feeling must be sought in literary productions from which it is impossible for cultivated people to derive any pleasure.

If we consider the *Oresteia* of Aeschylus, the only complete trilogy of his that we have, what may we conclude about the norms of the Athenians? Is it possible, for instance, that from these plays some evidence can be fairly drawn as to whether or not matriarchy has ever existed in human society, specifically, as George Thomson (1949, vols I and II. See also Thomson, 1941) and Kitto (1967) suppose, in the Aegean cultural area?

What actually happens in the plays?

In the first, *Agamemnon*, the King returns from the Trojan War, bringing with him his 'prize', the Trojan princess Cassandra. His wife Clytemnestra, who has been ruling Argos in his absence, knows of the fall of Troy immediately it happens, as she has arranged for a system of signal bonfires. The Chorus of elder citizens long for the return of the King, but Clytemnestra kills him in the bath in which he is purifying himself from the sins of war, and also kills Cassandra. She justifies this to the Chorus on the grounds that he sacrificed their daughter Iphigenia to get a good wind for the fleet on the way to Troy. Cassandra, before entering the house to her doom, foresees it and also describes to the Chorus the curse on the house of Atreus because Atreus, the father of Agamemnon, had killed his brother Thyestes' children and given Thyestes their flesh to eat at a banquet. The Queen's consort, Aegisthus, is the surviving brother of those children. The Chorus is cowed into accepting Clytemnestra and Aegisthus as joint rulers.

In the second play, the *Choephorœ* or *The Libation Bearers*, Agamemnon's son Orestes returns to Argos. He meets his sister Electra at their father's grave. Urged on by the Chorus, this time of female palace servants, they resolve to kill their mother and her lover. They appeal for help to their dead father and the underground deities, without apparently getting any reply, and finally conclude they must act alone.

Orestes in disguise enters his mother's palace as a guest, bringing the false rumour of his own death. He kills Aegisthus, and after some hesitation—he is in danger of weakening ('Pylades, what shall I do?')—his mother. The Chorus has meantime addressed the audience with a recital of the crimes of women. When Orestes kills his mother, he is immediately attacked by the Furies (seen by him alone) and driven from the stage 'with a cry of agony'. The Chorus wonders when the feud will end.

In the third play, the *Eumenides*, Orestes is tried for the murder of his mother. The play opens at the Temple of Apollo at Delphi, and the Temple is occupied by the Furies, fierce and hideous in appearance, at the moment sunk in an exhausted sleep, resting from the hunting-down of Orestes. Clytemnestra's ghost urges them on, Apollo protects Orestes, the Goddess Athena is summoned to preside at his trial, and a jury of twelve Athenian citizens decides. Their vote is evenly divided and Athena casts the deciding vote: Orestes is acquitted, on the grounds that he has not shed kindred blood and thus is unjustly hunted by the Furies (the mother is not related to the child), and that the male ought to be supreme in all things. The Furies are persuaded to give up their clan identity and incorporate themselves into the law-enforcement order of the City: they take the name of Eumenides ('the Gentle Ones'), a euphemistic term, propitiatory and at the same time recognising their function of protecting society by the execution of justice. A great period of peace and prosperity is foreseen, feuds are to end and homicides are to be settled by law in the Court of Homicide.

The final moral lesson, then, is the imposition of a new set of norms and the wiping out of old scores.

Are we then to conclude that the Athenians were normatively addicted to child murder, cannibalism, slaughter of nearest kin, and the interference of supernatural agencies in ordinary life? Or that their heroic models were psychopathic monsters, who would be deviant in any society? It seems that in interpreting these characters we must choose between the notion that they are intended to represent individual aberration, which would be very unlikely to be of great normative significance; and the notion that these persons and actions on the contrary have a social and symbolic meaning.

The progress of the plays is *from* the norms of clan-society, which is essentially the necessity of obtaining justice by clan-vengeance; the sacredness of the law of host and guest; and the sacredness of kindred blood, which must on no account be spilled: *to* the replacement of these by the impersonal punitive power of the State: that monopoly of force within a given area which Weber says is an essential attribute of the State, one which makes it possible for it to function and maintain its identity. The series of plays seems to have two themes: the substitution of the Court of Homicide for the blood-feud, and the apparently unrelated theme of the subjection of women. Why should the case which is symbolically claimed to be the first tried at the Court of Homicide be a case of matricide? Almost equally interesting, why does the sacrifice of Iphigenia, which is of central importance in the first play, drop out of sight before the end of the second? And why is no mention made of Orestes' breach of the law of host and guest when he enters his mother's house (in disguise) as a guest and then murders her?

Let us examine a little more closely the actions of the plays.

When her husband went to war, Clytemnestra seized control of the palace and the city. When she discovered that she had been tricked into letting her daughter go with the wily Odysseus, ostensibly to marry Achilles but really to be sacrificed to get the fleet a fair wind, she sent her son Orestes to another city; kept her daughter Electra at home; took as consort Aegisthus, a man who had a blood-feud with Agamemnon; and waited for the king to come home.

When he arrives, she coaxes him into treading, half unwillingly, on a richly woven cloth (thus demonstrating *hubris* or excessive pride, and setting the gods against him—a typical Greek trick) on his way into the palace; when she has entered she raises the cry of triumph: triumph at his return, but not as he or the Chorus understands it. While he is ritually bathing, to cleanse himself from the sins of war, she throws a net around him to entangle him, and stabs him to death. She makes it clear to the Chorus that this is not merely personal hatred, but a matter of punishment and power (*Agamemnon*, ll. 1377–9 and 1384–6):[2]

> For me this contest, sprung from an ancient quarrel
> has been matter for thought long since; but in
>   time it has come;
> and I stand where I struck, with the deed done.

> I struck him twice; and while uttering two cries,
> he let go, where he was, his legs; and after he had fallen
> I added a third stroke, a votive offering
> for the Zeus below the earth, the saviour of corpses.

The striking of the third blow as a thank-offering is analogous to
the third libation of wine the Greeks poured at a feast as thanks to
the gods. Lower-class Greeks to this day, when drinking at outdoor
tavernas, pour a little wine on the ground before drinking. Danish
workmen, similarly, if they are drinking bottled beer outdoors, as
they often are, throw a final splash of it on the ground—originally
to Odin the Ale-maker.

Clytemnestra makes it clear that the punishment is given not only
for Iphigenia, but for the other butchered children; it is hard to
avoid the picture of the Atreids as child-killers (ll. 1501–6):

> But in the likeness of this dead man's wife
> the ancient savage avenger
> of Atreus, the cruel banqueter,
> slew him in requital
> sacrificing a grown man after children.

She says plainly that she represents clan-justice, not individual
anger (ll. 1432–3).

> I swear by the justice I accomplished for my child,
> and by Ruin and the Erinys, to whom I sacrificed this man.
> [The Erinys are the Furies, later the Eumenides.]

According to my argument, in these actions, as well as the killing of
Cassandra and the display of both corpses to the Chorus and the
audience—justice must be seen to be done—she acts a social role,
not one of individual criminality. She is not, as stated by classicists
who lack 'the sociological imagination' an insulted but also un-
chaste wife, an outraged mother, and a jealous woman, but rather
the self-elected head of a clan, responsible in person for avenging
the death of her child. She, and not Aegisthus, struck the blow: she
retains the lead throughout. Cassandra, who foresaw the death of
Agamemnon and her own, was perfectly clear as to the social nature
of the deed (ll. 1125–30):

> Ah, ah! Look, look! Keep away the bull
> from the cow! In the robe

> she has caught him with the contrivance of the black horn,
> and she strikes; and he falls in the vessel of water.
> It is the stroke struck by the cauldron of cunning murder
>   that I speak.

To which the Chorus, with more than usual obtuseness, had replied (ll. 1131–2):

> I would not boast of being a master judge of oracles,
> but this seems to me like some evil thing.

Clytemnestra acts to avenge the shedding of kindred blood, that fundamental requirement of clan-based society, and also against male dominance in society, and is so understood, at least by Cassandra. Either she is inexplicable, or she is a strong, savage, and matriarchal chief.

Many scholars, including Philip Vellacott who made a highly readable translation (1956), regard her as a deviant individual, a 'masculinised woman', a misfit member of the patriarchal society, unfortunately married to a man inferior to her. But Agamemnon, King of Men, is not supposed to be inferior.

I think it far more likely that she represents, because she belongs to it, a different culture, a matriarchal society which was dominant in the area before the arrival of the long-haired Achaeans, of whom the Atreids (Kitto (1967, ch. 11) gives some tentative evidence) were a leading tribe or sept.

This culture was, according to these speculations, a matriarchy without marriage, without child-sacrifice (the children were the future of the clan, and belonged to their only parent, the mother), reckoning descent matrilineally; matrilocal; and especially without the subjugation of women.

Clytemnestra just before declaring her identity with Justice, denies her marital bond with Agamemnon (ll. 1498–9):

> You aver that this deed is mine.
> But do not consider that I am Agamemnon's consort!

—a natural enough remark, perhaps, about the husband she has just killed; but there is no question of her marrying Aegisthus either, and his short lived-attempt to seize leadership of the City founders on the resentment of the Chorus of Elders: they will accept her as ruler but not him, and they do not believe his claim to have been responsible for the killings.

There is another hint of her matriarchal allegiance in her defence of her sister, Argive Helen. The Chorus raises the traditional reproach to Helen, that so much Greek blood was lost for her at Troy (ll. 1455–7):[3]

> Ah, ah, mad Helen,
> you who alone destroyed the many, the very many
> lives beneath Troy.

Clytemnestra threatens the Chorus for this slander against her sister Helen—as if it was she who had made the Greeks go to war to recapture her (ll. 1462–7).

> Do not turn your wrath against Helen,
> calling her a destroyer of men, one who alone
> took the lives of many Danaan men
> and accomplished a woe none might resist!

Kitto mentions, as evidence of a former matriarchal culture, that even in classical times there were two places—Athens and Argos— which had female deities; Helen and Clytemnestra, sisters, of Argos, may reasonably be supposed to be socialised in this matriarchal society, which, even if it does not entirely reject marriage, allows female choice and change. If the Achaean Greeks had recognised the validity of Helen's matriarchal right to choose her consort, they would not have gone to war to recover what they, in their patriarchal norms, considered the female property of Menelaos: Clytemnestra is saying that they had only themselves to blame.

We are told that 'the historical existence of matriarchy has hardly a supporter in modern anthropology' (Magus, 1971, p. 84n). Nevertheless, although the speculations of Briffault (1927) and Engels (1884) may be dismissed by later research, based as they were on ideas of group marriage, there is no reason that I know of to dismiss the work of Thomson and Kitto, both of whom assume a clash of cultures, one predominantly male-dominated and the other female-dominated. The evidence is archaeological, linguistic, and mythic, including the existence of female deities and their replacement by male ones: a theme which opens the third play of the Oresteian trilogy, the *Eumenides*. The forced dynastic marriages by which the Olympian gods subjugated the local goddesses, according to Kitto, made the marriage-bond the most important social connection, and also the basis of the structure of the family, replacing the dyad of mother and child, or rather the dominant mother and her children. Children, then, the wealth and future of the tribe, would be reckoned by male descent and not through the matrilineal line, and this question of descent is essential to the question of the guilt or innocence of Orestes. The point is made by Apollo, in his plea at the trial of Orestes, that if women are allowed unpunished to kill their husbands, as Clytemnestra killed Agamemnon, the sacred marriage of Zeus and Hera will be dishonoured and lose its status as the central social relationship.

The confrontation of the two cultures apparently was the eventual result of the Achaean infiltration into the Aegean area over a long period, many hundred years, but particularly between 1300 and 1100 B.C. The sex war, or rather the cultural struggle between the two societies, must have been long-drawn-out. My contention is that the matriarchy was based on the female monopoly of agriculture and other arts, such as pottery and weaving, of which agriculture is the most important.

What has been called the Neolithic Revolution, which was essentially the establishment of agriculture as the basic economic activity, is quite generally assumed to be the result of a female invention, the product of the natural division of labour in which the men were mobile, engaged in hunting and fishing, while the women remained in more permanent settlements, caring for the children. Having discovered the fundamental principle, that seeds planted will grow and may be harvested with great increase, the women came to control the most reliable source of food. The basic centre of society would then be the groups of women and their children, in possession of the food, the arts, the future of the clan, making the laws and enforcing them through female deities—the Mother Goddess of the earth, in both Africa and Greece—and their agents, the Furies. The men then would be seen as circling around the stable base, being admitted to breed and to bring the results of their hunting or fighting.

Such a society is extremely vulnerable: it depends on the existence of enough space and a reasonably favourable climate to produce adequate food by very primitive gardening and agricultural methods; a not-too-big population; and no serious challenge by aggressive outsiders. If the Achaeans brought with them the invention of the plough, or if it arrived during their settlement, from the east or from Egypt, it would make it possible, almost at one stroke, for men to begin to dominate agriculture. Just as the discovery of gun-powder made the medieval castle obsolete as a means of defensive war, so would the use of the plough with a team of oxen or even horses make it impossible for women to control agriculture. A woman can, and still does in parts of Asia and Africa, dig the ground with a hoe or a digging stick, with one child on her back and another in her belly, and maybe one or two more around her feet. But she cannot, and never could, manage a team and plough under these conditions: for this, more strength is needed, and less distraction. Ploughing was in the Bronze Age a sacred male occupa-tion—in both Hellenic and northern European 'heroic' societies. 'Helleristingner'—pictures engraved on stone—in Scandinavia, show the ploughman engaged in the ritual of ploughing, sometimes with sacred sun-symbols, always ithyphallic and wearing his sword. The Achaeans, including the kings, knew how to plough. Agamemnon, King of Men, boasts in the *Iliad* that he can drive as straight a furrow as any man alive; and Odysseus was ploughing when they fetched him to the war.

Apparently the only basic productive arts which remained to women were pottery in Scandinavia and making thread and cloth in all places; and this last is consistently associated with women. The pre-Olympian Fates Clotho and Atropos are engaged in spin-ning the lives of men, and also determining the length of a man's life: they cut it off when it is time for him to die. Like Mother Kali in Hindu mythology, the woman gives birth and death. Women are associated with these arts in Greek myth, in Homer and in the dramas. Oedipus is identified by his woven swaddling-clothes, and Orestes partly by the band woven for him as a baby by his older sister Electra. The work-value of female slaves is their skill at weaving; Hector, when he speaks of Andromache's life as a captive after his death, speaks of her working at the loom in another woman's house. Agamemnon, with typical brutality, answers the priest Chryseis, who comes to ask him to return his daughter (Kitto, 1967, p. 46):

> I will not set free your daughter. Sooner than that,
> old age shall come upon her in my house in Argos,
> a long way from her own country; she shall walk to and
> fro at the loom, and she shall come to my bed.

Weaving is very much associated with the tricks used by women against men: Penelope's web is probably the best-known example, and Clytemnestra uses two woven things to kill the king: the cloth she entices him to walk on, and the net she entangles him in to make it possible to kill him.

To make sense of these plays, I think we must postulate Clytemnestra as morally committed to the (slowly) defeated matriarchy, acting for justice within the norms of her culture, rather than as a deviant or psychotic. In fact she convinces the Chorus of her right, both to kill Agamemnon and to rule the City, partly by making it clear that Agamemnon, as a person who had been justly punished, will get no funeral rites (ll. 1551–8):

> It does not fall to you to take thought for this duty;
>   by my hand
> he fell, by my hand he died, and my hand shall
>   bury him,
> to the accompaniment of no weeping from the house.
> But gladly Iphigenia,
> his daughter, as is fitting,
> shall meet her father at the swift
> ferry of sorrows
> and cast her arm round him and kiss him.

The Chorus, who had previously rehearsed the full horror of the death of Iphigenia—her father ordered her gagged to stop her pleading, the soldiers held her up and he cut her throat—accepts the lack of funeral rites (a serious matter to the Greeks)—'For the dead man's spirit to be deprived of its right to proper lamentation by the next of kin and of respectful burial was a grievous injury, according to Greek religious belief (Lloyd-Jones, 1970, *Agamemnon*, note to l. 1541ff.)—as proof that he deserved to die. They immediately reply (ll. 1560–4):

> Taunt is now met with taunt,
> and it is hard to judge;
> the plunderer is plundered and the slayer slain.
> But it abides, while Zeus abides upon his throne,
> that he who does shall suffer; for it is the law.

Their capitulation is strikingly reminiscent of that dictum of Durkheim, mentioned on p. 49, that *We do not punish it because it is a crime, but it is a crime because we punish it.* Society, in other words, determines what is right and wrong—moral = social—and we can tell how norms are changing by what sanctions—punishments—are invoked for what.

It is notable that the Furies do not trouble Clytemnestra for the killing. Orestes reproaches them with this at his trial, and gets the sufficient reply (*Eumenides*, ll. 605):

> She had not the same blood as the man she killed.

Moreover, we hear nothing of them attacking Agamemnon for the sacrifice of his daughter. She *must* be of kindred blood to him, according to our reckoning, and also according to the statute of purely paternal descent under which Orestes is acquitted of the murder of his mother; but not according to the reckoning of the Furies: they operate strictly within a matrilineal system. In matrilineal society she is the child of her mother; her father belongs to another clan, and marriage does not bring him into the clan of his wife and children ('husband', 'wife' and 'marriage' are non-concepts to them)—he remains for ever a stranger and may kill and be killed without arousing the Furies who avenge the shedding of kindred blood. Such killings do provoke blood-feuds, however.

In the description of the function of the Furies in the *Choephorœ* and the *Eumenides*, it is made clear that besides avenging kindred ('self-spilt') blood they punish two other kinds of crime: insults to the gods such as hubris and blasphemy, and infringements of the law of host and guest. These two latter crimes may seem to us to be treated with exaggerated importance, compared with matricide, child-murder, and the like, especially when we consider that the punishment of the Furies was to hunt the criminal out of society, destroying him by isolation and loathsome diseases—(the descriptions seem to be of leprosy, for which the victim is still traditionally isolated).

Blasphemy, however, includes some serious categories, ranging as it does from verbal defiance to cannibalism. Atreus had hoped to turn the gods against his brother by causing him unknowingly to eat 'the blasphemous food'—the flesh of his own children. The early Greek cosmology is full of cannibalism. Perhaps the strongest and earliest of taboos, relegating it exclusively to the gods, were instituted as a safeguard of society and associated with shedding kindred blood when clan-society became established.

The law of host and guest, however unimportant it seems in

modern industrial society—although this relationship is still regulated by customary behaviour—was surely one of the great social inventions. We find it formally established in all 'heroic' societies from Homer to the modern Bedouin, and persisting in diluted form throughout feudalism and in the Scottish clans right through the eighteenth century until the Clearances of the Glens.[4] The code required that those who asked for it should receive not only food and shelter but also sanctuary and defence: a kind of fictitious temporary kinship was established. (Here, too, the importance of symbolic roles appears: the guest adopts another *persona* for the time.)

All this was necessary because, before the State existed, when society was composed of many, distributed, and often hostile clans, it was impossible to move outside one's own village territory. The whole outside world was hostile. But by creating a fictitious kinship, the area of one's own kinship network is extended indefinitely, and travel, trade, and the dissemination of technology made possible. This host–guest bond was naturally precarious, as it was new and in every case might be formed at random, unlike the timeless and fixed relationship of real kinship; perhaps this is why it had to be made sacred, and guarded with a very strong taboo. One might find a deadly foe squatting on the hearth, and the temptation to kill him might be almost overpowering, for men habituated to kill, unless there were strong sanctions against it. Taboos, as Freud remarked in another connection, are not made against what no one wants to do. This is presumably why breaches of this law rank high in the Furies' catalogue of crimes, with hubris, blasphemy, and the shedding of kindred blood. Atreus, punished through his son Agamemnon, committed all three crimes: he shed kindred blood, caused blasphemous cannibalism, and all this while (*Agamemnon*, ll. 1587–8)

> as a suppliant at his hearth,
> poor Thyestes found a safety.

This significant final line of Aegisthus seems of little importance to us, but for the Athenians it would have capped the climax.

The first play, then, sees Clytemnestra justified, the law of clan society is justly, if brutally, enforced—and it is hard not to think that there are strong elements of matriarchalism in the society in question.

The second play, the *Choephorœ*, or *The Libation Bearers*, takes the feud into the next generation, as it brings the vengeance for the murder of Agamemnon. The tide is turning: Clytemnestra, who struck the third blow as a 'libation' of thanks, has to send real libations to Agamemnon's grave to appease his ghost. Her daughter Electra, with the libation bearers, a Chorus of female palace servants, comes with the offerings sent by Clytemnestra, 'she the godless woman' (*Choephorœ*, l. 42). She asks the Chorus what prayer shall accompany the libation, and they answer (l. 106):

> I revere your father's tomb as though it were an altar

and that she should pray for (l. 121):

> Express it plainly—one who shall take life for life!

Orestes appears as a stranger, identifies himself to his sister by comparing his hair with hers (he has left a lock of it on the tomb as an offering)—the brown-haired Achaeans are not yet mixed with the black-haired indigenous population, but remain a racially distinct ruling caste—and she also identifies him by a band of ribbon she wove for him long ago. Electra greets him as comprising her whole family—her father is dead, she hates her mother, and she gives him, besides the love that ought to go to them, the share of love (l. 241)

> that I bore the sister who was ruthlessly smitten.

This is the only allusion to Iphigenia in the *Choephorœ*, and the last time she is mentioned in the trilogy. Her case is dropped as if she had never existed, and the attitudes which the plays are now intent on establishing are those of patriarchal right: wrongs against females are forgotten.

Orestes reveals that Apollo has threatened him with the Furies if he fails to avenge his father's death. (This seems specious: as is later revealed, the Furies act instantly when they see occasion, and they have not made any gesture towards avenging the death of Agamemnon for ten years.) Orestes seems doubtful about this, for he says that even if he cannot trust the oracle (and, knowing Apollo, this is not unreasonable) (ll. 298–305. My italics),

> Even if I lack belief, the deed must be done.
> For many longings move to one end;
> so do the god's command and my great sorrow for my
> father;

and moreover *I am hard pressed by the want of my possessions*,
not to leave the citizens of the most glorious city upon earth,
the overthrowers of Troy with noble hearts,
thus *to be subject to a pair of women.*
For his heart is a woman's; whether mine is, he shall soon
   know.

Orestes and Electra try to rouse their dead father to help them,
and Orestes makes it clear which motive is in fact the strongest
(ll. 347–51):

Would you had died under the Trojan wall
My father, pierced with Lyceian sword or spear
Leaving your house enriched, your fame her boast,
Your children honoured by the eyes of all
In Argive streets;

Both Orestes and Electra are in some doubt as to whether they have
the right to kill their mother, since Zeus protects parents. Orestes
repeatedly appeals for support to the chthonian gods: these are the
underground (female) deities who regulate birth and death, whose
agents the Furies are (ll. 407):

When will you hear, thrones of the world below?

and they again appeal to their father (ll. 417):

What shall we speak to rouse the angry dead?

They recount the wrongs done to Agamemnon in all his masculine
roles (ll. 432–8, 441):

    Electra   A king, by no procession
               Through mourning streets attended
               A husband, laid unhonoured
               Unwept in a cruel bed.

    Orestes   Not alone on king and husband
               This deep dishonour lay
               But a father was dishonoured;

               . . .
               . . .
               She for this too shall pay;

They evidently do not feel that their invocations are answered, as

they continue them, reminding their dead father that children preserve a dead man's name and fame, promising him honour and
libations (Electra promises rich libations from her bridal feast).
Orestes persists in demanding his patrimony (ll. 480–1):

> My king, my father, dead by a death no king should die,
> Give me, I pray, this throne and kingdom, yours by right.

and they appeal again to the chthonian goddesses (ll. 490–502):

Orestes	O Earth, send up my father to survey the battle!
Electra	O Persephassa, grant him beauteous victory!
Orestes	Remember the bath in which you were murdered, father!
Electra	Remember the new sort of covering they devised!
Orestes	You were caught in fetters of no smith's working, father!
	[i.e. in woven stuff (made by women)]
Electra	And in the shroud of a vile plot!
Orestes	Do these shameful words not rouse you, father?
Electra	Do you not raise erect your beloved head?
Orestes	Either send Justice to fight by your dear ones' side
	or grant that we in turn get a like grip on them,
	if it is your will to atone for your defeat by victory.
Electra	Hear also this last cry, father!
	Look upon your nestlings here at your tomb,
	and pity alike my woman's and his man's cry.

Though reminded repeatedly of the female treachery and the dishonour of his death, Agamemnon apparently gives no sign, and
they are as far from being promised his sanction as when they
appealed in ll. 471–4 (ll. 472–5):

> not from others,
> without, but from its own children
> must it come, by means of cruel, bloody strife.
> To the gods below the earth this hymn is sung!

Orestes now takes command. He resolves to act, interprets Clytemnestra's dream that she gave birth to a serpent which attacked her,
and leaves the stage with Electra and Pylades, his friend. Electra is
not seen again.

The Chorus now recount to the audience a series of crimes committed by women. First that of 'sad Althea' who killed her son.
When he was born it was prophesied that he would live no longer

than the log on the fire burned; she snatched it out and carefully preserved it—until she heard that he had killed her brothers, when she threw it on the fire, it was consumed, and he perished miserably. Here we have a female figure who, like Mother Kali, gives birth and death; and moreover her basic allegiance is to her own matrilineal clan. Second, Scylla, who for a bribe 'a Cretan collar made of gold, that Minos made', cut off her father's golden hair while he slept, the hair which had made him immortal. Here again there is a reference to matriarchal culture—Minoan Crete with its snake-goddesses was the centre of it. And the third crime was the Lemnian massacre: the women of Lemnos killed their husbands and their husbands' concubines by agreement and reinstated the matriarchy. These were all, one would suppose, battles in the long sex-war between the two cultures, but the Chorus gives them as reasons for the necessary subjection of women (ll. 637):

> For none reveres what the gods detest.

This was a strong bid for the sympathy of the audience, to prepare them for what otherwise might be an intolerable traumatic shock in Orestes' slaying of his mother. In fact he himself hangs back and has to be urged by Pylades, who reminds him of the threats of Apollo. He manages the deed off-stage, and returns to show the Chorus the bloody web in which his father was murdered. The Chorus hails him with jubilation as the best of sons (to his father)—but the avenging Furies, whom he had tried in vain to summon to help him, appear to him alone, strike him with terror and drive him off the stage 'with a cry of agony'.

The feud is evidently not yet over—the Chorus once more reminds the audience of its origins, in the final statement of the play (ll. 1065–76):

> Now upon the royal house
> for yet a third time has the tempest
> blown and proved grievous!
> First came the eating of children's flesh,
> the cruel woes of Thyestes;
> then were the sorrows of the king, the husband,
> when slaughtered in his bath there fell
> the war-lord of the Achaeans;
> and now thirdly has there come from somewhere
>   a deliverer—

or shall I say a doom?
What shall be the decision, what the end,
of the might of destruction, lulled at last to rest?

Iphigenia has now entirely disappeared from the argument—her death does not count as a motivation in the feud, as we are now entirely in the area of patriarchal reasoning.

The third play, the *Eumenides*,[5] concludes the argument by proving the necessity of replacing clan vengeance and the blood-feud with the impartial Court of Homicide, and the matrilineal kinship system with the patriarchal family. George Thomson, a Marxist, feels that this was necessary for the development of democracy in Athens (1941, p. 288):

> And if we ask why the dramatist has made the outcome of the trial turn on the social relations of the sexes, the answer is that he regarded the subordination of women, quite correctly, as an indispensable condition of democracy.

It is hard to see why this should be so. On the contrary, it may very well be that the shortness of the duration of the glorious period of Athenian culture was due to the exclusion of women from public life.[6] They attended the theatre and were thus exposed to its normative influence, including such arguments as the cited address of the Chorus aimed at convincing them of the justice of their subordination. They saw not only tragedies but the extremely bawdy comedies: often, as Kitto points out, 'plays which we would certainly not allow our women to see' (!)—and of course women could discuss the norms with their husbands in the privacy of their homes, and they were certainly expected to transmit them to their children. But they were banned from the arena of rational discussion—the debating ground of tribal and city-state democracy—where issues were discussed and policies formed. They did not enter the Senate or the Law Courts, or the continuous informal discussion of the market-place. They could only obtain justice through their male relatives, and not against them. They were to receive and transmit norms, but not to form them.

The stability of the City required that clan conflict must be replaced by the impersonal punitive power of constituted authority, which in the case of Athens was the Court of Homicide. While the patriarchal Achaeans certainly had kinship groupings, their economy seems to have been based on the individual households of chiefs with their attached warriors. The clans which are specifically destined for oblivion in these plays seem to be matrilineal, matriarchal, perhaps communal agricultural societies, with female deities, now substantially overrun by the more aggressive and, it must be said, more productive male culture. This would be an important stage in the uneasy fusion of two cultures which was Greek society; since each culture had a different dominant sex, the conflict in norms could continue even when the two were fused by marriage.

The *Eumenides* opens with an invocation by the priestess of the Pythian oracle, now consecrated to Apollo. She calls on the Goddess Earth, first goddess of the temple and first author of prophecy; Earth's daughter Themis was second deity of the temple; the third was Phoebe, another Titan child of Earth—who gave the temple as a birthday gift to her brother Phoebus (Apollo). This must refer to the change in religion when the society changed: the shift from female to male deities accompanying the shift in dominance in human life. The priestess utters a cry of horror to find the Furies in the Temple: they are hunting Orestes, but slack in their task (perhaps a symbol of their failing powers also as a religious force), having to be goaded on by the ghost of Clytemnestra. The Furies repeatedly complain that younger masculine gods have arisen and driven them from their rightful honours and power.

They contend with Apollo for Orestes, as he is guilty of offences against the clan laws which it is their function to uphold (*Eumenides*, ll. 267–72):

> And if any other mortal who has wronged
> a god or a stranger,
> with impious actions, or his dear parents,
> you shall see how each has the reward Justice ordains.

They explain their special areas of action (ll. 354–9):

> For I have chosen the ruin
> of households; when violence
> nurtured in the home strikes a dear one down
> after it in pursuit we go,
> and mighty though the killer be,
> we put him in darkness through the fresh blood
>   on his hands.

Since he killed his mother, the unspeakable crime in matriarchal clan-society, they claim Orestes as their prey. Apollo argues against this, first on the grounds that he, Apollo, forced him to do it on Zeus' authority, and Zeus can never be wrong; second, that it was much worse for Clytemnestra to kill her husband than for Orestes to kill his mother (ll. 622–8):

> *Chorus* Was it Zeus, you tell us, gave you this oracle,
>   to tell Orestes here to avenge his father's murder
>   and to account nowhere the respect he owed his
>   mother?
> *Apollo* Yes, for it is not the same—the death of a noble man,
>   honoured by the Zeus-given sceptre,
>   and by a woman's hands at that, not by martial
>   far-darting arrows, as of an Amazon.

This measure of social value is echoed in a remark of Svend Ranulf, that social status is shown by the seriousness of the sanctions imposed for killing various types of people.

Apollo's third and deciding argument is that of patrilineal descent. Orestes has not in fact shed kindred blood because (ll. 658–64):

> She who is called the child's mother is not
> its begetter, but the nurse of the newly sown conception.
> The begetter is the male, and she as a stranger for a
> stranger preserves the offspring, if no god blights its birth;
> and I shall offer you a proof of what I say.
> There can be a father without a mother; near at hand
> is the witness, the child of Olympian Zeus . . .
>   [Pallas Athene]

Philip Vellacott, in the Introduction to his very readable translation of *The Oresteian Trilogy* (1956), summarily dismisses this decisive argument, saying (p. 35),

> Lastly, Apollo puts forward a far-fetched theory of parenthood: 'the mother is not the true parent of the child, she is a nurse who tends the growth of young seed', and so on. This again cannot possibly make an appeal to any audience, for it denies outright the intimate bond between mother and child.

The above-quoted statement is a textbook example of the dangers of ethnocentric, non-sociological reading of literature: the tacit assumption that all audiences have the same norms, and that great literature is equally valid at all times. I think we must assume that Aeschylus knew what he was doing in making this appeal, and it most certainly was not as strange to the Athenians as it is to us (especially to Vellacott). It was, as Thomson points out, the standard Pythagorean argument of paternal descent. The Greeks believed in the proof offered by Apollo: that Athene sprang full-armed from the head of Zeus. (Why is that stranger than the virgin birth of Christ?) Furthermore, the Pythagorean philosophy has a dualism along sex-lines: a creative, light-coloured, life-giving male principle in conflict with a dark, evil, destructive female principle. Aeschylus, too, has not presented this argument as a sudden improvisation when he was writing the third play: he had already 'planted' the idea of the child/plant similitude in the *Agamemnon*, in the words of Clytemnestra in a speech where she is defending herself for using (typically female) trickery (ibid., ll. 1524-9):

> The guile I used to kill him
> He used himself the first:
> When he by guile uprooted
> The tender plant he gave me,
> And made this house accurst.

The patrilineal argument, far from being an insignificant bit of casuistry, is the crux of the play. Because descent is patrilineal, Orestes is not related by blood-kinship to his mother, and therefore he is acquitted of shedding kindred blood and leaves the court a free man, 'again an Argive'.

Athena summons a jury of twelve Athenian citizens to judge the case, their vote is equal for death or acquittal, and she casts the deciding ballot in favour of Orestes. She carries the argument of patrilineal descent to its extreme and logical conclusion (ibid., ll. 734-40):

> *Athene* It is now my office to give final judgement;
> and I shall give my vote to Orestes.
> For there is no mother who bore me;
> and I approve the male in all things, short of accepting marriage,
> with all my heart, and I belong altogether to my father.
> Therefore I shall not give greater weight to the death of a woman,

> one who slew her husband, the watcher of the house;
> Orestes is the winner, even should the votes be equal.

Professor Hugh Lloyd-Jones (1970, p. 58n) tells us that, 'at the actual trials conducted by the Areopagus, if the votes were equal the defendant was acquitted by means of the so-called "vote of Athena", which was always on the side of mercy'. One function of this play is to 'explain' the origin of the Areopagus, the Court of Homicide; Athena (ibid., 681–82) addresses the

> people of Attica,
> you who are trying your first trial for the
> shedding of blood.

The Furies, enraged in defeat, threaten to desolate the land with pestilence and unfruitfulness, but are persuaded by Athena into conciliation with the new male-dominated society, in which the City and not the clan is the basic centre of loyalty. Their tribal function of instant, internalised punishment is changed to one of embodying the terror of the law, and they retire to caves under the Acropolis, with promises of due institutionalised honour and the significant change of name to *The Gentle Ones*.

The trilogy, then, which contains one of the most powerful female figures in all literature, Clytemnestra, as well as a female deity who has highest status on Olympus next to Zeus—the goddess Athena—thus turns out to be an argument, not only for the rule of law rather than the blood-feud, but for the necessary subordination of women. The female party is defeated on all counts, even Cassandra is butchered as an indirect consequence of breaking her word to Apollo. If a mighty creature like Clytemnestra, with the provocation she has in the murder of her child Iphigenia, has not the right to take revenge, what woman has? If the first trial at the new Court of Homicide proves that matricide is not a blasphemous crime because no matrilineal relationship exists, what better argument for sole patrilineal descent?

Athena, the deity of the City, retains the matriarchal trait of refusing marriage; but declares herself in all other things in favour of male supremacy. This is a masterly bit of cultural diplomacy; it is very important in an institutional shift that a leading figure of the defeated party is seen to accept the new power. Athena's declaration found an echo fifteen hundred years later in Iceland, when the Althing debated the introduction of Christianity. The decision was delegated to an old pagan, whom many thought would declare for Thor, but on the contrary he clearly decided in favour of White Christ, from whom he said many people had had good help, and such was his prestige that his decision was accepted without question. If Kitto is right, and Athena was (with Hera of Argos) one of the only two female deities remaining from the matriarchal period, she fills the same role as that old pagan, and her action is very persuasive. Also, as the deity of the City of Athens, she was of particular religious importance to the Athenians, and her vote would be decisive. With Athena declaring for male supremacy and the Furies tamed and brought into the service of the City, it seems that the norms which Aeschylus exemplifies for the Athenians must be conclusively accepted. The action of the trilogy, by dramatic ritual participation of the audience, has brought them from full consent to the justice of Clytemnestra's case in the first play, to a point where her daughter is forgotten, her ghost is eclipsed, and her case is non-existent, because women do not have those rights and attributes which she had claimed.

Aeschylus wrote his play in the fifth century B.C., but placed it in the period of the Trojan Wars, 800 years before, which was also the period of the chief Achaean infiltration and presumably of the greatest cultural clash. It may seem strange that the conflict of the sexes, and the defeat of women, was still enough of a live issue to dominate the moral debate of one of the greatest playwrights and one of the greatest audiences of all time. To this one can only reply in general that the tenacity of institutional norms is remarkable, and in particular to the fact that Thomson produces evidence that some aspects of female dominance still, or again, were in evidence in the area in the eighteenth century, 2,300 years after Aeschylus wrote and 3,100 years after the Achaean patriarchal infiltration of the Aegean matriarchal area (Thomson, 1948, pp. 202–3):

> Lastly, it is worth noting that in a number of Aegean islands, including Lesbos, Lemnos, Naxos and Kos, matrilineal succession to real property was the rule at the end of the 18th century A.D. The facts are reported by an English traveller, John Hawkins, who wrote:
>
>> At the close of the year 1797 I transmitted to Mr. Guys as the result of those enquiries which it had been in my power to make: that in a large proportion of the islands of the

Archipelago the eldest daughter takes as her marriage
portion the family house, together with its furniture, and
one third or a larger share of the chief means of subsistence;
that the other daughters, as they marry off in succession,
are likewise entitled to the family house then in occupation
and the same share of whatever property remains; finally,
that these observations were applicable to the islands of
Mytilin, Lemnos, Scopelos, Skyros, Syra, Zea, Ipsera,
Myconi, Paros, Naxia, Siphno, Santarini, and Cos, where I
have either collected my information or had obtained it
through others.

(Hawkins in Walpole, p. 392).

I am not in a position to explain this remarkable survival or
revival. That could be done only by embarking on the
unexplored subject of Greek land-tenure under the Byzantine
and Ottoman empires. I mention it, because those scholars
who find it impossible to believe that anything so un-Greek as
matriarchy ever existed even in the prehistoric Aegean may be
reassured to know that it was flourishing there in their
great-grandfathers' time.

It may be added that at the present time Greek brothers are not to
marry before their sisters: perhaps because they are obligated to
support them before supporting a wife, perhaps because the sisters
take their dowry first. E. C. Banfield, in *The Moral Basis of a Backward Society* (1967), reports that girls are rather favoured in inheritance, which they receive in the form of a dowry; in the very poor
Calabrian section of southern Italy 'A house is a necessary part of a
dowry, and therefore most labourer families own them' (p. 53). Of
a poor girl: her parents 'would give her their house and move into a
rented one, if they could pay rent' (p. 55). Of peasants (p. 72):

The elder son gets the education. The daughter gets half the
family's land as a dowry; this (with what her husband has) sets
her branch of the family up well. The younger son, then, gets
less education than his brother and less capital than his sister.

And again, about a young man who had to give up his apprentice-
ship to earn money for his sister's dowry (p. 111):

from the standpoint of the family, it was more important that
she made a good marriage than that he become an artisan.

These customs of securing the marriage of the feminine line are undoubtedly co-existent with a very general and severe restriction of women's rights and activities, and seem to operate on opposing principles, whether or not these are the remnants of a pre-existing female dominance. It is notable that the women are favoured in the matter of houses and land, and the men are favoured in sexual matters and legal domination in marriage. The overall effect is to continue the family, by securing the economic well-being of one male and of one female descendant.

But a possible explanation for the extraordinary tenacity of matriarchal institutions and attitudes, if that is what is here represented, a tenacity which made it necessary for Aeschylus to devote the full force of his genius to combat it, must lie in the fact that a cultural conflict based on division of norms by sex has no chance of a final solution by elimination of the conquered. However much women may be shown to be essentially wicked and only deserving of a subordinate position, they must be *there*, half the population, necessary for the continuance of society and with a monopoly of the socialisation of young children. Patriarchal warrior societies, up to and including the British upper class, take the boys away from their mothers and train them in male superiority as soon as possible;[7] but one half of the population, once infected with matriarchal ideas, is potentially dissident and must be restrained from acting in a rebellious way, by the power, as Athena says, of Holy Persuasion. This is what we see in these plays supplementing more down-to-earth sanctions such as discriminatory laws and customs. It is curious that the areas where women are most ritually subjugated—the Mediterranean area and Africa—are the very areas where there is a traditional belief in former female dominance.

Scandinavia has in the saga literature a body of epic poetry comparable in quality and theme with the Homeric poems. There are many similarities in the societies depicted, with one very large exception: the position of women, which is consistently much higher in the North. It is impossible to imagine Skrap-Hedin, the most savage of Bergthora's sons in *Njal's Saga*, telling her to leave the room because now the men were about to talk of serious matters, as Telemachus tells his mother Penelope in the *Odyssey*. On the contrary, contemporary witnesses, such as Tacitus in *Germania* (*c.* A.D. 110), describe women in conspicuously decisive roles in the Germanic tribes; their plans for war are often based on the oracular decisions of grey-haired priestesses, and the 'armies' often follow a maiden, who on horseback leads the tribe and decides which way to ride. These acts, of course, may be simply a ritual manifestation of fatalism, as when Danish peasants in the twelfth century determined the site of churches by following a horse and building where it stopped.

Certainly in Scandinavia, from numerous examples in the sagas, we see women in the role of determining the course and extent of the blood-feud. It is often they who determine whether blood-vengeance is to be taken, and force the men to do it, by shaming them into it. In this it is tempting to see them as the descendants of the Furies, who (before the establishment of the City and the Areopagus in Athens) directed the punishment of breakers of taboo, with consequent bloodshed; there is much insistence on the essentially female nature of the Furies. But this attribute of the structure of the blood-feud, that the women essentially direct it, while the men do the killing, is not confined to Scandinavia; it may be a necessary division of labour along sex-lines, without which the blood-feud would disappear. Thus quite recently (April 1972) when Crazy Joe Gallo had been gunned down in Umberto's Clam House in New York, it was his sister who, over his coffin at the funeral, declared the feud: 'Blood will flow in the streets, Joey!' and flow it did, as the Mafia 'Families' escalated the killings. This, incidentally, is quite different from the situation as described by Puzo in *The Godfather*, where the women are entirely ignorant of the men's activities, let alone making any decisions regarding them.

It corresponds exactly, however, to what Norman Lewis, in one of the first open and informative books about the Mafia, *The Honoured Society*, tells us about Sicilian feuds (1964, p. 25. My italics):

In 1872, Giuseppi Lipari, a member of the Fratuzzi clan, committed what the Mafia calls *infamitá* by denouncing a Stoppaglieri to the police. The Stoppaglieri sent an emissary to their opponents describing what had happened, and calling upon the Fratuzzi to observe Mafia Law and execute Lipari. This the Fratuzzi failed to do, and the feud was on. Within a short time all the close relations of the original disputants had been killed, and as more remote degrees of kinship were forced into the vendetta, the whole population began a terror-stricken rummaging back into its ancestry in search of dangerous ties of blood. By 1878 *a man might be approached by some enshrouded, tragic crone he had never seen before—the female head of one of the clans—who would inform him that he was now the surviving head* of the Fratuzzi, or the Stoppaglieri, and that he *must consider himself in a state of ritual vendetta* with some cousin he had never heard of and who might even have had the foresight to take refuge in Tunisia or the United States.

These old women may be more messengers than instigators, but they have the symbolic power of enforcing the taboo, through activating others, if not by direct hounding down like the Furies. This was also Electra's role in the *Choephorœ*, when she egged on her brother Orestes to do the actual deed of revenge. In the Scandinavian tradition there are very many examples, one of the most striking of which is in *Njal's Saga*, when Bergthora, Njal's wife, forces her sons to take blood-vengeance for an illegitimate son of Njal's, when they were thinking of accepting compensation in money: 'I wonder at you men! For unimportant matters you grow very angry, but something like this you will cover up with money!' There is a famous scene too in *Heiðarviga Saga* (Hallberg, 1965), considered one of the oldest and best-preserved sagas. Its general theme is of the duty of revenge, and it contains a number of humorous provocations which finally induce the dull-witted Barði to avenge his brother (ibid., p. 111):

> At a meal, old mother Y'Huridor puts an enormous chunk of beef in front of each of her three sons, including Barði. When they complain about these great lumps of meat she tells them their brother Hallr was hacked into even bigger pieces, without the brothers seeming to think *that* was anything to complain about. To make her meaning even more clear, she lays a good-sized stone on top of each of the portions of meat, telling them that they have swallowed worse things than stones, since they haven't yet avenged their brother Hallr. After this they jump up and run for their horses.

And about time too, according to the norms of the blood-feud.

It seems paradoxical that in a society in which women have no rights independent of their male kin, they direct and manipulate them for life or death in the feud. But, as noted above, since this is endemic to blood-feud societies (at least as recorded in literature)

12

it may be a necessary component—functional to the system working. The men perhaps would not kill unless they were shamed into it. This is supported by the fact that the literature in which these egging-on scenes are recorded are from the transitional period between the clan- and blood-feud society and the establishment of the monopoly of force by the State. The men may see some hope of abandoning that expensive way of maintaining justice, which demands the continual slaughter of élites. It may also, certainly, be a remnant of female authority from a matriarchal period in which women perhaps directly ordered the men to kill, without the circumlocutions required by appeals to honour and reputation. Or, more likely, two or more discrete causes may be operating.

Female deities are well known in the Mediterranean and in the African matrilineal belt, and Tacitus describes with some horror the worship of the goddess Nerthus among the northern Germanic tribes in the second century. In the spring, the goddess, who symbolises, or is, returning summer, fertility, and vegetation, is drawn in her wagon through the countryside, greeted everywhere with dancing and festivity; having made the round, the slaves who attended her, and her male companion are killed, and the ceremonial wagon taken apart and sunk in the bog. The archaeological discovery of parts of two wagons that could easily be the ones used gives support to this theory. And such prominence of a female deity, with which other Bog finds agree, indicates that women had a very high status in Scandinavia from the remotest antiquity. According to the Danish cultural historian V. Broby-Johansen (1968), women's graves in the Bronze Age were more elaborate and contained richer grave-gifts than those of men.

P. V. Glob, the eminent Danish archaeologist, describes in *The Bog People* (1969) the archaeological evidence for the dominance of the rites of Nerthus in the early Iron Age (from *c.* 400 B.C.) in Scandinavia, which again supports the evidence of Tacitus. He also gives a quantitative measure of the social importance of women: they are depicted with increasing frequency in the religious representation of deities, and offerings to the supreme female goddess of Fertility also predominate (ibid., p. 117):

> The Danish Bronze Age is divided into six periods, and a
> study of the many hundreds of Bronze-Age sacrificial deposits
> shows the goddess gradually supplanting her male partner. In

the first period masculine objects are supreme. In the second
they represent only about 40 per cent of the material found,
and in the fifth and sixth periods only 25 per cent and 10 per
cent, whereas the percentage of feminine objects in these last
two periods rises to 75 per cent and 90 per cent. These
statistics agree with the evidence of Bronze-Age human
representations. While male figures appear in the second period,
female figures do not appear until the fourth. We should not
place too much stress on the evidence of plastic representations
of the human figure, since so few survive. We can none the
less say that female subjects are far more numerous than male
in the second half of the Bronze Age.

Yet this goddess was being worshipped as far back as the
Neolithic Period, as we know from depictions of her on
pottery vessels. . . .

Torcs or necklets found in the bogs, often twisted like
ropes, are evidence for the cult of this goddess, in the Bronze
and Iron Ages alike. The torcs become so heavy in the Iron
Age that they cannot all have been intended for human use.
They were probably made specially as offerings for the goddess
and deposited by women praying that they might have a child,
or wanting to give thanks for a safe delivery.

Her symbol indicates how highly the goddess was esteemed
in the Iron Age and how great the significance with which she
was invested. . . . Female amulets, which are known from both
Jutland and the Danish islands, are highly stylized, but the
sex is strongly indicated in the breasts and belly, while the
collars are merely indicated.

It is indeed tempting to identify the twisted torcs of the northern
bogs with the snakes of the goddesses and priestesses of the Minoan
matriarchal culture of Crete, and conclude that the cultural similarities are due to cultural diffusion and that the matriarchy once
stretched from the south to the north of Europe. Professor Glob,
speaking for Denmark, concludes that (ibid., p. 132):

At the beginning of the era of the bog people it was not a male
but a female god that was dominant; and her servant, who
fulfilled the role of the male deity, had to be sacrificed at the
completion of the journeyings so that the cycle of nature might
be supported and helped forward.

If we speculatively equate the killing of Agamemnon with the sacrifice of the male pendant of the female deity, the Oresteian Trilogy is seen to be, not a study of psychological maladjustment, but a telescoped ritual narrative of the change in society and in religion, from female to male dominance. One might conclude that Aeschylus' anti-matriarchal trilogy suggests, by the use of this theme, the historical reality of matriarchy as a remembered epoch in the past and a possible threat to the stability of the Athenian city-state.

On the other hand, the fact that the masterpiece of one of the greatest of all dramatists, presented with total participation to the optimal audience, did not have the total normative effect that was intended—to wipe out all traces of matriarchal culture—may give some comfort to those who dread the total manipulation of modern industrial populations by the mass media. Literature is normative but not omnipotent.

Notes

1 There are other ways of joining the human race and the family: one of them is sharing food. A mighty factor in the law of host and guest is that breaking bread with someone is equal to establishing a quasi-familial relationship.

2 Hugh Lloyd-Jones translations (1970), *Agamemnon, The Libation Bearers (Choephorœ)*, and *The Eumenides*, by Aeschylus, are presented in as literal version as possible, and all citations are taken from this modern version. Professor Lloyd-Jones emphasises the pre-eminence of the Chorus, an interesting coincidence with my notion of participation.

3 Indignation against Helen had not subsided by the time of the patriarchal Renaissance. Shakespeare, in *Troilus and Cressida*, is still insisting that the Trojan War was Helen's fault, and not the fault of Menelaus or the other Greeks. He has Diomedes say of Helen, when reproached for being bitter to his countrywoman (Act IV, Scene I):

> She's bitter to her country. Hear me, Paris:
> For every false drop in her bawdy veins,
> A Grecian's life hath sunk; for every scruple
> Of her contaminated carrion weight
> A Trojan hath been slain.

4 The Massacre of Glencoe, 1692, aroused a real sense of horror, also in England, because the British soldiers who slaughtered the clansmen had been living with them as guests for some time before.

5 It is interesting that this play, like the *Choephorœ* or *The Libation Bearers*, takes its name from the social function of the Chorus. This seems to support the importance of the Chorus, as noted in the 'Introduction' to the Greek

Drama Series (see note 2 above) and also emphasises the didactic nature of the Trilogy.

6 I owe this idea to Professor S. L. Andreski, who raised it in conversation.

7 See Iris Andreski (1970). In many African manhood ceremonies, the boys ritually attack and beat their mothers. This signifies a break with the women's world in which they have lived hitherto. Orestes' killing of his mother may be a similar mythic statement of rejection of the mother's world, and entering into the father's; or, it may be a symbolic retelling of social history, when power passed from women to men.

Chapter 6

Normative attitudes of spies in fiction*

The spy in British fiction, like the real-life British spy, used to be a gentleman, or at the very least, he was governed by a gentlemanly ideal and life-style. Ashenden, the British agent, W. Somerset Maugham's fictional representation (1928) of his own spying career during the First World War, did his work comfortably at hotels in Switzerland, living in his usual style as a gentlemanly man of letters. And Sidney Reilly, the real-life master-spy of the same period, explained to his Control 'C' (Lockhart, 1967, p. 27),[1]

> that if 'C' had not heard from him for a year it had been
> because he had had to acquire money and a proper background.
> He pointed to his recently acquired British wife and flat in
> Westminster. He complained that Secret Service pay was too
> meagre to enable him to undertake intelligence work really
> successfully. He now had ample private means.

When Kipling's Kim looked in from the dark at the dining-table of the Commander-in-Chief of the British Army in India, it was the glitter of the silver and glass, the jingle of spurs, and the proud bearing of these gentlemanly warriors which captivated him, and made them his ideal. Now, however, the spy in fiction is a very different animal: he is rather seedy, tough, and lower middle class (Le Carré's Leamas in *The Spy Who Came in from the Cold* (1965) is the prototype, and it covers most of Le Carré's and Deighton's characters) or even working class (Turner, in *A Small Town in Germany* (1968), or 'Callan', in an excellent and popular British TV series). Le Carré's gentle scholarly middle-class spy, George Smiley, quit the service in disgust.

Kipling's Kim, the prince of all British fictional spies, whose influence on life and literature is noticeable to this day,[2] was certainly not a gentleman. Orphaned (but legitimate) son of an Irish colour-sergeant ('but his mother had been nursemaid in a Colonel's family'), his origins were low enough; he was raised by a 'bazaar-woman', which puts him right outside the lowest area of the caste-system of the British Army in India. Nevertheless, he is shown to be sincerely admiring the 'gentlemanly ideal'—rank, power, and arrogance when dealing with the Indians. This comes to him as a revelation when he overhears the C-in-C planning reprisals against some dissident princes (1965, p. 46):

> 'Warn the Pindi and Peshawur brigades. It will disorganise all the summer reliefs but we can't help that. This comes of not smashing them thoroughly the first time. Eight thousand should be enough.'
> 'What about artillery, sir?'
> 'I must consult Macklin.'
> 'Then it means war?'
> 'No. Punishment.'
> . . . 'Send off those telegrams at once . . . I don't think we need keep the ladies waiting any longer. We can settle the rest over the cigars. I thought it was coming. It's punishment —not war.'

and Kim, lost in admiration, reflects (p. 47),

> 'Every time before that I have borne a message it concerned a woman. Now it is men. Better.'

His ambition thenceforth is tied to the maintenance of the machinery of power, and he is chosen as having a special talent to be 'one of those who hunts out men who have done a foolishness against the State'. There is nothing he wants more than to have a number in the files and a price on his head—to be one of those who play 'The Great Game which never stops night or day'.

It is significant that Kipling/Kim calls espionage The Great Game. This is a common similitude in the upper-class British 'secret world'. Thus Norman Holmes Pearson, in a foreword to J. C. Masterman's account of the double-cross system of 'turning agents round', has this to say (1972, p. ix):

> Work with double agents was a game made for one amateur—J. C. Masterman—who was a university don and an enthusiastic cricketer. His mind was tuned to the pitch of the ball in this

sport whose hazards were so real and whose rewards were so immense. This was the greatest test match of the century. It is by no mere rhetorical flourish that Masterman can refer to two masters of cricket when he remarks of two masterly double agents, 'If in the double-cross world SNOW was the W. G. Grace of the early period, then GARBO was certainly the Bradman of the later years'.

And Masterman himself, in his historical-analytical description of the actual operation of the network by means of which, as he says, 'we actively ran and controlled the German espionage system in this country' (ibid., p. 3), puts it all in terms of cricket (ibid., p. 90):

> Running a team of double agents is very like running a club cricket side. Older players lose their form and are gradually replaced by newcomers. Well-established veterans unaccountably fail to make runs, whereas youngsters whose style at first appears crude and untutored for some unexplained reason make large scores. It is not always easy to pick the best side to put into the field for any particular match. With our double agents the object was always to have a thoroughly well-trained and trustworthy team, changing the personnel to the best advantage and ready always to take the field for what might be a decisive match. In addition some of the players required a good deal of net practice before they were really fit to play in a match. The prime difficulty was that we never knew the date when this decisive match would take place, and our best batsmen and the ones we had most carefully trained might be past their best or even deceased before the date of the final game.
> The first big change in the team came early in 1941 with the collapse of SNOW (who had always till then batted at number one).

To describe the situation in these terms is to make it absolutely acceptable. Gentlemen play games, especially elegant, dangerous, and exciting games, but they don't do dirty work for pay. Writers of contemporary spy fiction, on the other hand, emphasise that this is what their spies are doing all the time, on a petty scale: Leamas, for instance, wants an interest-free loan. In Kipling's time, all who on the English side engaged in spying are animated by both patriotism and gentlemanly, sporting instincts: this even includes natives like Mahbub Ali and Hurree Babu. The enemy, however, are beastly outsiders with no gentlemanly instincts at all. They are despised by their very coolies. Pretending to be on a shooting trip, they buy the heads they are supposed to have shot, they have no retinue of servants, and are even stingy enough to cook their own food. They are also over-familiar with natives—Kipling is very specific in observing that no British officer would offer a native a drink, but then neither would he strike him. Gentlemen do not lose their heads or their tempers.

Kipling, of course, was a major apologist for imperialism when *Kim* was published (1901). Just then the British Empire was reaching its greatest extension of territory, power, and prestige. Kipling favours anything which will consolidate this position. Somerset Maugham, in *Ashenden; or the British Agent* (1928), a book based on his own experiences in the First World War, takes to the job of spy quite naturally, regarding it as a patriotic duty, perfectly compatible with being a literary figure and an educated man from an upper-class milieu. One of the particularly fascinating aspects about the spy in British fiction is the exceptionally close connection between fact and fiction (Page *et al.*, 1969, pp. 134–5).

> The administrative reality has been overlaid by thick fictional and semi-fictional accretions. The vogue for books about espionage is today at such a point that the spy ranks as one of the most potent images of mid-twentieth-century life; but the stream of works in English about espionage, intrigue and secret service goes back at least to the latter part of the nineteenth century, and there is a curious inter-relationship between secret service work and literature. . . . The list of writers of fiction who have worked in one way or another for British secret organizations includes some of the most widely read of our time, like John Buchan, Compton Mackenzie, Somerset Maugham, Graham Greene, Dennis Wheatley, Ian Fleming and John Le Carré (and even, perhaps, Rudyard Kipling).

That there is 'a stream of works in English' about spying is perfectly true; but it is also true that the gentleman-as-spy is peculiarly English, never American. Americans read spy stories with avidity, but they read Le Carré, Fleming, and Deighton, not an American equivalent of these. A new mass-produced American spy story has appeared, which will be discussed below, but it has little claim to literary or psychological interest.

The lack of the gentleman-spy as a serious protagonist in the American thriller is due to two things: the populist tradition in classic American literature, and the actual position with respect to real espionage in American society, and the consequent low tolerance of the image of the spy-as-hero.

Unlike British fiction, American literature has never taken its heroes from the gentry or even the middle class until very recently. Who are the heroes of Cooper, Melville, Mark Twain, and Dreiser? The commonest of common men. Hawthorne and Poe, to be sure, avoided these protagonists, but the ones they chose were psychotics. Faulkner divides his attention between the cabin and the mansion-house, but the chief thing he says about the latter is that it is falling down. Hemingway's heroes are serious middle-class professional people, who find themselves among the rich and their hangers-on, with a sprinkling of upper-class Bohemia and exceptionally skilled lower-class 'friends'—but he was an expatriate, like the only two American writers who reverence the rich, Henry James and Scott Fitzgerald. (And a case for extreme ambivalence could be argued for both: in *The Golden Bowl* and *Gatsby*, for instance.) The middle-class and upper-class protagonist has only recently become a legitimate character in American fiction, and this development is in marked contrast to the English literary tradition, which has consistently projected gentlemanly or middle-class heroes; if they are poor (Tom Jones, Oliver Twist,[3] Tess d'Urberville), some kind of social displacement is at work—they are really lost heirs, belonging rightfully to the upper classes after all.

The different social situation has probably at least as much influence on types of protagonists as differing literary traditions. England had an Empire, and an upper class consciously devoted to maintaining it by all means. As Le Carré says in the Introduction to *Philby*, membership in the upper class was identified with loyalty. The loyalty is understood to be not only to the country, but also and specifically to the Empire as such: Chapter 2 of *Philby*, entitled 'The Boyhood of Three Spies', is headed by a sentence taken from the dossier on Donald Maclean. The occasion was his playing childish games with his younger brother, to amuse him when ill. The significant remark reads as follows:

'Why shouldn't the Indians win? After all, it's their country.'
Donald Maclean, aged 17.

America has never had an Empire in this sense—one not only acknowledged but acclaimed, and viewed as a just cause rightly demanding loyalty manifested in any and every service. With the fading of the Kennedy–Johnson dream it seems unlikely that she ever will. Americans go abroad to make money, to acquire culture, to promote a cause, to avoid the draft, but not by any means to put in thirty years in some awful desert, swamp or jungle to serve the Queen, God bless her!

America has certainly national money-making interests abroad, but has only lately developed a spy network which gentlemanly writers could join and use as a literary source, even if the ideal did prevail. American espionage never enjoyed anything like the scope and public acceptability of the spy network in Great Britain or of continental European countries. Alexander Orlov, a Russian defector who was formerly a general in the NKVD, mentions in his *Handbook of Intelligence and Guerrilla Warfare*, the deficiencies of American Intelligence which lagged (1963, pp. 2–3):[4]

> far behind those of other countries. General George C. Marshall frankly admitted at the Senate Committee on Military Affairs (Oct. 18, 1945) that until World War II the American Intelligence abroad was 'little more than what a military attaché could learn at dinner, more or less, over the coffee cups'.* When in 1941 President Roosevelt asked Col. Wm. J. Donovan to organise an intelligence service (the O.S.S.) he told Donovan: 'You will have to begin with nothing. We have no intelligence service.'† Dwight D. Eisenhower also deplored the 'shocking deficiency' of American Intelligence at the outset of the war, and General Omar Bradley‡ stated that 'the British easily outstripped their American colleagues in military intelligence'. The state of the so-called diplomatic intelligence was no less deplorable.

Orlov attributes this state of affairs to what he calls *The American doctrine of intelligence*' (ibid., p. 8). The basic error, in his opinion, is dependence on the massive collection of data from (ibid., p. 7),

* William Donovan, 'Intelligence; Key to Defense', *Life*, 30 October, 1945.
† *Crusade in Europe*, 1948, p. 32.
‡ *A Soldier's Story*, 1951, p. 33.

legitimately accessible sources, such as library research, foreign newspapers, military and scientific journals, foreign parliamentary debates, encyclopaedias and statistics. According to a reliable source, the American intelligence agencies monitor as many as five million words daily from foreign radio broadcasts alone (which equals fifty books of average size) and condense them into a few short pages . . . the intelligence officers and trained analysts derive, process, and distill much information about foreign countries, their economies and finances, industries, agriculture and trade, populations and social trends, education, political systems, structure of governments, and biographical data on political and military leaders. . . . Admiral Ellis, who was deputy chief of Naval Intelligence in World War II, wrote that in the Navy 95% of peacetime intelligence was derived from legitimately accessible sources, 4% from semi-open sources, and only 1% was procured through secret agents.*

Orlov estimates that in fact between 10 and 20 per cent of US Intelligence comes from secret sources, but he amply demonstrates, by his use of public statements by high-ranking officials, that this is played down: no acceptably devious image of the spy in constant danger, playing the Great Game with a lone hand, emerges. He seems rather to be a bureaucratic personality, buried beneath a mountain of paper work. The years since Orlov's *Handbook* was published (1963) have not changed the official image. The *New York Times* of 22 June 1969, gives substantially the same picture (Benjamin Welles, Special, ibid.):

The bulk of the agency's (CIA) work consists of gathering intelligence from radio broadcasts, from agents and other sources all over the world and then evaluating it for the President. . . . The CIA and the Atomic Energy Commission between them, he added, probably lead the government in the use of computers and data retrieval procedures. By contrast, other sources say, the clandestine work or 'dirty tricks' side as it is called inside the agency, plays far less a role than is popularly supposed. 'Every covert action must first be authorized by a top-level White House committee. . . .

Captain Ellis M. Zacharias, USN, *Secret Missions: the Story of an Intelligence Officer*, pp. 117–18.

'Moreover,' he added, 'James Bond to the contrary—
absolutely no one is authorized, licensed, permitted or
encouraged to kill anyone.'

This soothing image of the bureaucratic spy is evidently desired by
the public and actively promoted by those in a position to judge
the true nature of espionage. Orlov, a Continental, is strongly in
favour of the secret-agent type of spy: he quotes with contempt
General MacArthur's explanation of the lack of intelligence at the
start of the Korean War: *There is nothing, no means or methods,
except spy methods . . . that can get such information as that.* Orlov's
point is that spy methods are what ought to be used (op. cit., p. 12).

Important state secrets, and especially clues to the intentions
and plans of potential enemies *cannot be found in libraries and
encyclopaedias*, but only where they are being kept under lock
and key. The task of intelligence services is to acquire the
keys and lay the secrets before their governments and thus
provide them with *foreknowledge*.

Whether Orlov was aware of electronic spying devices such as U-2
and *Pueblo*, not to mention the activities of Michigan State University, located eighty miles from the University of Michigan, which
published his book, not to mention the spying activities of US
academics abroad, is immaterial. He was trying to popularise and
legitimise the image of the non-bureaucratic spy, engaged as often
as not in 'dirty tricks', to a public opinion which rejected that
image. Without the image there was no possibility of developing a
literature of espionage in America comparable to that in Britain,
where the spy was acknowledged, admired, and identified with the
exemplary upper class.

One interesting question about the spy in British fiction is, how
and why has his social status slipped downhill so disastrously that
now, far from being a gentleman, he expresses a great deal of
conscious and subconscious aggression towards the upper class?
The TV series, 'Callan', mentioned above, ended abruptly when
Callan (working class) is brain-washed into shooting his (upper-
class) Control, and is shot down himself.

It used to be different. Maugham and his Ashenden, who took
so naturally to the job of agent, were gentlemen *par excellence*.
Ashenden was much higher on the stratification scale of the outside

world than M., his superior in the service. M. lacks social grace; he is far from well-bred and finds himself ill at ease in the smart restaurants to which Ashenden spitefully takes him, mostly to gloat over M.'s discomfort: his incompetent way of appearing 'a little too much at ease', and his naive pleasure in sharing the same room with so many celebrities, pointed out by Ashenden. Ashenden's insistence on his social superiority would make most modern readers uneasy, but he himself is quite complacent about it. He has another source of superiority: as a professional man of sensibility, a writer, it is more or less his duty to note the human qualities of the people he is tracking down. Caypor, the English spy, is devoted to his wife and dog and charming to an elderly couple in the hotel, but it is a significant point against him that he has no money and is therefore not genuinely upper class: Ashenden sneeringly says of him that he is 'not only betraying his country for £40 a month', but has 'lived his furtive life in shabby side-streets'.

In one of the stories there is an interesting beginning of a conflict between sensibility and loyalty. M. sets Ashenden on to trap Chandra Lal, a man 'who has done a foolishness against the State' —an Indian nationalist who is stirring up a good deal of trouble for the British in India during the War. Ashenden conceives quite a romantic admiration for this man, for which he is rebuked by M., who tells him not to get sentimental because Chandra Lal should not be considered a heroic patriot, but only a common criminal who must be put down. Nevertheless, Ashenden is struck by this little fat, middle-aged man, who besides tackling the total might of the Empire more or less single-handed, has a genuine and passionate love affair with an equally ridiculous actress/prostitute, the 'Giulia Lazzari' of the title. It should be said that real and reciprocal love is one of the few human situations that Maugham (in fiction) truly admires; he gives it the respect appropriate to a miracle. Ashenden, however, on instructions, traps the Indian by bullying his lover into betraying him. How he avoids the self-disgust which would immediately overwhelm a Le Carré or Deighton character is most revealing. Chandra Lal has committed suicide to avoid arrest, and Maugham has Giulia come to Ashenden and ask for the return of his wristwatch, which she had given him for Christmas: 'It cost £12.' This of course lets Ashenden off the moral hook—these low-class wogs are hardly human.

Perhaps the most interesting story for our purpose, however, is the last one in the book. On this occasion Ashenden is sent to Moscow (1917) to prevent the Revolution. He remarks that the reader will be aware that in this he did not succeed, but he can't help feeling that if he had been sent a little earlier. . . .[5]

This is an expression of the prime myth of the British upper class, the delusion that it is a genuine élite, distinguished by an 'effortless superiority'. It does everything better, with no trouble, than the lower orders do with great effort. This belief, which might be called the Pimpernel syndrome, is persistently displayed in British thriller fiction. It includes the maintenance of ritual frivolity, which proves that the superiority is really effortless. A typical example is the correspondence of Lord Peter Wimsey, the model aristocratic detective of the 1930s, with a friend in the Foreign Office, about a possible foreign agent (Sayers, 1932, p. 277):

Dear Clumps,
    Here's a cipher message. Probably Playfair but old Bungo will know. Can you push it off to him and say I'd be grateful for a construe? Said to hail from Central Europe but ten to one it's in English. How goes?
                                    Yours,
                                    Wimbles.

The answer is as follows (ibid.):

Dear Wimbles,
    Got your screed. Old Bungo is in China, dealing with the mess-up there, so have posted enclosure off as per instructions. He may be up-country, but he'll probably get it in a few weeks. How's things? Saw Trotters last week at the Carlton. He has got himself into a bit of a mess with his old man, but seems to bear up. You remember the Newton-Carberry business? Well, it's settled, and Flops has departed for the Continent. What-ho!
                                    Yours ever,
                                    Clumps.

This baby-talk, which infuriated Orwell, is part of the upper-class image of 'the inspired amateur'. Lord Peter, of course, sets to and solves the cipher in about twenty minutes with the aid of his girl-friend, an academic (MA, Oxon.) writer of thrillers, the well-known Miss Harriet Vane. Whatever the modern reader may think, and here, as with Ashenden, standards of admiration have certainly changed, the intention is to present Lord Peter as totally admirable for his superiority in every single human activity and emotion, throughout the series of books in which he figures. Lord Peter is of course incredibly well-connected—there is even the odd hint of R——y now and then—and well-mannered (including necessary insolence); he plays cricket for England (Wimsey of Balliol, legendary figure at Lords), punts, rides and all that, is a leading expert on incunabula, wines, the metaphysical poets, philosophy and history, has decent enough Latin and Greek, is a fencer and full of unexpected wiry strength, can talk to farmers about agriculture, is a great connoisseur of women ('il tient son lit en grand turque' and 'he had once owned the finest contralto voice in Europe'), is often engaged in delicate diplomatic missions for the FO, is the world's greatest detective as a hobby, and withal is a man of extraordinary sensitivity, capable of a serious and sustained passion and deeply meaningful personal relationships, with that special shy charm so characteristic of Leslie Howard in his best-known roles. His American counterpart was summed up by Ogden Nash in the immortal distich:

> Philo Vance
> Needs a kick in the pance

but Lord Peter is presented (oh yes, I forgot that he habitually wears a monocle and has complete knowledge (of course) of the correct modes of address to titled persons) absolutely straight, for the admiration of the reader. And this glorification of the ruling aristocracy is typical of thriller fiction as well as spy fiction right through the 1930s and up to 1945. The 'mess-up' in China to which Clumps refers, was the Shanghai Massacre of Communists by Chiang-Kai-shek, the Battle of Nanking, and the beginning of the Long March to Yenan by the Chinese Red Army under the leadership of Mao Tse-tung. Perhaps if old Bungo had been sent a little earlier . . .?

Doubtless the belief in upper-class ability led to staffing high posts, including the secret service, with upper-class people. It was accompanied by another assumption, and one much more rationally founded, of the total identification of class with loyalty. Le Carré points out, in his introduction to *Philby* (Page *et al.*, 1969), that this assumption made the service continue to employ Philby long after it had more than enough evidence to get rid of him. The assumption of loyalty is not only based on the obvious material interest which members of the upper class have in maintaining the status quo—plenty of people are capable of putting larger interests above their own—but on the fact that the British ruling class runs its affairs as if it were a primary group. There is great emphasis on personal acquaintance with family and social background, the interlocking web of alliances by birth, education, and marriage, which constitute a 'clan' of rulers having almost a relationship of blood kinship. Whatever their surface characteristics they can be assumed to be basically loyal. There is necessarily a great tolerance of eccentricity of various kinds. Thus it did not count against Maclean that he was a drunkard, or against Burgess that he was demonstratively homosexual and Bohemian (although the Consul at Cairo is reported to have said, when he saw Burgess's fingernails, 'Can he really be one of us?'); or against Philby that he was, as his dossier records, 'a bit of a bastard with the girls'. Neither did youthful left-wing tendencies count against anyone: they were presumed to be outgrown, and were in any case a normal stage in the development of young gentlemen of the brighter sort. Malcolm Muggeridge assumes that blindness to this particular trait was due to a breakdown in the instinctual detection apparatus of the 'clan' (1966, p. 187):

> A ruling class on the run, as ours is, is capable of every
> fatuity. It makes the wrong decisions, chooses the wrong
> people, and is unable to recognise its enemies—if it does not
> actually prefer them to its friends.

And there may be something in this, since the recognition of friends was based on two false premises: ability and loyalty as inevitable class characteristics. But the reason there was such an outburst of fury in Britain over the defection of Burgess, Maclean, and especially Philby, was that they had shown themselves to be true deviants, not merely eccentrics, by challenging the existence of their own clan: a crime tantamount, in clan society, to shedding kindred blood. This explains the prominence given, by the authors of *Philby*, to the remark of the seventeen-year-old Maclean, cited above: it shows that he was rotten to the core, a criminal deviant, and not merely a generous-hearted boy, as anyone outside the Empire ideology might suppose.

The secret service is the part of the ruling clan most exactly like a primary group—the inner core of the family. The method of recruitment supports this hypothesis. Graham Greene, for instance,

13

was asked in a BBC interview, 'How was it you went into intelligence work?' Answer: 'I was recruited by a relation. They wanted somebody who had a little knowledge of Africa' (*Listener*, 21 November 1968). Ashenden had a long chat with a highranking officer at a party, and was asked to go to a seedy house in Kensington, where he was recruited. This seedy house in Kensington still haunts British spy-fiction: see, for instance, the opening of Len Deighton's *Funeral in Berlin* (1964). The point of it in Ashenden's time was that it was so incongruous for gentlemen to be there; not so now.

Given the social assumptions set out above, it is not surprising that in the late 1930s and during the war, Intelligence was recruited on the basis of class membership. Page, Leitch, and Knightley give extensive and very funny documentation of this. Leitch (Page *et al.*, 1969, pp. 124–5) for instance, reports the following conversation with

an amiable gentleman who passed the war excitingly in a series of very clandestine operations.

They were discussing the quality of the intake in those hectic days of the early forties, and the exchange was as follows:

Leitch: 'An amazing amount of crooks seem to have got into S.O.E., S.I.S. and all those outfits during the war, don't you think?'

Veteran: 'Well, have to take what you can get in wartime, don't you?'

Leitch: 'They seem to have got most of these chaps out of the bar at White's, so far as one can see.'

Veteran: 'Yes, well, you wouldn't find anything except crooks there, would you?'

Leitch: 'Where were you recruited?'

Veteran: 'Boodle's.'

White's, we are informed (ibid., p. 146), 'is usually bracketed with the Turf at the apex of the subtle hierarchy of London clubland'. Boodle's is lower down, but not by much (ibid.).

During the war, an etiquette grew up among members of White's that one was not to bother Menzies and Koch de Gooreynd when they were together at the bar, because it was understood that they were 'running the secret service, or something'. It would hardly have struck anyone at White's as odd that the club should occasionally be a sort of partial, alternative headquarters of the secret service; rather the reverse, in that the major clubs of the West End are, quite unselfconsciously, citadels of the British ruling orders.

By 1945, then, the upper class, in real life as in fiction, had moved in and taken over the executive posts in the secret service; they were no longer gentlemanly outsiders, patriotically offering their services as a duty, which might entail the laughable requirement that they take orders from their social inferiors. Now the gentlemen are running the Game, including the 'dirty tricks'—'I can see them working it out, they're so damned academic,' says Leamas in a burst of bitterness; 'I can see them sitting round a fire in one of their smart bloody clubs.'

From admiration of the gentlemanly imperial ideal to the bitterness and sometimes hatred towards gentleman-superiors which is shown again and again by the best British spy-writers—Le Carré, Deighton, Adam Hall *(The Quiller Memorandum)*—is a considerable distance. I think the watershed in that change of attitude is the post-war ambience most accurately presented in Michael Innes's masterpiece, *The Journeying Boy.*

This delightful book, first published in 1949, is extraordinarily cheerful. Besides being a tour-de-force of donnish writing, it is full of the post-war optimism which was general in England at the time, before everything began to go wrong (for this Sissons and French (1963)). Mr Thewless, the tutor, muses not about social superiority but about 'the building of a better England. For the achieving of that, after all, how many people more talented and powerful than he must passionately care!' This hope and attitude implies a downgrading of mere wealth as a moral value. Thewless,[6] outside the door of Sir Bernard Paxton, who is 'beyond doubt the greatest of living physicists', is visited by sharp misgivings, and this despite being, 'as he sometimes told himself, a sober and self-respecting snob, just as by vocation he was a hanger-on of people themselves no more than desperately hanging-on' (Innes, 1968, p. 6):

Often enough before he had been in this sort of house, but never with comfort for very long. Positive opulence was something which he found uncomfortably to jar with the spirit of the time; the poet whose social occasions obliged him to spend a day at Timon's villa was not rendered more uneasy by its splendours than was Mr. Thewless by anything resembling their latter-day counterpart. And why—the question suggested itself even as he raised his hand to the doorbell—yes, why in the world should a really great man take the trouble to surround himself with so emphatic a material magnificence?

The social assumption in this context is that society is really changing. The 'idle rich' are disappearing—'no more than desperately hanging-on'—there is to be a true aristocracy of merit and moral worth. It counts against Sir Bernard that he indulges himself in a display of wealth; nevertheless it is Mr Thewless's duty to help him because of his scientific genius, which is used for the public good. The values are not to be gross material gain and the brutal exercise of power, as with Kipling and Ian Fleming, or the arrogance of hereditary superiority, as in the whole snob school of thrillers from Maugham through John Buchan and the snob murder-queens: Dorothy Sayers, Agatha Christie, Margery Allingham, and Ngaio Marsh (their American counterparts are Elizabeth Daly and Mary Roberts Rhinehart). On the contrary, in *The Journeying Boy* the admired values are intelligence, social responsibility, and honourable behaviour directed at promoting the good of the whole society. In this situation idealism is consonant with patriotism, which may account for the optimistic tone. The privileges of the upper stratum are noted, but allowable because of superiority due to great effort, not by right of birth. They have constantly to make hard moral decisions, and their consciousness of kind is based on virtue not class. The villains, unlike those of Kipling, Maugham, and Fleming, are neither foreign nor low-class, but cousins of Sir Bernard's late wife, in hot pursuit of unenlightened self-interest.

We encounter frequent jabs at the gentlemanly snob ideal—phrases like 'our faded institutions of privilege'—and this attitude is not exclusive to this particular book and author, but general in the tone of thriller literature of the time. Thus even in a contemporary work of Allingham, an eccentric countess who has used the prerogatives of rank to move the body and generally interfere is castigated, the other character noting that 'ninety-nine per cent of the world's population were in agreement' as to the non-acceptability of this Old Girl Privilege.

But the optimal social situation reflected in *The Journeying Boy* came quickly to an end. The resumption of Parliamentary power by the Conservatives in 1951 made it clear that, some social gains notwithstanding, the New Jerusalem had not been built in England. So far as the Secret World was concerned, its upper-class administrators had remained uninterruptedly in command since the War, and beginning with Graham Greene's *Our Man in Havana* (1958), a new type of mocking, disillusioned spy literature appeared; in this first instance, the attack was on the delusion of the effortless superiority of the 'inspired amateurs' in command, whose gullibility and incompetence are the target. There is also an implied attack on the whole wrong-headed mystique of spying, which ignores the real miseries of the island (Cuba), but is infatuated with fake photos of a vacuum cleaner.

With the appearance of Le Carré's *Call for the Dead* (1961; later reprinted as *The Deadly Affair*) and *A Murder of Quality* (1962), and Len Deighton's *Ipcress File* (1962), a really jeering attack on the upper class is mounted, and the new type of spy fiction is established. The distinguishing features are: the detestation of the middle- or lower-class spy in the field for his upper-class administrative superiors; emotional attachment, sometimes only consciousness of kind but sometimes real affection, of the spy for his enemy opposite number; revulsion at the dirty work of spying in general, and in particular at having to kill his enemy/friend; and finally, a basic loyalty after all to his own country and service, not because it is superior but because he happens to have been born in it.

The alienation of operatives in the field from superiors in safe spots is not unknown in real life. Vilhelm Aubert, the Norwegian sociologist, discusses this in 'Secrecy: the underground as a social system' (1965), with respect to the members of the Norwegian Resistance who remained in Norway during the Occupation, running the risks and doing the work, while the Norwegian exile government attempted to direct them from London. By the end of the War their distrust and dislike had turned to real hatred: most of them contemptuously refused the decorations they were offered by the exile government. There may also have been an element of age and class antagonism. Field commanders were necessarily unknown and young, and Norwegians of high rank and influence in ordinary life could not be used for Resistance work as they were watched. In the world of espionage, as in the Resistance, the important people in the field in World War II were those low on the ordinary ladder of social stratification. Sidney Reilly made a point of mingling with élites, and in fact insisted often on élite status and income to make it possible. But modern times call for modern remedies. Masterman is most explicit (1972, p. 32. My italics).

> It is a mistake to suppose that the well-placed person friendly, let us say, with a Cabinet Minister or an official in the Foreign Office or a highly-placed staff officer is necessarily in the highest grade of agents. The indiscreet remarks of ministers or generals do not carry much conviction, and it is a truism of historical research that when dealing with diplomatic conversations and the rumours of embassies we are in the very realm of lies. . . . It was of far more value to . . . learn, for example, that a certain division had moved to the area of one of the northern ports, or that it had had instruction in mountain warfare, or that it had been issued with arctic equipment, than it was for him to hear that 'Lord So-and-So in the Cabinet told me in the utmost confidence that an invasion of northern Norway was being discussed by the Chiefs of Staff'.
>
> It follows from this that *the highest-grade agent is often a low-grade man.* A seaman or a wireless operator can give much more useful information with regard to convoys than the most expert or well-informed spy of the traditional pattern.

These important informants would almost necessarily have to be of working-class origin and orientation, which would certainly emphasise the social distance and potential, if not actual, dislike between them and their gentlemanly Controls. The enormous success of sabotage efforts in Denmark (*'De* ringer og kalder, *Vi* kommer og knalder')[7] is due to the numbers of skilled Danish workmen involved, few indeed of whom were on Danmarks Frihedsraad—the Council of the Resistance Movement, composed of élites.

In Norway, according to Aubert, upper-class and prominent Norwegians who stayed in the country took orders from the young commanders; but they were naturally in command if they were in London, and if they were in the government they were upper-class or professional people.

Aubert gives no indication that the Resistance fighters felt any attraction towards the Germans; on the contrary, their emotional involvement was all with each other. People were recruited if deemed to be trustworthy by their friends, and it was necessary for the confidence to be well founded, as the penalty for mistaken judgment was extreme: to be taken by the Gestapo. Friendship among themselves alone was the single available reward and solace, and Aubert reports that it was sometimes impossible to resist the temptation of telling one's real name, as a mark of trust, although this was of course contrary to security and good sense. It marked the total cut-off in intimate life, not only from the Germans but also from the general population.

The invaluable Orlov, however, reports a different attitude among Soviet intelligence officers, an attraction for their professional opponents which is similar to that described in the new spy fiction. He says (1963, p. 23. My italics):

> The fifth line of Soviet intelligence is *Infiltration of Security Agencies and Intelligence Services of Foreign Countries.* This activity contains a special challenge to Soviet intelligence officers and holds for them a peculiar kind of fascination. Although they regard foreign intelligence officers as professional spies (they think of themselves as revolutionaries carrying out dangerous assignments of the party) *they do have a feeling of kinship with them* and react to a suddenly encountered foreign intelligence agent with the same thrill and curiosity with which two enemy pilots sight each other over the wide spaces of the sky. The general attitude of the Soviet intelligence officer towards his foreign counterpart is hostile, but *it is sincerely friendly from the moment the foreign intelligence man becomes an informant for Russia.*

Kinship, sympathy, attraction, fascination, admiration: these sentiments of a spy towards his opponent are heavily emphasised in contemporary spy fiction. Ashenden's romantic admiration for Chandra Lal, the Indian nationalist, is a prefiguration of this change. George Smiley in *The Deadly Affair* (Le Carré, 1961, p. 145), having killed his enemy/friend (a former student, to be sure), resigns from the service (but not for ever).

> Dieter was dead, and he had killed him. . . . And Dieter had let him do it, had not fired the gun, had remembered their friendship when Smiley had not. . . . They had come from

different hemispheres of the night, from different worlds of thought and conduct. Dieter, mercurial, absolute, had fought to build a civilization. Smiley, rationalistic, protective, had fought to prevent him. 'Oh God,' said Smiley aloud, 'Who was then the gentleman?'

Leamas and Fiedler, in *The Spy Who Came in from the Cold* (Le Carré, 1963), are similarly bound in sympathy—'We're all the same, you know, that's the joke,' says Fiedler. All the same, that is, not only in their kinship and attraction for each other, but in their help-less and hopeless relationship to their superiors. Leamas explains this to Liz (and to the bewildered reader) at the end (p. 230):

'They used us,' Leamas replied pitilessly. 'They cheated us both because it was necessary. It was the only way. Fiedler was bloody nearly home already, don't you see? Mundt would have been caught; can't you understand that?'

'How can you turn the world upside down?' Liz shouted suddenly. 'Fiedler was kind and decent; he was only doing his job, and now you've killed him. Mundt is a spy and a traitor and you protect him. Mundt is a Nazi.'

Well, yes, it's all true. In fact it is part of the game of cricket so antiseptically described by Masterman: spy books like *The Spy Who Came in from the Cold* are an expression of disgust at the game, as Leamas says (p. 226):

'I'll tell you. I'll tell you what you were never, never to know, neither you nor I. Listen: Mundt is London's man, their agent; they bought him when he was in England. We are witnessing the lousy end to a filthy, lousy operation to save Mundt's skin. To save him from a clever little Jew in his own department who had begun to suspect the truth.'

Leamas, sickened though he is, defends these operations as neces-sary 'so that the great moronic mass that you admire can sleep soundly in their beds at night'. Nevertheless, he in effect commits suicide when Liz is killed.

Len Deighton's 'I', in *Funeral in Berlin*, makes a collegial defence of Johnny Vulkan to his own Control (1964, p. 20):

'Protection', I said. 'What sort of protection have we ever offered him? The only protection he ever had from us was old-fashioned money. People like Vulkan are in danger—

physical danger—every moment of every day. The only weapon they have is money. If Vulkan is always asking for more, it's worth considering the motives.'

Vulkan is a double agent, and 'I' finally kills him; nevertheless in this early conversation 'I' is shocked ('I didn't think old Dawlish could make me shiver') when Dawlish makes it clear that Vulkan's life is not exactly sacred: 'If we decide not to continue with Vulkan's contract there is no question of leaving him available for the highest bidder.' And a systematic search of the literature would yield many more examples, even excluding the old-fashioned commonplace of sexual involvement. Attraction to the literally mortal enemy seems to be a characteristic trait of modern spies, based not just on occupational identification but also on a genuine emotional involvement. One of the few bright moments in the TV series 'Spy-Trap', mentioned in Chapter 2, was the beginning of the interrogation of the Russian master-spy, when he walked forcefully across the room, crashed into a chair, and when asked 'Your profession?' gave a smile of extreme, even seraphic, sweetness and warmth, to which there was a small responsive smile from the interrogator, although this was more like seeing a shark turn under water, about ten feet down. Nevertheless, there was the implication that if no one else did, these two really understood each other. It never took more than an episode, or two at most, to turn spies around on this series, though whether this had any relation to the coincidental publication of *The Double-Cross System in the War of 1939–1945* and what Professor Hugh Trevor-Roper (*Sunday Times*, 5 March 1972) describes as a spate of such books (*Gehlen—Spy of the Century* by E. H. Cookridge, published on 29 November 1971; *The Game of the Foxes* by Ladislas Farrago, published on 30 March 1972; *Network* by Heinz Höhne and Hermann Zolling, published on 20 March 1972; *Codeword: Direktor* by Heinz Höhne, published on 1 November 1971; *Der Dienst* (1971) by Reinhard Gehlen) I cannot say.

As Orlov shows, the phenomenon is not confined to fiction, and it is not confined to Russia, either. We are told in *Philby* (1969, p. 259) of:

William Skardon, the crack MI5 investigator, who with his usual deceptive gentleness, had extracted an enormous amount of information from Klaus Fuchs (to whom he always referred as 'dear old Klaus').

The ability to lead a convincing double life is of course the basic operational necessity of an agent, and although this must give an area of tolerance to the fascination with real enemies recorded by Orlov (and made much of in the brilliant American film *The President's Analyst*, which features a very nice Russian spy named Kropotkin), it must also lead to the operational inconvenience of agents becoming double-agents. I suppose that every spy is at least potentially a double-agent, just as every portrait is a self-portrait.

The agent attracted to the enemy, and the double-agent serving two Powers at the same time, whether or not with equal enthusiasm, is not the opposite but of a different kind from the old-fashioned spy as seen in Kipling, or the Norwegian Resistance fighter. There the commitment to one's own side is absolute. It is unthinkable for Kim to give the despised and detested enemy a few secrets, for money or any other consideration. Their employment was a devotion to what they knew to be right. The bright nostalgic quality of *The Journeying Boy* derives from a more sophisticated version of the same allegiance: one's own side is, in fact, virtuous, and the others are villains of the deepest dye; no confusion of moral issues here. Ashenden speciously preserves this façade by an unfair moral degradation of the enemy. The unspeakable James Bond reverts to the social morality of Kipling's Empire, the personal morality of the toughest American private-eye and gangster literature, and the most vulgar possible one-up-manship in material possessions and their conspicuous consumption, as well as connoisseurship and womanising. He is a kind of mad parody of Lord Peter Wimsey, in an age when 'effortless superiority' can hardly be made credible. The fact that books and films about him break all records shows that the sensitive and introspective agent, doing his distasteful duty despite moral revulsion, does not by any means dominate the field, even today. There is a demand by a more sophisticated audience for hardheaded recognition that much espionage is morally repulsive, but necessary out of tribal loyalty. But there is a larger demand, measured in the standard mass-culture measure of sales, for approval of any kind of brutality whatsoever, provided it is associated with expensive consumer goods and machinery, and directed against political enemies, national or ethnic aliens, or women.

An interesting mass-culture phenomenon is the spy-fiction factory recently reported in the *New York Times* book review section. As indicated above, American culture has no immediate imperial or literary connection with espionage such as that which involved British writers of respectable talents and serious intentions. But the market has been created, and an entrepreneur named L. Kenyon Engel employs sixty-four writers to fill in the outlines of plots and characters as directed by him. As with James Bond, the values revert to an earlier type: the principal figure is Nick Carter, a railroad detective created in the 1870s, tales about whom were manufactured for years by the publishers Street and Smith. It is safe to bet that no moral issues arise in these productions, no self-doubt, no detestation of superiors.

Whether real or fictional spies are right in distrusting their administrators, and vice versa, may perhaps be partially illuminated by the following jocular exchange between a couple of their ultimate employers (quoted in Deighton, 1964, p. 1):

Allen W. Dulles (then director CIA): 'You, Mr. Chairman, may have seen some of my intelligence reports.'

Mr. Khrushchev: 'I believe we get the same reports—and probably from the same people.'

Mr. Dulles: 'Maybe we should pool our efforts.'

Mr. Khrushchev: 'Yes. We should buy our intelligence data together and save money. We'd have to pay the people only once.'

News Item, September 1959.

Notes

* This chapter first appeared, in somewhat different form, in *Mass Culture Revisited*, eds B. Rosenberg and D. M. White, Van Nostrand Reinhold, New York, 1971.
1 Lockhart, like Maugham and perhaps Dorothy Sayers, entertains the delusion that with just a little bit more luck the British agent could have 'freed the Russian people from the yoke of Bolshevism' and that then the 'whole course of history might have been changed' (p. 79).
2 See Page *et al.* (1969). 'Kim' Philby's real name was Harold Adrian Russell Philby, but he was nicknamed after Kipling's hero. His early life was passed in India, he played with Indian boys and spoke Hindi before he spoke English. There has been speculation as to whether his father, the Arabist and somewhat estranged British Civil Servant, Harry St John Bridger Philby, who took the name of Abdullah ('slave of God') and later Al Hajji, meaning he had made the pilgrimage to Mecca, had 'dedicated' his son from childhood to spying against Britain. It seems pretty certain, though, that he was recruited at Cambridge, like Burgess and Maclean. John le Carré, in the

Introduction has some illuminating speculations about the unknown recruiter:

> He understood us better than we understood ourselves: was he our countryman? He recruited only gentlemen: was he himself a gentleman? He recruited only from Cambridge: was he a Cambridge man? All three recruits would travel far on the reputations of their families alone: was he too a man of social influence?

3 See Orwell's essay on 'Dickens' (1940).

4 Preface to this US edition:

> Before World War II, when I was one of the chiefs of the Soviet intelligence, I lectured at the Central Military School in Moscow on the tactics and strategy of intelligence and counter-intelligence. In 1936 I wrote down the basic rules and principles of Soviet intelligence in the form of a manual which was approved as the only textbook for the newly created NKVD schools for undercover intelligence officers and for the Central Military School in Moscow. Because intelligence has gained considerable importance in world affairs and has become a regular subject in the curricula of American and other Western military colleges, the University of Michigan Press has commissioned me with the reconstruction of the intelligence manual. I did it in a way that I thought would be suitable for the specialist and the layman alike.

Can this be the same man as that 'Vladimir Orloff, a Tsarist who under the name of Orlinsky had infiltrated into the Cheka and had become a senior official at the Cheka's headquarters in Petrograd', where he worked with 'Sidney Reilly', according to Robin Bruce Lockhart, op. cit., p. 65? I suppose it is not impossible that he could infiltrate as a young man in 1918, lecture at the Central Military School fifteen or twenty years later, and defect ten years after that as a General in the NKVD, reassuming his original name.

5 See note 1.

6 Innes amuses himself by using the names of characters to define their roles, in the manner of a medieval Morality and in the literary tradition of Dickens and Henry James (see discussion of significant naming in Chapter 3). Not only is the tutor named Thewless, but Paxton's researches are presumably to be used for peace; the lady secret agent is called Miss Liberty; the two men from Homicide are called Cadover and Morton; a psychiatrist named Lord Polder is mentioned (polder: 'a piece of low-lying ground reclaimed from the sea. (Du.)'); even the village where the crime takes place is called Killyboffin, and boffin = scientist in England, since Dickens created the first Boffin in *Our Mutual Friend*.

7 Toward the end of the Occupation the panache of the Danish sabotage groups was such that they posted the cited slogan like a commercial advertisement. It means '*You* ring us up, *we'll* come and blow it up', and is typical of Copenhagen working-class wit in being a parody of typical commercial language, defiant, amusing, and having an evident sexual connotation.

Bibliography

ACHEBE, CHINUA (1958), *Things Fall Apart*, Heinemann, London.

AESCHYLUS (1956 edn), *Oresteian Trilogy*, trans. by P. Vellacott, Penguin, Harmondsworth. (1970 edn), *Agamemnon, The Libation Bearers, The Eumenides*, trans. and with an introduction by Hugh Lloyd-Jones, Prentice-Hall, New York.

AMIS, KINGSLEY (1954), *Lucky Jim*, Gollancz, London; Doubleday, New York.

AMIS, KINGSLEY (1971), *The Green Man*, Panther, London; original ed. 1969, Cape, London.

ANDERSEN, HANS (1970 edn), *Little Claus and Big Claus*, Kaye & Ward, London.

ANDRESKI, IRIS (1970), *Old Wives' Tales*, Routledge & Kegan Paul, London.

AUBERT, VILHELM (1965), 'Secrecy: the underground as a social system' in *The Hidden Society*, Bedminster Press, New York.

AUDEN, W. H. (1951), *The Enchaféd Flood—or, The Romantic Iconography of the Sea*, Faber, London.

AUDEN, W. H. and MACNEICE, LOUIS (1937), *Letters from Iceland*, Faber, London.

AUERBACH, ERICH (1953), *Mimesis: the representation of reality in Western literature*, Princeton University Press.

AUSTEN, JANE (1814), *Mansfield Park*.

AUSTEN, JANE (1815), *Emma*.

AUSTIN, JANE (1818), *Persuasion*, published posthumously.

BANFIELD, E. C. (1967), *The Moral Basis of a Backward Society*, Free Press, New York.

BBC REPORT (1970), *Violence on Television*, London.

BLACK, PETER (1972), 'Coming through a door with a gun forever', *Encounter*, April.

BOHANNAN, LAURA (1966), 'Shakespeare in the bush', *Natural History*, 75, 7.

BONE, ROBERT (1958), *The Negro Novel in America*, Yale University Press, New Haven.

BRANDELL, GUNNAR (1963), *Freud og hans Tid*, Gyldendal, Copenhagen; from Swedish *Freud och Sekelsluttet*.

BRIFFAULT, ROBERT (1927), *The Mothers. A study of the origins of sentiments and institutions*, W. H. Allen, London.

BROBY-JOHANSEN, V. (1968), *Oldnordisk Stenbilleder*, Gyldendal, Copenhagen.

BROWNE, SIR THOMAS (1643), *Religio Medici*.

BURLING, ROBBINS (1970), *Man's Many Voices; language in its cultural context*, Holt, Rinehart & Winston, New York.

CARTER, HUNTLEY (1924), *The New Theatre and Cinema of Soviet Russia,* Chapman & Dodd, London.

CHESNEY, KELLOW (1970), *The Victorian Underworld,* M. T. Smith, London.

CHILD, FRANCIS JAMES (1883–98), *English and Scottish Popular Ballads,* Boston.

CHILDE, GORDON (1942), *What Happened in History,* Penguin, Baltimore, rev. edn, 1960.

CHINOY, ELY (1967), *Society: an introduction to sociology,* Random House, New York.

COMMITTEE ON BROADCASTING (1960), *Report* (Pilkington Report), Cmnd 1753, HMSO, London.

CONNOLLY, CYRIL (1945), *The Unquiet Grave,* Harper, New York.

COOKRIDGE, E. H. (1971), *Gehlen—Spy of the Century,* Hodder & Stoughton, London.

COSER, LEWIS (1963), *Sociology Through Literature: an introductory reader,* Prentice-Hall, Englewood Cliffs.

CRITCHLEY, T. A. (1970), *Conquest of Violence,* Constable, London.

CRYSTAL, DAVID (1971), *Linguistics,* Penguin, Harmondsworth.

CUNLIFFE, MARCUS (1954), *The Literature of the United States,* Penguin, Harmondsworth.

DAVIS, KINGSLEY (1940), 'Extreme social isolation of a child', *American Journal of Sociology,* vol. 45, January.

DAVIS, KINGSLEY (1947), 'Final note on a case of extreme isolation', *American Journal of Sociology,* vol. 50, March.

DAVIS, KINGSLEY (1966), *Human Society,* Collier-Macmillan, New York.

DEFOE, DANIEL (1719), *The Life and Strange Surprising Adventures of Robinson Crusoe.*

DEFOE, DANIEL (1722), *The Fortunes and Misfortunes of the famous Moll Flanders.*

DEFOE, DANIEL (1927 edn), *A Tour through the Whole Island of Great Britain,* Everyman, Dent, London and Toronto. Originally published in three volumes, 1724, 1725, 1726.

DEIGHTON, LEN (1962), *The Ipcress File,* Hodder & Stoughton, London.

DEIGHTON, LEN (1964), *Funeral in Berlin,* Cape, London.

DENNIS, F., HENRIQUES, F. and SLAUGHTER, C. (1956), *Coal is our Life,* Eyre & Spottiswoode, London.

DEUTSCH, MARTIN (1959), 'In nuclear research' in *Evidence and Inference,* ed. Daniel Lerner, Free Press, Chicago.

DOUGLASS, DAVID (1971), *Pit Life in Co. Durham,* History Workshop Pamphlet No. 5, Ruskin College, Oxford.

DOUGLASS, FREDERICK (1882), *Life and Times of Frederick Douglass: written by himself,* Park Publishing House, Hartford, Conn.

DOWLING, JOHN H. (1968), 'Sharing by hunters', *American Anthropologist,* vol. 70.

DURKHEIM, ÉMILE (1912), *Elementary Forms of the Religious Life,* trans. from *Les formes élémentaires de la vie religieuse,* Allen & Unwin, London.

DURKHEIM, ÉMILE (1969 edn), 'The normality of crime' in *Sociological Theory: a book of readings,* eds B. Rosenberg and L. Coser, Collier-Macmillan, London.

Egil's Saga, ed. N. M. Petersen (1969); Copenhagen, Thaning & Appels Forlag.

Elder Edda, The, trans. W. H. Auden, Faber, London, 1969.

ELDRIDGE, J. E. T. (1971), ed. and with an introduction, *Max Weber: the interpretation of social reality*, Nelson, London.

ELIOT, T. S. (1939), *Family Reunion* (drama), Faber, London.

ENGELS, F. (1884), *The Origin of the Family, Private Property, and the State.*

FARRAGO, LADISLAS (1972), *The Game of the Foxes*, Hodder & Stoughton, London.

FAST, HOWARD (1944), *Freedom Road*, Duell, Sloan & Pearce, New York.

FAULKNER, WILLIAM (1929), *Sartoris*, Harcourt, Brace, New York.

FAULKNER, WILLIAM (1930), *Absolom, Absolom*, Random House, New York.

FAULKNER, WILLIAM (1948), *Intruder in the Dust*, Random House, New York.

FIEDLER, LESLIE A. (1966), *Love and Death in the American Novel*, Criterion Books, New York.

FIELD, MARGARET (1957), 'Religion and magic of the Ga people', quoted in Parrinder (1963).

FIELDING, HENRY (1743), *Jonathan Wild,* London.

FIELDING, HENRY (1749), *Tom Jones,* London.

FINLEY, M. I. (1954), *The World of Odysseus*, Viking Press, New York.

FINNISH TOURIST BUREAU (1971), *Look at Finland*, Helsinki.

FISCHER, ERNST (1963), *The Necessity of Art: a Marxist approach*, Penguin, Harmondsworth: trans. from *Von der Notwendigkeit der Kunst*, Dresden, 1959.

FITZGERALD, F. SCOTT (1925), *The Great Gatsby.*

FITZGERALD, F. SCOTT (1934), *Tender is the Night.*

FLAUBERT, GUSTAV (1857), *Madame Bovary*, Paris.

FORSTER, E. M. (1910), *Howards End,* London.

FRANKLIN, BENJAMIN (1733–58), *Poor Richard's Almanac*, publ. periodically.

FREUCHEN, PETER (1961), *Book of the Eskimos*, Fawcett Publications, Greenwich, Conn.; ed. Dagmar Freuchen and selected from his early writings: *Eskimo-Fortællinger og andre Noveller* (Nordiske Lands Bogforlag, 1944); *I al Frimodighed* (1953); *Blandt Polareskimoer* (Carit Andersen, 1959); *Erindringer* (Gyldendal, 1963).

FROMM, ERICH (1963), *Sigmund Freud's Mission: an analysis of his personality and influence*, Grove Press, New York.

GALSWORTHY, JOHN (1963 edn), *The Man of Property*, London (first novel in *The Forsyte Saga*, 1906–27).

GAY, JOHN (1728), *The Beggar's Opera* (comedy with incidental music).

GEHLEN, REINHARD (1971), *Der Dienst*, Hasse & Kuhley, Frankfurt.

GESELL, ARNOLD (1939), *Biographies of Child Development; the mental growth careers of eighty-four infants and children*, Harper, New York.

GESELL, ARNOLD (1941), *Wolf Child and Human Child*, Harper, New York, Methuen, London.

GIMPEL, JEAN (1969), *The Cult of Art*, Weidenfeld & Nicolson, London; trans. from *Contre l'art et les artistes ou la naissance d'une religion*, Éditions du Seuil, Paris, 1968.

GLOB, P. V. (1969), *The Bog People: Iron-Age man preserved*, Faber, London; trans. from *Mosefolket: Jernalderens mennesker bevaret i 2000 Ar.*, Gyldendal, Copenhagen, 1965.

GLUCKMAN, MAX (1965), *Custom and Conflict in Africa*, Blackwell, Oxford.

GOLD, MICHAEL (1930), *Jews Without Money*, Liveright, New York.

GOLDMANN, LUCIEN (1967), 'The sociology of literature: status and problems of method', *International Social Sciences Journal*, vol. 19, no. 4.

GOLDMANN, LUCIEN (1964), *The Hidden God*, Routledge & Kegan Paul, London; trans. from the French *Le Dieu Caché*, Gallimard, Paris, 1955.

GOODLAD, J. S. R. (1971), *A Sociology of the Popular Drama*, Heinemann, London.

GORKY, MAXIM (1969), *My Childhood*, first publ. 1913–14; Penguin, Harmondsworth.

GOULDNER, ALVIN W. (1971), *The Coming Crisis of Western Sociology*, Heinemann, London and Basic Books, New York, 1970.

GREENE, GRAHAM (1958), *Our Man in Havana*, Viking Press, New York.

GRIEST, GUINEVERE L. (1970), *Mudie's Circulating Library and the Victorian Novel*, Indiana University Press.

GRÖNBECH, WILHELM (1922), *Vor Folkeæt i Oldtiden*, V. Pio's Boghandel, Copenhagen, vol. 4.

HALL, ADAM (pseud. of Elleston Trevor) (1965), *The Quiller Memorandum*, Simon & Schuster, New York.

HALL, EDWARD T. (1966), *The Hidden Dimension*, Doubleday, New York.

HALLBERG, PETER (1965), *De Islandske Sagaer*, Gyldendals Uglebøger, Copenhagen (Summary of *Heiðarviga Saga*).

HANSEN, BENTE (1972) *Den marxistiske litteraturkritik*, Reitzel, Copenhagen.

HARRISON, JANE (1962), *Themis: A study of the social origins of Greek religion*, Meridian Books, London; P. Smith, Gloucester, Mass.; 2nd ed. Merlin Press, London, 1963.

HAVELOCK, ERIC A. (1970), Introduction, *The Oresteian Trilogy*, Prentice-Hall, New York.

HIMMELWEIT, H. T., OPPENHEIM, A., and VINCE, P. (1958), *Television and the Child*, Oxford University Press, London.

HOBSBAWM, J. A. B. (1969), *Bandits*, Weidenfeld & Nicolson, London.

HÖHNE, HEINZ (1971), *Codeword: Direktor*, Secker & Warburg, London.

HÖHNE, HEINZ and ZOLLING, HERMANN (1972), *Network*, Secker & Warburg, London.

HOLBERG, LUDWIG (1723), *Jeppe paa Bjerget*.

HOLBERG, LUDWIG (1744), *Moralske Tanker*.

HUACO, GEORGE A. (1965), *The Sociology of Film Art*, Basic Books, New York/ London.

INNES, MICHAEL (pseud. of J. I. M. Stewart) (1968), *The Case of the Journeying Boy*, Penguin, Harmondsworth; Gollancz, London, 1949.

JACKSON, SHIRLEY (1948), 'The Lottery', *New Yorker*.

JAMES, HENRY (1898), *The Turn of the Screw*.

JAMES, HENRY (1904), *The Golden Bowl*.

JARRELL, RANDALL (1954), *Pictures from an Institution*, Knopf, New York.

JOHNSON, DR SAMUEL (1750–2), *The Rambler*, written almost entirely by him.

JOHNSON, DR SAMUEL (1930 edn), *A Journey to the Western Islands of Scotland*, Oxford University Press, London.

JONES, B. E. M. (1933), *Henry Fielding, Novelist and Magistrate*, Allen & Unwin, London.

JOYCE, JAMES (1914–15), *A Portrait of the Artist as a Young Man*, publ. serially in *Egoist*.

JOYCE, JAMES (1922), *Ulysses*, Paris.

KETTLE, ARNOLD (1951–3), *An Introduction to the English Novel*, 2 vols, Hutchinson, London.

KIPLING, RUDYARD (1965 edn), *Kim*, Macmillan, London.

KITTO, H. D. F. (1964), *Form and Meaning in Drama. A study of six Greek plays and Hamlet*, Methuen, London.

KITTO, H. D. F. (1967), *The Greeks*, Penguin, Harmondsworth.

KNIGHT, EVERETT (1970), *A Theory of the Classical Novel*, Routledge & Kegan Paul, London.

KRISTENSEN, EVALD TANG (1891), *Gamle Folksfortællinger om det Jyske Almueliv, 6. Afdeling*, Gyldendalske Boghandel, Copenhagen.

KRISTENSEN, EVALD TANG (1931), *Dansk Sagn som de har lydt i Folkemunde, Ny Række, III. Afdeling, Kjæmper, Kirker, Kilder*, Woels Forlag, Copenhagen.

KRISTENSEN, EVALD TANG (1936), *Dansk Sagn som de har lydt i Folkemunde, Ny Række, VI. Afdeling, Djævelkunster, Kloge Mænd og Koner, Hekseri, Sygdom*, Reitzels Forlag, Copenhagen.

KRISTENSEN, SVEND MØLLER (1970), *Litteratur-sociologiske essays*, Munksgaard, Copenhagen.

LARSEN, O. N., ed (1968), *Violence and the Mass Media*, Harper & Row, New York.

LAWRENCE, D. H. (1913), *Sons and Lovers*.

LAWRENCE, D. H. (1958 edn), *Studies in Classic American Literature*, first publ. 1923; Doubleday, New York.

LE CARRÉ, JOHN (pseud. of D. J. M. Cornwell) (1961), *The Deadly Affair*, orig. publ. as *Call for the Dead*, Gollancz, London.

LE CARRÉ, JOHN (1962), *A Murder of Quality*, Gollancz, London.

LE CARRÉ, JOHN (1965), *The Spy Who Came in from the Cold*, Pan, London.

LE CARRÉ, JOHN (1968), *A Small Town in Germany*, Coward-McCann, New York.

LEWIS, NORMAN (1964), *The Honoured Society; the Mafia conspiracy observed*, Collins, London.

LEWIS, OSCAR (1959), *Five Families; Mexican case-studies in the culture of poverty*, Basic Books, New York.

LEWIS, OSCAR (1962), *The Children of Sanchez: autobiography of a Mexican family*, Random House, New York.

LEWIS, OSCAR (1966), *La Vida: a Puerto Rican family in the culture of poverty*, Random House, New York.

LIDMAN, SARA (1968), *Grube*, Gyldendal, Copenhagen; from Swedish *Gruva*.

LLOYD-JONES, HUGH (1970), Introduction, ed. and notes, *Agamemnon, The Libation Bearers, The Eumerides*, Prentice Hall, New York.

LOCKHART, ROBIN BRUCE (1967), *Ace of Spies: the incredible story of Sidney Reilly*, Hodder & Stoughton, London.

LONDON, JACK (1914), *The Valley of the Moon*.

LOWENTHAL, LEO (1960), *Literature and the Image of Man: studies in the European drama and novel 1600–1900*, Beacon Press, Boston.

LUKÁCS, GEORG (1960), *The Historical Novel*, 'composed during the winter of 1936–7 and published in Russian soon after completion . . . today [1960] I present it to the English reader without any changes . . .' (GL, Preface to first English edition, Merlin Press, London).

14

LUKÁCS, GEORG (1971), *The Theory of the Novel*, Merlin Press, London: first publ. by P. Cassirer, Berlin, 1920.

MCCARTHY, MARY (1961), *On the Contrary*, Farrar & Strauss, New York.

MCDOUGALL, WILLIAM (1920), *The Group Mind*.

MACHIAVELLI, NICCOLO (1532), *The Prince*.

MCQUAIL, DENIS (1969), *Toward a Sociology of Mass Communications*, Collier-Macmillan, London.

MAGUS, BRANKA (1971), 'Theories of women's liberation', *New Left Review*, 66, March–April.

MALSON, LUCIEN (1972), *Wolf Children and the Wild Boy of Aveyron*, New Left Books, London; trans. from *Les Enfants sauvages*, Union Générale d'Éditions, Paris, 1964.

MANNONI, O. (1971), *Freud; the theory of the unconscious*, New Left Books, London: Éditions du Seuil, Paris, 1968.

MAO TSE-TUNG (1942), *Talks at the Yenan Forum on Literature and Art*.

MARX, KARL and ENGELS, FRIEDRICH (1951 edn), *The Communist Manifesto* in *Selected Works* Moscow, Foreign Languages Publishing House, 1951, vol. 1.

MASTERMAN, J. C. (1972), *The Double-Cross System in the War of 1939–1945*, Yale University Press, New Haven.

MAUGHAM, W. SOMERSET (1928), *Ashenden: or the British Agent*, Doubleday, New York.

MAUGHAM, W. SOMERSET (1963), *Ten Novels and their Authors*, Heinemann, London.

MICHENER, JAMES (1971), *Kent State, What Happened and Why*, Random House, New York.

MITCHELL, MARGARET (1936), *Gone With The Wind*, Macmillan, New York.

MITFORD, NANCY (1946), *The Pursuit of Love*, Hamish Hamilton, London.

MITFORD, NANCY (ed.), (1956), *Noblesse oblige: an enquiry into the identifiable characteristics of the English aristocracy*, Hamish Hamilton, London.

MITFORD, NANCY (1960), *Don't Tell Alfred*, Hamish Hamilton, London.

MUGGERIDGE, MALCOLM (1966), *Tread Softly for you Tread on my Jokes*, Collins, New York.

MUSGRAVE, P. W. (1969), 'How children use television', *New Society*, 20 February.

NAPIER, JOHN (1971), *The Roots of Mankind*, Allen & Unwin, London.

NASH, WALTER (1972), *Our Experience of Language*, St Martin's Press, New York.

Njal's Saga, or *Burnt-Njal's Saga*, the longest and most famous of the Icelandic Sagas, transcribed and recorded in the thirteenth century by (perhaps) Snorri Sturlason; trans. Magnus Magnusson (1970), Penguin, Harmondsworth.

NOVAK, M. E. (1962), *Economics and the Fiction of Daniel Defoe*, University of California Press.

O'BRIEN, CONOR CRUISE (1967), *Camus*, Fontana, London.

OPIE, IONA and PETER (1969), *The Lore and Language of Schoolchildren*, Oxford University Press, London.

OPIE, IONA and PETER (1969), *Children's Games in Street and Playground*, Clarendon Press, Oxford.

ORLOV, ALEXANDER (1963), *Handbook of Intelligence and Guerrilla Warfare*, University of Michigan Press, Ann Arbor.

ORWELL, GEORGE (1940), 'Dickens', 'The Boy's Own Weekly', 'The decline of the English murder' and other essays from *Inside the Whale*, Gollancz, London.

ORWELL, GEORGE (1946), *Critical Essays*, Secker & Warburg, London.

PAGE, BRUCE, LEITCH, D., and KNIGHTLEY, P. (1969), *Philby, the Spy who Betrayed a Generation*, Penguin, Harmondsworth.

PARRINDER, GEOFFREY (1963), *Witchcraft, European and African*, Faber, London.

PEI, MARIO (1914) *Voices of Man*, Allen & Unwin, London.

PICKARD-CAMBRIDGE, A. W. (1927), *Dithyramb, Tragedy and Comedy*, Oxford University Press, London.

PICKARD-CAMBRIDGE, A. W. (1953), *Dramatic Festivals of Athens*, Oxford University Press, London.

PUZO, MARIO (1969), *The Godfather*, Putnam, New York, 1969.

RANCH, HIERONYMUS JUSTESEN, *Karrig Niding*, a Jutland comedy from *c.* 1600.

RANULF, SVEND (1936), *The Jealousy of the Gods and Criminal Law at Athens*, Gyldendal, Copenhagen: from *Gudernes Misundelse og Strafferettens Oprindelse i Athen*, Historisk-Filologiske Meddelelser, Copenhagen, 1930.

REAGE, PAULINE (1970), *Story of 'O'*, Olympia Press, London.

RIBBLE, MARGARETHA ANTOINETTE (1944), *The Rights of Infants*, Columbia University Press, New York.

RICHARDSON, SAMUEL (1740–2), *Pamela, or, Virtue Rewarded*.

RICHARDSON, SAMUEL (1747–8), *Clarissa Harlowe*.

ROSENBERG, C. (1878–85), *Nordboernes Aandsliv fra Oldtiden til vore Dage*, Samfundet til den danske Litteraturs Fremme, Copenhagen, 3 vols.

ROSS, JAMES B. and MCLAUGHLIN, MARY, eds (1949), *The Portable Medieval Reader*, Viking, New York.

SAINTSBURY, GEORGE (1916), *The Peace of the Augustans*, Bell, London.

SAYERS, DOROTHY (1932), *Have His Carcase*, Gollancz, London.

SELBY, HUBERT, JR (1964), *Last Exit to Brooklyn*, Grove Press, New York.

SHILS, EDWARD A. (1960), 'Mass society and its culture', *Daedelus*, vol. 89, no. 2.

SILLITOE, ALAN (1958), *Saturday Night and Sunday Morning*, W. H. Allen, London.

SILLITOE, ALAN (1970), *A Start in Life*, W. H. Allen, London.

SINCLAIR, UPTON (1906), *The Jungle*.

SISSONS, O., and FRENCH, E. (1963), *Age of Austerity*, Hodder & Stoughton, London.

SPEARMAN, DIANA (1966), *The Novel and Society*, Routledge & Kegan Paul, London.

STEINBECK, JOHN (1939), *The Grapes of Wrath*, Viking Press, New York.

STENDHAL (1822), *On Love*, trans. from *De l'amour*.

STOWE, HARRIET BEECHER (1852), *Uncle Tom's Cabin*.

STYRON, WILLIAM (1966), *The Confessions of Nat Turner*, Random House, New York.

SUTHERLAND, JAMES (1971), *Daniel Defoe: a critical study*, Harvard University Press, Boston.

SYMONS, JULIAN (1972), *Bloody Murder: from the detective story to the crime novel*, Faber, London.

TACITUS, *c.* A.D. 55–*c.* 117, *Germania*, 'a description of the Germanic peoples and their institutions'.

THOMPSON, HUNTER S. (1966), *Hell's Angels*, Random House, New York.

THOMSON, GEORGE (1941), *Aeschylus and Athens: a study in the social origins of drama*, Lawrence & Wishart, London.

THOMSON, GEORGE (1948), *The Pre-historic Aegean*, Lawrence & Wishart, London.

THOREAU, HENRY DAVID (1854), *Walden*.

TROLLOPE, ANTHONY (1855), *The Warden*.

TWAIN, MARK (pseud. of Samuel Clemens) (1884), *The Adventures of Huckleberry Finn*.

VELLACOTT, PHILIP (1956), Introduction, *The Oresteian Trilogy* (Aeschylus), Penguin, Harmondsworth.

VAN GHENT, DOROTHY (1967), *The English Novel, Form and Function*, Harper, New York.

VICO, GIAMBATTISTA (1744), *The New Science*, trans. from the Italian by Thomas G. Bergin and Max H. Fisch, Cornell University Press, Ithaca, New York, 1948.

WAIN, JOHN (1954), *Hurry On Down*, Knopf, New York.

WATT, IAN (1957), *The Rise of the Novel*, Chatto & Windus, London.

WEBER, MAX (1949), *Max Weber on the Methodology of the Social Sciences*, trans. and ed. by E. Shils and H. A. Finch, Free Press, Chicago.

WELLS, H. G. (1909), *Ann Veronica*, Unwin, London.

WHALE, JOHN (1969), *The Half-Shut Eye*, Macmillan, London.

WOOLF, VIRGINIA (1925), *Mrs Dalloway*, Hogarth Press, London.

WOOLF, VIRGINIA (1941), *Between the Acts*, Hogarth Press, London.

WOOLF, VIRGINIA (1966), *Collected Essays, 1920-45*, Chatto & Windus, London.

WYLD, H. C. (1920), *A History of Modern Colloquial English*, Blackwell, Oxford.

ZWEIG, FERDYNAND (1965), *The Quest for Fellowship*, Heinemann, London.

Index

Of topics, concepts, historical persons including authors of works cited, and fictional characters. Real persons are listed alphabetically by surname, fictional characters alphabetically by first name or title. Books, plays, journals and films are italicised, short stories, articles and TV series are indicated by quotation marks, TV series identified as such. Thus, Fielding, Henry, the author, under F; *Tom Jones*, the novel, under T; Tom Jones and Squire Western the fictional characters under T and S respectively.

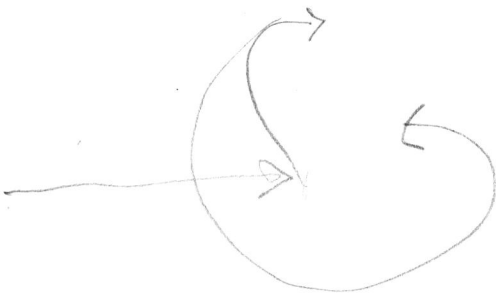